Born to Work
Child Labour in India

Born to Work

Child Labour in India

Neera Burra

DELHI
OXFORD UNIVERSITY PRESS
CALCUTTA CHENNAI MUMBAI

Oxford University Press, Great Clarendon Street, Oxford OX2 6DP

Oxford New York
Athens Auckland Bangkok Calcutta
Cape Town Chennai Dar es Salaam Delhi
Florence Hong Kong Istanbul Karachi
Kuala Lumpur Madrid Melbourne Mexico City
Mumbai Nairobi Paris Singapore
Taipei Tokyo Toronto

and associates in

Berlin Ibadan

ISBN 0 19 564097 7

Typeset by Rastrixi, New Delhi 110070
Printed in India at Rekha Printers Pvt. Ltd., New Delhi 110020
and published by Manzar Khan, Oxford University Press
YMCA Library Building, Jai Singh Road, New Delhi 110 001

For Sundar . . .
without whom this book could never have been written

Contents

Contents

Foreword

Just one hundred years ago, in the last decade of the nineteenth century, an American non-governmental organization called the National Child Labor Committee (NCLC) conducted a series of studies on child labour in U.S. industries. These studies — which now occupy several feet of shelf space in Harvard's Weidner Library — documented the plight of America's working children. The social activists and scholars who prepared these studies described the conditions for children in the textile, cigarette, glass, and other industries throughout the country. The NCLC used these studies as part of its campaign to appeal to the conscience of Americans and to lobby state legislatures to extend the age of compulsory education (in 1900 education was compulsory up to age fourteen in only 31 states) and to ban the employment of children. Through their efforts state governments extended the years of compulsory schooling and introduced the system of 'working papers', or employment certificates which permitted young people to work only after they had completed at least six years of schooling and were over fourteen years of age. The NCLC was also instrumental in getting national legislation passed to supersede weak state government laws on child labour.

A similar campaign is now under way in India to pass stricter child labour laws and to introduce compulsory primary school education. While there is no national Non-Governmental Organization (NGO) in India to compare to the NCLC, a small band of social activists, journalists, scholars, and film makers have been hard at work appealing to the conscience of officials and to the Indian public. Meera Nair, in a much acclaimed prize winning film, *Salaam Bombay*, poignantly portrayed the life of Bombay's street children. Smithu Kothari, Manu Kulkarni and Harbans Singh have described conditions for children in the notorious match industry in Sivakasi. Sheela Barse and Debasish Chatterji have written articles on children in the glass industry. Articles on the plight of children have appeared in *Frontline*, *India Today*, and in India's leading dailies. But few people have been as persistent and indefatigable in describing the conditions of working children as Neera Burra, a research scholar earlier on the staff of the International Labour Organization and now the Coordinator of the Sub-Regional Programme, South Asia, for United Nations Volunteers. Since 1986 she has been study-ing the lives of children in some of the major industries that employ child labour: the brass ware industry in Moradabad, pottery making in Khurja, gem polishing in Jaipur, lock making in Aligarh, and glass factories in Firozabad. These studies pro-vide us with the most documented account we now have of child labour in India.

The book you are about to read draws from her remarkable field investigations. Burra spent weeks in each of her sites, interviewing children, employers, and officials, carefully de-scribing the industrial processes on which children labour, the hours they work, the wages they are paid, and the health and safety hazards which they endure. She has pulled together the best data available on the number of children in each industry, their age on entering the labour force, and what happens to them as they grow older. Her prose is factual and unemotional, but her central theme is unmistakable: child labour in India is rampant and state policies to protect children are poorly con-ceived and badly enforced.

Children in India, at any age, are legally permitted to work in small scale industries, though there are supposed to be restrictions on their employment in hazardous work. In each industry she surveyed, Burra found children engaged in work that is unsafe and unhealthy. In the lock industry children work with potassium cyanide, trisodium phosphate, sodium silicate, hydrochloric acid and sulphuric acid. They inhale noxious fumes, are exposed to electric shocks, and suffer from tuberculosis, bronchitis, asthma and other diseases. In the brass ware industry, children work at high temperature furnaces and inhale the dust produced in polishing. In pottery, too, children suffer from respiratory illnesses from inhaling clay dust. The glass industry is particularly hazardous since children carry molten glass and work around furnaces with intense heat. Even when children are not employed in hazardous work, the environment itself often puts children at risk. Household employment is not normally dangerous, but children as domestic servants are often beaten and sexually abused, and children employed in *dhabas* are at the mercy of their employers.

Officials and employers argue that the children are serving as apprentices, acquiring needed skills for adult employment, contributing to the income of their families, and are mainly employed as part of family labour. They further argue that the employment of children sustains India's traditional craft-oriented industries and that child labour makes India's exports more competitive. Neera Burra's case studies refute each of these arguments.

In the lock industry in Aligarh and in the brass ware industry in Moradabad she reports that children are not working side by side with their parents. Though unit owners claim that they employ their own children, Burra finds that this is rarely so. Children supplementing family income? In the pottery industry, she reports children are employed in spite of high levels of adult unemployment. Here and in other industries adults are being displaced by children, who are invariably paid less. 'Simply put,' she writes, 'employers prefer child labour because it is cheaper than adult labour and because children, unlike adults, cannot question the treatment meted out to them. Evidence indicates that the child's wage in any industry is a third to half that of an adult for the same output, with the child working for as many, if not more, hours than the adult.' It is often because wages are kept low for adults that families are forced to send their children into the labour force.

Training? 'These children are not being trained, they are being used,' she quotes a master craftsman in the gem industry in Jaipur. In the industries she studied, artisans have been transformed into factory workers. Glass bangle-making and glass blowing are no longer hereditary occupations and the children employed in them are not acquiring special skills. In the lock industry children work on buffing machines, electroplating, spray painting, filing components, making springs, assembling and packing locks. No skills are required that could not be easily learned by adults. She also reports that there is no evidence that children are capable of weaving better carpets than adults and no evidence that children (with their so-called nimble fingers) are better able to perform tasks in any industry better than adults. One of her most heart rending findings is that early entrance into the labour force has shortened the working lives of many young people who, now as adults, are too ill to remain in the labour force. Adults in Firozabad who used to work around the furnaces in the glass industry as children, said that they had to send their own children into the labour force since they themselves were now unable to work. The children of the poor, she writes, have become 'an expendable commodity.'

One of her most interesting findings is that child labour is not enhancing India's ability to compete in exports, an argument used by government officials to justify the creation of government centres for the training of children as weavers in the carpet industry, and for the employment of children in the brass ware and gem industries, three of India's most successful export industries. Burra compares a brass ware factory in Moradabad with a brass ware factory she visited in Bangkok, a highly successful export-oriented factory where children were not employed and where the level of technology was more sophisticated than in Moradabad. Unlike Thai businessmen, she reports, Moradabad businessmen have no incentive to acquire new technologies since they can employ low wage children. Child labour in India has reduced the need for technological innovation, so essential to the expansion of exports.

Finally, she reports that child labour is keeping children out of school, and contributing to the growth of illiteracy, especially among girls. Employers in the carpet industry, with government support, compete with the schools for the children. School-age children are recruited by *dalals* or middlemen who belong to the same villages and earn a commission for bringing child workers. In Moradabad, she reports, practically none of the children she met had ever attended school. Employers are particularly eager to employ young girls, since they are paid less than boys, and are often employed at younger ages. In the match industry in Sivakasi, most of the child workers are girls below the age of fourteen, and their wages are well below the agricultural wages in the region. In every industry she studied, in coir, *papads*, gems, *beedis*, locks, carpets, embroidery, girls are paid less than boys and are employed in the jobs requiring the lowest skills.

Given the low female attendance in primary schools, is it any wonder that female literacy is so low in India? The 1991 census reported that the percentage of adult female literates to the total female population remained under 40 per cent in Andhra Pradesh (33.7 per cent), Orissa (34.4 per cent), Madhya Pradesh (28.4 per cent), Bihar (23.1 per cent), Uttar Pradesh (26.0 per cent), Rajasthan (20.8 per cent) and Arunachal Pradesh (29.4 per cent), states with a high incidence of child labour. There is, writes Burra, a web of illiteracy and exploitation — uneducated parents send their children to work, who as illiterate adults then send their own children to work.

India is the largest producer of non-school-going child workers. Estimates of the number of children under age fifteen in the labour force range from an official government figure of 17.4 million to a high of 44 million by a respected non-government research organization. Most child workers in India are illiterate while in nineteenth century England and in the United States, child workers were at least able to read and write since they were generally in school for six years, the period of compulsory education. In India most child workers have never attended school or have dropped out before completing four years of schooling, the minimum needed to acquire literacy.

What can be done to end child labour in India? Burra does not spell out detailed policy solutions, but, frankly, she need not. A government that is committed to removing its children from the labour force and placing them in primary schools can do it. It has been done before by other poor countries — by many European countries in the eighteenth century, by Japan at the end of the nineteenth century, and in our time by Korea, Taiwan, the Peoples Republic of China, Singapore, Thailand, Indonesia, and Malaysia. Primary school budgets can be increased (perhaps at the cost of free higher education for India's middle classes), primary schooling can be made compulsory, and child labour laws can be extended and enforced. In India, concludes Burra, 'universal primary education is not given the importance it deserves. Instead many government programmes offer palliatives like adult literacy programmes and the establishment of model schools catering largely to the rural elite, rather than tackle frontally the need for a good basic education.' The Indian government has the capacity to make education compulsory and to bring an end to the kind of child labour conditions described in this book. What is lacking is the political leadership that is prepared to do what is necessary.

Ford International Professor of Political Science   MYRON WEINER
Massachusetts Institute of Technology
Cambridge
Massachusetts

Acknowledgements

My professional interest in the issue of child labour was kindled because of Dr Walter Fernandes of the Indian Social Institute who gave me the opportunity to study child labour in India. He asked me to write a report based on secondary sources on the subject. But soon it was clear, that we had to go beyond. The Government of India was preparing for a new legislation to protect children which we thought was untimely. Walter gave me complete freedom to take whatever direction I wanted. He not only gave me the opportunity to get involved, but supported a field trip to study the glass industry of Firozabad. I am indebted to him.

The late Tara Ali Baig and Professor Dharma Kumar have been my mentors in the field. Tara Ali Baig encouraged me at a time when child labour issues were not particularly media-worthy: she gave my findings publicity in the various governmental committees of which she was a member. Professor Dharma Kumar not only took the trouble of reading several versions of the manuscript, but needled me frequently about publishing the research. Her comments were very valuable. And if the book is now in print, I owe it largely to Dharma who kept the pressure on!

I am deeply indebted to UNICEF, ILO, DANIDA and UNESCO for supporting my research on child labour. UNICEF supported the research on child labour in the lock industry of Aligarh and child labour in the gem polishing industry of Jaipur. ILO/ARTEP supported the study on child labour in the brass ware industry of Moradabad. DANIDA supported the research on child potters of Khurja and UNESCO commissioned me to write a report on child labour and education in Asia. Without the financial support of these agencies, this research would not have been possible.

Some of these reports have appeared in abridged forms in the *Economic and Political Weekly*. EPW gave me the opportunity to share some of my earlier findings at a time when not much was being written about child labour. I am grateful.

The opinions expressed in this book are my own. I cannot pretend to have all, or even some of the answers. What I have tried to do is to present the material in ways which would avoid sensationalism. I have very strong feelings about the role of compulsory education in the elimination of child labour, a feeling not shared by many. I hope that this book can encourage a debate on this issue.

NEERA BURRA
New Delhi 1994

Glossary

agarbatti	incense sticks
amani	monthly wages
auraton-ka-kaam	women's work
bakerywala	owner of the bakery
beedis/bidis	local cigarettes
belan	rolling pin
belanwala	the man who rotates the belan
bhatti	furnace
bigha	a unit for measuring land
bindai-ka-kaam	piercing holes in beads
charpai	bed
chilai	scraping
chimta	tongs
chulha	stove
coolies	porters
dalals	middlemen/brokers
darja	box moulding system
darja bhatti	box mould furnace
dhabas	small way-side eating places
dhalai	moulder
dhalaiya	moulder
dhol	drum. This is a term used for drum polishing
dibbi	a term used to describe a flat and small box

duniya dari	ways of the world
gali	lane
gali-moballa	all-embracing term used to describe a residential locality and its lanes and by-lanes (see *moballa*)
ghadiya	crucible
ghadiyawala	the person who melts the raw material in the graphite crucible
ghat	rough cut stone
ghat bananewala	the person who makes the rough shape
gulli	round ingots
halwai	sweetmeat shop owner
hath-gadi	hand cart
haveli	mansion
hookah	tobacco-pipe with a long tube passing through water for cooling the smoke
inam	gift
jagaiya	the person whose responsibility it is to wake up workers on night shifts. He is also the man who recruits labour for the factory owner
jeeta/jeeta gadus	a term used to refer to bonded labourers mainly in South India
jindra	an instrument used for polishing gem stones
jotedars	a term used for landlords in Bengal
judai	to join
judai addas	unregistered small units where bangles are joined over acetylene flames
kabana	bow used for the polishing of gem stones
karkhana	workshop, also used for a factory
karkhanedar	owner of a karkhana
katai	work on the jigger jolly machine

katai addas	unregistered units where designs are cut on bangles
kataiwala	the worker who makes pots on the jigger jolly machine
kathai	a particular type of polishing work done
kathai-ka-kaam	polishing work
khandani pesha	(hereditary) traditional occupation
khet mazdoor	agricultural labourer
khula mazdoor	casual labourer
kulhads	clay cups
kumbhars	potters
labya	the 7-foot iron rod used for carrying molten glass
loam	molten glass
lungis/thehmats	a long cloth wrapped around the waist, worn by men
malik	employer/owner
marking karnewala/ nishan laganewala	the person in charge of grading and marking the gem stone
masala	a term used for describing a mix of ingredients
mohalla	residential locality, usually a closely clustered group of houses, in the older parts of cities and towns
munim	accountant
muthauthanewala	the man who removes the spring of hot bangles from the *belan*
nagine ka karigar	gem stone artisan
netagiri	politicking
nimbu	lemon
pakai bhatti	a unit where bangles are baked in layers on metal sheets covered with silica sand
pakaiwala	the person who places trays of bangles into the furnace and also stokes it

paldaras	casual labourers
panja	the fork used for weaving
pankha	literally means fan. In this context it is the rotation of the wheel which is called a pankha to keep the furnace fire burning
pankhawala	the persons who fans the furnace
pannaiyal	a term used to describe bonded labour in the southern States of India
papad	an Indian savoury
phanti	piece of wood on which five or six moulds are kept
phantiwala	the boys who carry the phanti
polishwala	polisher
pudias	small packets
purdah	the seclusion of women amongst the Muslims
rotis	whole wheat bread
saggars	fire resistant containers in which unbaked pots are baked
sakuras	small clay pots
seth	a term used to describe the rich, a term often used for landlords, owners of workshops and factories
shoe-polish-ka-samaan	a shoe polishing kit
sigri	small coal stove
silli	oblong ingot
surahis	earthen pitchers used for keeping water for drinking
taarkash	the man who threads hot glass onto a rolling pin
tehsil/taluka	an administrative unit of the district
thandibattiwala	the person who carries the molten glass after it is beaten into shape, back to the furnace

thehmats	see under lungis
theka	contract
thekedars	contractors
toras	strings of 312 bangles
truckwala	truck driver
unionbaji	unionizing
ustad	master
uthai rakhai	pick up and put down
zari	gold thread embroidery

Child Labour in Some Sectors in India

Industry	Location	Total Workers	Child Workers	Percentage of Child Workers to Total Workers
Slate Pencil	Mandsaur, Madhya Pradesh	12,000[a]	1,000[b]	8.3
Slate	Markapur, Andhra Pradesh	15,000[c]	app. 3750	25
Diamond-cutting	Surat, Gujarat	100,000[d]	15,000[e]	15
Agate-cutting	Cambay, Gujarat	30,000[f]	not known	–
Gem polishing	Jaipur, Rajasthan	60,000	13,600[g]	22.6
Powerloom	Bhiwandi, Maharashtra	300,000	15,000[h]	5
Cotton hosiery	Tiruppur, Tamil Nadu	30,000	8,000[i]	33.3
Carpet-weaving	Mirzapur-Bhadohi, Uttar Pradesh	200,000	150,000[j]	75
Carpet-weaving	Jammu and Kashmir	app. 400,000	100,000[k]	25
Carpet-weaving	Rajasthan	30,000	12,000[l]	40

Industry	Location	Total Workers	Child Workers	Percentage of Child Workers to Total Workers
Lock-making	Aligarh, Uttar Pradesh	80,000 – 90,000	7,000[m] – 10,000	8.7 11.1
Pottery	Khurja, Uttar Pradesh	20,000	5,000[n]	25
Brass Ware	Moradabad, Uttar Pradesh	150,000	40,000[o] – 45,000	26.6 30.0
Match	Sivakasi, Tamil Nadu	not known	45,000[p]	–
Glass	Firozabad, Uttar Pradesh	200,000	50,000[q]	25
Silk and silk products	Varanasi, Uttar Pradesh	11,900	4,409[r]	37
Textile	Varanasi, Uttar Pradesh	3,512	1,108[s]	31.5
Knives	Rampur, Uttar Pradesh	not known	3,000[t]	–
Handicrafts	Jammu amd Kashmir	90,000[u]	26,478	29.42[v]
Silk weaving	Bihar	not known	10,000[w]	–
Brocade and Zari industry	Varanasi and other centres, Uttar Pradesh	not known	300,000[x]	–
Brick-kilns	West Bengal	not known	35,000[A]	–

Industry	Location	Total Workers	Child Workers	Percentage of Child Workers to Total Workers
Beedi	India	3,275,000	3,275,00[B]	10
Circus industry	40 major circuses		12% of the entire labour strength[C]	
Handloom and Handicraft Industry	Jammu and Kashmir	116,000	28,348	25[D]

SOURCES:
a. Singh, N.K., 'Slate-pencil industry: Deadly bondage' in *India Today*, 30 September 1986, p. 159.
b. Rao, A., 'Silicosis deaths of slate workers' in *Economic and Political Weekly*, vol. XV, no. 44, 1 November 1980, p. 1883.
c. 'Slated to toil to make children literate', *Patriot*, 11 April 1983.
d. Jani, G., 'Child workers of diamond-cutting industry in Surat: Some observations', Paper presented at Workshop on *Child Labour in India* (New Delhi: Indian Social Institute), 9 August 1986, p. 2.
e. Jani, G., 'No sparkle in gem workers' lives', *The Hindustan Times*, 26 July 1987.
f. 'Agate dust causes lung diseases, says survey', *Indian Express*, 22 December 1986.
g. Burra, N., 'A report on child labour in the gem polishing industry of Jaipur, Rajasthan, India' (New Delhi: Prepared for UNICEF, October 1987, pp. 6–7 (unpublished).

h. Barse, S., 'Child labour hit by powerloom closure', *Indian Express*, 15 November 1985.

i. Venkatramani, S.H., 'Tamil Nadu: Vested interests' in *India Today*, 15 July 1983, p. 60.

j. Juyal, B.N., *Child labour and the exploitation in the carpet industry* (New Delhi: Indian Social Institute), 1987, p. 26.

k. Gupte, S. 'Child Labour', *ICCW News Bulletin*, vol. XXXIII, no. 3, September 1985, p. 9.

l. Gupta, M., 'We cut out fingers but no blood falls: Child labour in the carpet industry in Rajasthan' in Manju Gupta and Klaus Voll (eds), *Young hands at work: Child labour in India* (Delhi, Lucknow: Atma Ram and Sons), 1987, p. 37.

m. Burra, N., 'A report on child labour in the lock industry of Aligarh, Uttar Pradesh, India' (New Delhi: Prepared for UNICEF), March 1987, p. 1 (unpublished).

n. Burra, N., 'A report on child labour in the pottery industry of Khurja, Uttar Pradesh, India' (New Delhi: Prepared for DANIDA), November 1987, p. 1 (unpublished).

o. Burra, N., 'Child labour in the brass-ware industry of Moradabad, India' (New Delhi: ILO/ARTEP Working Paper), 1988, p. 2.

p. Kothari, S., ''There's blood on those matchsticks': Child labour in Sivakasi' in *Economic and Political Weekly*, vol. XVIII, no. 27, 2 July 1983, p. 1191.

q. Burra, N., 'Glass Factories of Firozabad II: Plight of child workers' in *Economic and Political Weekly*, vol. XXI, no. 47, 22 November 1986, p. 2033.

r. Juyal, B.N. et al, *Child labour: The twice exploited* (Varanasi: Gandhian Institute of Studies), 1985, p. 20.

s. Ibid.

t. 'Children being exploited in Rampur', *National Herald*, 8 August 1985.

u. Garg, R.B.L. 'Fair deal for children', *Patriot*, 28 November 1980.

v. Pandit, M.L., 'Child Labour in Handicrafts of Kashmir Valley', (unpublished, manuscript) (n.d.).

w. Ibid.

x. Srinivasan, Nirmala, 'Little hope for little hands', *Indian Express*, 30 January 1984.

A. Gothoskar, Sujata, 'Where will they be on Children's Day?' in *Femina*, 8–22 November 1986, p. 28.

B. 'Changes in Factories Act under study', PTI News, 18 November 1986.

C. Sen, Ashoke Mohan, 'Exploitation of children: Grim consequences' in *Mainstream*, vol. XVII, no. 47, 21 July 1979, p. 23.

D. Nangia, Sudesh, 'Child workers in carpet weaving industry in Jammu and Kashmir (with a special emphasis on girls)', (Project sponsored by UNICEF Regional Office for South Central Asia, New Delhi), 1988, p. 12.

1

How it all started . . .
Government Policy and the Law

It was for the first time in 1985 that the issue of child labour attracted public attention and debate in India. There had been government-appointed committees in the past to look into the question of child labour and make recommendations; but these committees did not receive media coverage, nor were their recommendations discussed in public. The occasion for the debate was the drafting of a Bill dealing with child labour by a Non Governmental Organization (NGO) based in Bangalore city. Briefly, the group argued that poverty was the main cause of child labour and that, therefore, the attempt should be to regulate the conditions under which children work rather than to prohibit such work.

The group, whose experience was largely confined to the urban centre of Bangalore, felt that working children should be unionized and made aware of their rights. They had come across cases where children suffered accidents but would be denied compensation because employers would not officially recognize these children to be on their rolls. The group believed that prohibiting child labour would be counter-productive and urged that there be no minimum age for children to enter employment.

The general approach of the Bill was endorsed by the Central Government. In particular, there was frequent recourse to the argument that poverty was the cause of child labour and that hence, it could not simply be legislated away. Widespread public discussion in workshops, seminars and the media was to follow.

Broadly, there were two schools of thought. One supported the governmental position of regulation and the other argued for the prohibition of child labour. The public debate continued in different fora for almost a year. The Government of India came out with a position paper on the proposed comprehensive legislation. The paper was ambivalent about the Government's position as to whether there should be a minimum age for employment; it also took the view that in order to provide protection to children it would be better to make the law realistic and permit children to work under regulated conditions. With respect to the carpet industry, the position paper seemed equivocal: on the one hand, it toyed with the proposition that child labour be permitted in certain non-hazardous operations but, on the other hand, said that industries thriving on child labour should not be encouraged. The position paper gave sufficient warning of governmental intention and revealed the basic approach to child labour.

The Child Labour (Prohibition and Regulation) Act came into force towards the latter half of 1986. It listed particular processes in certain industries as being banned for children below the age of fourteen years with the proviso that such a ban would not apply to those children working as part of family labour or to those working in any State-funded or State-supported institutions. It is interesting to note that the provisions of the 1986 Act were almost identical to those in the Employment of Children Act, 1938, with reference to the ban referred to above. The only significant difference between the laws of 1938 and 1986 was that the latter envisaged the constitution of a Child Labour Technical Advisory Committee which was to investigate, on a continuing basis, processes in different industries in order to determine whether they were hazardous or otherwise. While debate on the legislation was still taking place, the Government of India announced a National Child Labour Policy (NCLP). According to this policy, some industries were identified for priority action to tackle the problem of child labour[1] through non-formal education, employment and income-generation schemes for poor parents of working children.

What was curious about the discussion that took place was that it seemed as if the issue of child labour had come up for the first time in India. That was not so. The International Labour Organization (ILO), set up in 1919 under the League of Nations, had felt that there should be some international guidelines by which the employment of children under a certain age could be regulated in industrial undertakings. It therefore suggested that the minimum age of work be twelve years.

This Convention had to be ratified by the Government of British India. During the Legislative Assembly debates concerning ratification, the question of raising the minimum age from nine to twelve years created a furore. The Honourable Sir Thomas Holland said in the Legislative Assembly in February, 1921, that if the minimum age were raised, it would upset the organizational set-up of most textile mills which were the principal employers of children: their machinery was made specifically with child workers in mind and any change would render it obsolete. He suggested that children who were already working should be allowed to continue to do so but fresh recruitment should not be permitted.

On the other hand, there were those who felt that the answer to the problem lay in compulsory primary education. Discussing this issue at length, Sir Holland pointed out that there was reluctance on the part of local authorities to insist

---

[1] The ten project areas are:
1. The match industry in Sivakasi, Tamil Nadu.
2. The diamond polishing industry in Surat, Gujarat.
3. The precious stone polishing industry in Jaipur, Rajasthan.
4. The glass industry in Firozabad, Uttar Pradesh.
5. The brass-ware industry in Moradabad, Uttar Pradesh.
6. The hand-made carpet industry in Mirzapur-Bhadohi, Uttar Pradesh.
7. The hand-made carpet industry in Jammu and Kashmir.
8. The lock-making industry in Aligarh, Uttar Pradesh.
9. The slate industry in Markapur, Andhra Pradesh.
10. The slate industry in Mandsaur, Madhya Pradesh.

upon primary education even where the Provincial Councils had passed Acts. He in fact argued that it was very unlikely:

> . . . that ratepayers will be very keen on paying for education which will also steal from them the cheapest form of their labour. If you stop their labour first, we may hear more about primary education in our industrial areas (Govt. of India 1921: 281).

And further:

> It is no use saying that until you can provide primary education, the children are much better off in the mills. Unless you turn them out of the mills, you will never provide primary education for them (ibid.).

L.P. Watson argued that factory owners like himself actually looked after the interests of the child. He pointed out (ibid.: 284) that the working children of the poor were the mainstay of their families and not allowing them to work would lead to greater hardship and misery for them. He also argued that India should not ratify the Draft Convention of the ILO regarding the minimum age as conditions in India were vastly different from those in Western countries. Watson objected strongly to raising the minimum age of children working in industry because he felt that young children worked very fast and were more intelligent and since there was no universal primary education, work was good for children. He felt that if children below twelve years were forced to remain outside the work-force, it would have very serious consequences for the country as a whole. Another member, Rahimtoola Currimbhoy, said that large employers of labour like himself were not opposed to compulsory education but to ban child labour below the age of twelve years in order to force the pace of compulsory education was all wrong (ibid.: 285). Compulsory education should first be introduced and only then should the minimum age be introduced, he went on to say. Other members claimed that the parents of working children wanted their children to work and the State ought not to interfere in the rights of parents: this was used as an argument for maintaining the status quo. In other words, Watson's plea, like that of many other factory owners, was that introducing a minimum age for children in industry would be detrimental to the interests of the children, the people and the country (ibid.: 287).

As a result of this debate, the House was divided with thirty-two members voting for raising the minimum age of child labour to twelve and forty voting against it. Ultimately, the Assembly recommended to the Governor-General-in-Council that the Draft Convention fixing the minimum age of admission of children in industrial employment should be ratified with certain reservations. It was stated that this would not apply to factories employing more than ten but less than twenty persons. However, the local government could formulate transitional regulations to regulate the labour of children between the ages of nine and twelve who were already employed in factories.

It is of interest to note that the question of compulsory education was linked to that of the abolition of child labour as early as 1921.

The Royal Commission on Labour in India was established in 1929 to enquire into and report on the existing conditions of labour in industrial undertakings and plantations in British India, on the health, efficiency and standard of living of workers and on the relations between employers and employed, and to make recommendations. The Commission travelled all over British India, visited various industries, interviewed employers, workers and children, looked into the health hazards in different industries, modes of recruitment of children, conditions of work, wages, etc., and finalized its report in 1931. Though its canvas was much larger, the Report brought to light many inequities and the shocking conditions under which children worked. The Commission's painstaking, empirical labours were important for what they revealed about the situation of children.

Describing the conditions of work in shellac manufacture, which they found mainly in the States of Bihar and Orissa, the Commission reported that 10 per cent of the work-force was made up of children and they were largely to be found inside the stove room which 'in the opinion of the Director of Public Health of the Central Provinces, was harmful to them because of the excessive heat. Even the adult melters reported that "great exhaustion is felt at the end of the day, and debilitation is often experienced after three or four months of regular work" ' (Govt.of India 1931: 95–6). The Commission also pointed out that the employers, although educated people, had not responded to suggestions on improving working conditions.

The *beedi* (local cigarettes)industry was another industry the Commission investigated and found that it was spread throughout the country and most establishments 'are small airless boxes, often without any windows where the workers are crowded so thickly on the ground that there is barely room to squeeze between them' (ibid.: 96). The Royal Commission was concerned about child labour in the *beedi* industry, particularly in the Madras Presidency, where 'there is reason to believe that corporal punishment and other disciplinary measures of a reprehensible kind are sometimes resorted to in the case of the smaller children' (ibid.: 96). 'Workers as young as five years of age may be found in some of these places working without adequate meal intervals or weekly rest days, and often for ten or twelve hours daily, for sums as low as 2 annas in the case of those of tenderest years. This recalls some of the worst features of child apprenticeship in England at the time of the agitation prior to the passing of the first Factory Act, particularly when it is realized that many of the parents of these child workers are in debt to the employer. As a result they are not in a position to enquire too closely into the treatment meted out to their children or to do other than return an absconding child' (ibid.: 96). Although it was difficult for the Commission to estimate the exact numbers involved, the numbers were large enough ' . . . in certain areas to constitute an evil which demands immediate remedy' (ibid.: 97).

Another industry which the Commission investigated was the carpet-weaving industry of Amritsar. According to their report, in the carpet factories of Amritsar these children are employed not directly by the factory owner but by the weaving masters, who are responsible both for engaging them and for paying their wages. The manager concerns himself solely with the master weaver who is paid on a contract basis, *i.e.,* so much for each carpet, according to its size, quality and design. There is for the most part no limitation on the children's hours, other than that imposed by the exigencies of daylight . . . No girl labour is employed. For the most part boys start at nine years of age, though in some cases, it may be as low as six years (ibid.).

The essential requirement for the recruitment of this child labour is:

> where the child is not the son or a near relative of the weaving master, he is normally the child of a man who, in return for a loan of money from the weaving master, contracts out the labour of his child at so many rupees (seven, nine, etc., according to the age of the child) per month. The duration of the contract, which is sometimes set out in a formal document, would appear to be determined by the repayment of the loan. It is not without significance that one witness, who was Managing Director of a leading carpet manufacturing firm, declared, when shown such a document found by us on his premises and drawn up only a few weeks previously, that that was the first time he had ever heard of the existence of written contracts of the kind, excusing his ignorance on the ground that he had "nothing to do with the children" and dealt only with the master weavers (ibid.).

The Commission found children working in the same factory and said that 'it was clear to us from the evidence that these children were in a position of being obliged to work any number of hours per day required of them by their masters' (ibid.: 97–8).

The children in the carpet weaving industry worked long hours without any intervals and were even subjected to corporal punishment. The condition of child labour in the carpet industry came to the attention of the local government as early

as 1923 and later in 1927 there was another enquiry held but
the conditions of work remained unchanged. The factory
owners were prepared to accept a minimum age of eight years
and to provide educational facilities, but the opposition of the
master weavers prevented any agreement. The Royal Commission was convinced that as in the *beedi* industry, official inter-
vention was necessary in order to protect the interest of child
workers (ibid.: 98).

The pledging of children by parents to employers in return
for small sums of money was another issue that was of great
concern to the Royal Commission. The Commission was of the
view that the system of mortgaging the labour of children was
indefensible and

> . . . it is worse than the system of indentured labour, for the
> indentured labourer is, when he enters on the contract a full
> agent while the child is not . . . The giving of advances to
> secure the labour of children and the execution of bonds
> pledging such labour could both be made criminal offences
> (ibid.: 102).

The Commission recommended that a bond 'pledging the labour of any person under the age of fifteen years, executed for
or on account of the receipt of any consideration, should be
void' (ibid.). This recommendation was meant for all sectors.

I have quoted long extracts from the Commission's Report
both in order to bring out the quality of their fieldwork as well
as to show how relevant their enquiries are even today. They
made several recommendations regarding the prohibition of
child labour in certain industries, the raising of the minimum
age for the employment of children as also legislation to curb
the pledging of children. These recommendations were to be
subsequently discussed in the Legislative Assembly Debates and
the Children (Pledging of Labour) Act, 1933, was passed on the
basis of the Commission's findings. The Report also formed the
basis of a new law, the Employment of Children Act, 1938,
which had a number of provisions for the protection of
children. All the industries that the Commission members had

visited and in which children were found working under appalling conditions were listed as banned in the Schedule appended to the Act.

I have dwelt at some length upon the Report of the Royal Commission on Labour because it is a good example of how law needs to rest upon a comprehensive investigation of the reality in the field. In sharp contrast, the Child Labour (Prohibition and Regulation) Act of 1986 was not preceded by or based upon empirical investigation. The Schedule in the 1986 Act of processes banned for children is virtually identical to that of the 1938 Act! Surely, in a span of nearly fifty years there would be other industries to be added and perhaps some to be deleted.

When I began researching the issue of child labour at the time the 1986 legislation was on the anvil, it was apparent that there was little systematic data on the situation of children in different industries. The five case studies presented in this book were, in part, an attempt to fill that void. I have sought in the case studies to look at each industry as a whole, to understand the motivation of employers, parents and children and, most importantly, the place of children in the structure of the industry as also the conditions under which they are toiling. The industries were selected out of the list which the Government of India wanted to tackle on a priority basis, except for the pottery industry, which I decided to study because of reports I had read about child labour in the pottery industry in early nineteenth-century England. Apart from the case studies, the book deals with issues like the extent and nature of the problem, modes of recruitment and methods of retention of children. The 'nimble fingers' argument, the impact of work on the health and education of children, the special problems of the female child and the policy implications for law and governmental programmes that emerge from a study of the reality on the ground are other areas covered in what follows.

As would be expected, the distinction between adult and child labour rests upon age. The Census of India uses fifteen years and above as the cut-off age for child labour. In the Indian Constitution, the age of fourteen years forms the dividing line

between adult and child labour. Article 24 of the Indian Constitution, which states a Fundamental Right, says:

> No child below the age of fourteen years shall be employed
> to work in any factory or mine or engaged in any other
> hazardous employment.

Artice 45, a Directive Principle of State Policy, enjoins the
State to provide free and compulsory education for all children
until they complete the age of fourteen years. Different labour
laws like the Factories Act, 1948 and the Child Labour (Prohibition and Regulation) Act, 1986, use the same criterion of age.
Moreover, one of the Directive Principles of State Policy (Article
39 (e) and (f) provides that the tender age of children should
not be abused, that citizens should not be forced by economic
necessity to enter avocations unsuited to their age or strength
and that childhood and youth be protected against moral and
material abandonment.

In the Census of India, 1981, work is defined as 'participation in any economically productive activity'. Main workers are
those who worked for the major part of the year (183 days)
preceding the date of enumeration and whose main activity
was cultivation or agricultural labour or household industry or
other paid work. Marginal workers are those who have done
some work but cannot be classified as main workers (Census
Commissioner and Registrar General 1981: xiii). The Census of
India of 1991 also uses the same definitions.

2

Where are Children Working?

There are broadly four kinds of child labour. First are those children who work in factories, workshops and mines. They are usually to be found in semi-urban and urban areas in both the unorganized and organized sectors. Second, are those children who are under bondage to their employers, whether in agriculture or industry. The third category of working children are the street children — those who live on and off the streets — and are to be found in the service sector of semi-urban and urban India. Children who work as part of family labour in all the contexts of agriculture, industry, home-based work, etc. belong to the fourth category. These are not exclusive categories, they are often combined in different ways.

DEMOGRAPHIC PROFILE

According to the 1981 Census, there are 263 million children aged fourteen years or under in India comprising 39.5 per cent of the total population of the country. Nearly 78 per cent of the child population is in the rural areas. The share of males in the child population is 51.64 per cent (Census Commissioner and Registrar General 1981). Approximately 11.2 million children are notified as main workers and 2.4 million as marginal workers. Main workers are those involved in full-time economic activity and marginal workers are those who are not working full-time. Table I below gives the percentage of children zero to fourteen in the workforce (all ages) according to the 1981 Census.

Table I

Percentage of the Workforce aged under 15 Years, 1981

	Persons	Males	Females
1. Main Workers			
Total	5.02	4.17	8.35
Rural	5.78	4.88	8.86
Urban	2.12	1.80	4.58
2. Marginal Workers			
Total	10.97	19.34	9.38
Rural	11.32	21.29	9.59
Urban	5.02	5.59	4.56

SOURCE: *Census of India 1981*: 'Report and Tables based on 5 per cent Sample Data', Series-I, Part II, Special, pp. 2–3.

Interestingly, a comparison of the work participation rate (WPR) of male and female children shows that between 1971 and 1981 there has been an increase in the WPR of girls as compared to boys. (The WPR of children is the percentage of child workers to the total child population. There is an increasing trend in sending more girls than boys to work. Sumanta Banerjee says, girls outnumber boys in many sorts of work. There are twice as many girls as boys working in mines and in quarrying and also in factory work (Banerjee 1979: 26).

Table II gives the WPR of girl workers (main) by sex for both the 1971 and the 1981 Census, showing an increase in the WPR of girls and a decrease in the WPR of boys. However, some observers have noted that female participation rates tended to be under-estimated in the 1971 Census since women respondents did not consider household work as productive work (Nayyar 1987: 2207).

Table II

Work Participation Rates for Child Workers (Main) by Sex,
1971 and 1981

	Males		Females	
	1971	*1981*	*1971*	*1981*
Total	6.65	5.46	2.63	2.95
Rural	7.56	6.30	3.05	3.53
Urban	2.75	2.46	0.82	0.88

SOURCE: *Census of India 1981*: 'Key Population Statistics based
on 5 per cent Sample Data', Paper 2 of 1983, Series-I,
India, p. 26.

The definitions used by the *Census of India, 1991*, for main
and marginal workers were the same as in the 1981 Census.
However, there was a significant change in the 1991 Census in
that, for the first time, an effort was made to compute unpaid
work on farms or in family enterprises so that women and
children's work could be better reflected (*Census of India
1991*, Series-1, Paper 3 of 1991: 4). Thus, participation in any
economically productive activity also included unpaid work on
farms and in family enterprises (ibid.: 5). However, since the
1991 Census figures are provisional, only broad figures are
available and data on the number of child labourers are yet to
be published.

The Operations Research Group (ORG), an organization
involved with market and social research, was commissioned
by the Ministry of Labour to undertake an All-India Child Labour
Sample Survey in 1980–1. They surveyed about 40,000 households spread all over the country using questionnaires. These
households were spread in 238 urban centres and 805 rural
centres in seventy-seven districts excluding the north-east.
Their survey was conducted zone-wise rather than state-wise.
According to them:

A working child is that child who was enumerated during the survey as a child falling within the five to fifteen age bracket and who is at remunerative work may be paid or unpaid, and busy any hour of the day within or outside the family . . . . The estimated working children in our country are around 44.0 million. Out of these about 21.0 per cent are in urban areas and the rest are rural based (Khatu et al 1983: 69).

Other than the decennial Censuses and the National Sample Survey no other report, except for that of ORG, appears to have any systematic data base for their estimates on child labour. According to a 1991 UNICEF report, 'Going by the official "medium projection" of a total population of 820 million by 1990, the number of children of the preschool age, three to six years, would be over 60 million; and those of the primary school age, six to eleven years, would exceed 100 million' (UNICEF 1991: 48). If the figures for the age group eleven to fourteen years are added, the figure goes well above the 100 million mark. The report clearly states that 'as of 1981, there was an estimated 75 million children between six to fourteen years out of school (of the total population of around 140 million in that age group)' (ibid.: 57). According to the UNICEF report, 'most of the children of school age who are not at school may be expected to be put to some work, in the home or outside, unpaid or paid in cash or kind. India has probably more working children than any other country' (ibid.: 60). It will be seen that estimates range from 13.59 million (Census Commissioner & Registrar General 1981), to 17.36 million (NSS 1983) and 44 million (Khatu et al 1983). The differences in the estimates of child labour are partly attributable to the differences in the definitions employed as also the year in which any estimate was made. While it is true that one needs to have a roughly accurate estimate of the size of the problem, I would argue that the different definitions used above are not useful from the point of view of analysing the problem and understanding its varied dimensions. Such an understanding would be the first step towards framing policies and devising programmes for different categories of child labour.

CHILD LABOUR

The table on page xxii lists industries and occupations with estimates of the numbers of total workers, as also child workers. In some cases, figures are not known, since the writers of the articles from which this information has been gleaned have not mentioned any figures. Even where the figures have been mentioned, they represent estimates arrived at by different writers on the basis of local interviews and discussions and not necessarily on the basis of household surveys. However imperfect these statistics might be, they indicate the diversity of industries and the range of geographical locations where child labour is to be found.

Apart from factories and workshops, children are also employed to work in mines. One report says that:

> . . . in Meghalaya, children work in mines of private companies, in trenches ninety centimetres wide and one metre high, where adults could only 'crawl'. As soon as their size is no longer profitable, they are thrown on to the streets (*The Indian Worker*, 4 April 1980: 3).

A report on child labour in Rajasthan (Thanga Raju 1977: 369) pointed out that children in the age-group of five to fourteen comprised about 4.5 per cent of the total labour force in the mining and quarrying industry in that State.

BONDED CHILD LABOUR IN INDUSTRY

Mode of Recruitment and Retention in the Workforce

This is clearly the harshest form of child labour as very small children, sometimes only eight or nine years old are separated from their parents for life.

A large segment is made up of those children whose parents pledge them to factory owners or their agents or middlemen in exchange for small consumption loans (Juyal et al 1985: 73; Ganguly 1984; Singh et al 1980; Menon 1979; GOI 1981: 18). These children work for long years for the industrialists, and

are paid at well below the minimum wage. Loan repayment cal-
culations are engineered to the severe detriment of their illiterate parents. The industries in which this type of transaction is
widespread are the *beedi* industry in the States of Andhra Pradesh, Madhya Pradesh and Tamil Nadu (Mehta 1983: 15; Mohandas 1980), the carpet industry of Mirzapur-Bhadohi in the State
of Uttar Pradesh (Prembhai 1984; Gangrade and Gathia 1983:
4–5; Ninan 1984a, b, c, d, e; Devi 1984a, b; and Chowdhury
1984a,b), the match industry of Sivakasi in the State of Tamil
Nadu (Sarma 1979: 346; Menon 1979; *The Indian Worker*, 17
September 1979: 4), the slate industry of Mandsaur in the State
of Madhya Pradesh (Rao 1980: 1883; Singh 1986: 159) and the
silk industry of Varanasi in the State of Uttar Pradesh (Juyal et
al 1985: 84). One difficulty in assessing the numbers of children
bonded to industries is that most journalistic accounts are
descriptive rather than quantitative.

Beedi Industry

Of all the industries employing children, the *beedi* industry in
India and the carpet industry of Mirzapur-Bhadohi-Varanasi are
the most notorious. In the report of the Task Force on health
prepared for the National Commission on Self-Employed Women, *beedi* workers in Tamil Nadu told of their pitiable condition where they had to mortgage their children in order to
survive. One middle-aged woman told Prayag Mehta, the then
Director of the National Labour Institute:

> I have mortgaged my seven-year-old girl, and eight-year-old
> boy to a Sheth three years ago for a loan of Rs 200 (Rs 100
> on each child). Two years later, my husband was mortgaged
> to the same Sheth for a loan of Rs 200. My two children and
> their father roll 4000 *beedis* a day. They work all the time for
> the master. Their total wage should be at least Rs 20 a day.
> However, the Sheth has been paying them each Rs 2.50 a
> day, out of which he deducts half the money every day (Mehta
> 1983: 15).

Another woman said:

All of us are forced to mortgage our children. What else can we do? When we mortgage other items to the Sheth, we lose control over those items, like our utensils and jewellery. We don't have these any more. We have only children. When we mortgage them, we lose control over them, as we lose control over other items (ibid.: 15–16).

Saroja, another woman, said:

Our grand-children are also mortgaged. We are like bonded labour. We are slaves. We just give birth to children and then leave them to work for the moneylenders. We can ask no questions. We have to follow them like slaves. Husband, children and grand-children all work in this way. All are slaves (ibid.: 16).

Mehta writes:

In voices choked with emotion, they described how mercilessly their children are beaten by the moneylender employers. Most of the children are very young when mortgaged. It is difficult for them to work all the time. Sometimes they do not go. The Sheth then beats them severely. Their fingers are injured by caning (ibid.).

Most of the mortgaged children said that they became bonded over very small sums of money. They had in fact paid back both the principal and the interest but since they and their parents are illiterate, they did not understand the basis of calculation. Even after ten or fifteen years of work, when they want to leave, the employers demand the principal and the interest.[1]

If the *beedi* industry is oppressive, the conditions of children in the carpet industry are worse.

Carpet Industry

Gangrade and Gathia's study of carpet weavers in Varanasi reveals that:

To keep the production cost low the middlemen often suggest

[1] See also *New Age*, 4 September 1986: 6; Purushotham 1983: 18–23.

to the families to engage children under twelve years of age.
They even pay advances of Rs 400 to Rs 500 for some family
function and thus tie the child to work for them indirectly
(Gangrade and Gathia 1983: 4-5).[2]

In some cases, the parents ask for advances against the child.
But there is ample evidence that often employers take advantage
of the poverty of the families and offer large loans against
children knowing that the parents will never be able to pay off
the debt. Sevanti Ninan, writing about child weavers in Bhadohi
in Uttar Pradesh, says:

> The latest 'Carpet Bulletin' which is published from this
> region moans that advances are killing exporters. But the
> proprietor of one of the bigger units in Bhadohi, Ratin Chand
> and Sons, says candidly,'they don't need advances, we thrust
> it upon them' (Ninan 1983).[3]

The carpet industry has become notorious for its bonded
child labour (Kapoor 1992; Dasgupta 1992; McDonald 1992;
Times of India, 4 August 1992; *Financial Express*, 11 August
1992). Even the Uttar Pradesh Government report on child
weavers admits to the incidence of bonded children (GOUP
1986b: 3).[4]

Prembhai, a social activist who was appointed Commissioner by the Supreme Court to investigate the incidence of
child bonded labour in the carpet industry, found that out of a
sample of 858 children who were interviewed, 414 or 48 per
cent had received small loans from their employers. Eighty-three
per cent of the children had received about Rs 500 which had
been adjusted against wages after a few months (Prembhai
1984: 53). Many of them had in fact worked for more than five
years. Prembhai's interviews established that out of the 858
children from Bihar, 572 or 67 per cent had to do free work
for employers such as grazing the cattle, working in agriculture,

[2] See also Ninan 1984a, b, c; Devi 1984a,b; and Chowdhury 1984a.
[3] See also Das 1985: 3.
[4] See also Chowdhury 1985; Tiwari 1985.

fetching water from the well and other odd jobs over and above the time spent on weaving (ibid.: 62). Prembhai says: 'If they tried to escape or go to another loom owner who promised better payments, they were caught, brought back and punished' (ibid.: 63).

Many children were kidnapped to weave carpets (ibid.: 90; *Down to Earth*, 15 September 1992: 50–1). According to Juyal, about 50 per cent of the hired child labour force, which is two-thirds of the total labour force, has been sold to the loom-holders (Juyal 1987: 30).

Prembhai visited Chhichori village in Palamau district of Bihar which is located twenty kilometres from the district head-quarters, Daltonganj. The children and the parents were inter-viewed in depth. The investigation revealed that:

> . . . in all thirty-two children were taken away from this village in four batches by Shiva Kumar (barber) and his brother Sudama Thakur of the same village. Shiva Kumar Thakur was working with Shri Pannalal, the carpet loom owner of village Belwaria (Mirzapur) and acted as his agent. He lured the children distributing toffees, making promises of showing cinemas, etc. He recruited them for Pannalal and his brother on the false promises that the children will be given food (three meals per day) plus clothes and Rs 10 to 20 per day as wages. Most of them were taken without the consent and knowledge of their parents. Shiva Kumar had warned them not to tell the parents about their going with him to cinema or otherwise (Prembhai 1984: 89–90).

An important fact that came out of this investigation was that at least eleven children were studying in the local school. Parik Ram said that he was promised by Shiva Kumar that every afternoon after 4 o'clock, arrangements would be made for education. He was also told that he would be given three good meals, clothes and Rs 20 a day as wages and that if he were to feel unhappy, he could go back home. Other children — Mogul, Kodu and Virendra — were similarly lured and taken to Belwaria village.

Koiler Bhuian, aged ten, said that he and other children were forced to work from dawn to late at night. Petromax lamps were used for night-work. All the children were locked up at night and when they went out for their morning ablutions in the open field, they were escorted by two persons. Koiler Bhuian said:

> I tried to escape three times but I was caught and severely beaten. My feet and hands were tied together and I was slung onto a jackfruit tree in front of Pannalal's house. I was tied with a rope and repeatedly lifted and thrown on the ground. I was beaten with sticks and shoes and sometimes even with an iron *panja* (the fork used for weaving). Once my thigh was branded with a hot iron rod when I tried to escape and was caught. Four other children were also branded: Shyam Mochi in the armpit, Munni on the hand, Inder Mochi and Vinod on the leg (ibid.: 91).

Seven children were taken in the third batch: Inder Mochi, Rajchani Bhuiya, Vinod Bhuian, Vijai Bhuiya, Nathuni Thakur and Anil were between seven and eleven and Madan looked about fourteen years. These children reported that they were often beaten with a bamboo if there was any fault in weaving, that they were only given one or two *rotis* (whole wheat bread) for food, and were beaten up if they asked for more. Shiv Kumar and Sudama Thakur threatened to set their houses on fire and beat them if they disobeyed. When some of them tried to escape, they were captured and severely beaten (ibid.: 92).

Some of the parents went to the village where these children were working and asked the loom-owner to release their children. But the loom-owners demanded Rs 500 for the release of each child against the cost of food consumed as well as the yarn the children were supposed to have damaged while they were learning. As the parents had no money, they had to return home without the children. Many parents had sold all their possessions in order to be able to purchase a bus ticket to come to get their children back. Many of them found that their children had disappeared and in some cases were later told that the child had died (ibid.: 91–101).

This is not merely the story of thirty-two children but of hundreds and thousands of them, many of them kidnapped or lured away or pledged by their parents for paltry sums of money. Most of them are kept in captivity, tortured and made to work for twenty hours a day without a break. Little children are made to crouch on their toes, from dawn to dusk everyday, severely stunting their growth during formative years. Social activists in the area find it hard to work because of the strong mafia-like control that the carpet loom owners have on the area. Any whisper of an investigation of child weavers means that the children are just whisked away from the area (*Proceedings & Resolution of First National Workshop on Eradication of Child Labour in Carpet Industry* 1991). According to the Anti-Slavery Society, which made a representation to the United Nations Working Group on contemporary forms of slavery in Geneva, there are about 100,000 children employed to work in the carpet industry in conditions of slavery (Puri 1984).

Most of the children working in the carpet industry belong to the Scheduled Castes and Scheduled Tribes and many of them come from the perennially drought-prone areas of Bihar, particularly from districts like Palamau. They are children of landless labourers, many of whom have been deprived of their lands by the landlords of the village. Ironically, in spite of the conditions of semi-slavery in which these children were working, after they were restored to their parents, they returned to work for the same masters. Mahasveta Devi, a social activist, interviewed some parents who had knowingly sent their children to the looms. One person was brutally frank and said: 'We cannot feed our children. What is the use of keeping them with us and seeing them die? Let them earn a living, let them eat' (Devi 1984a: 751).

Glass Industry

I was told by many workers that a large number of children were working as bonded slaves in glass factories. In Chandwar village, just outside Firozabad, there is a *pakai bhatti* (a unit where bangles are baked in layers on metal sheets covered with silica sand). Two little boys work here. One was about twelve years old and the other was eight years. Their job was to arrange bangles on the trays which the *pakaiwala* (the person who places trays of bangles into the furnace and also stokes it) would put into the furnace. The heat was unbearable as the temperature soared to 800° C. These two boys have been left behind by their parents. The older boy was studying in school till a few months prior to my interview. When his father had an accident working on a thresher and lost his arm, the boy was withdrawn from school and brought to Firozabad. His father had taken an advance from the *thekedar* (contractor) and the boy was to pay off the loan from his wages.

The other boy comes from Tundla village in Agra district. His father left his little boy behind for an advance of Rs 500 from the *thekedar*. On being asked whether he had any brothers and sisters, the boy put his head down and started crying. The old man sitting next to him explained that the boy was feeling homesick as his father had just come a few days ago to collect the child's wages and had gone back to the village. These two boys live alone in the *pakai bhatti* unit and cook their food on the silica-covered trays.

Other Industries

Slate Pencil Industry: Cases of bonded labour have also been reported in the slate pencil industry of Mandsaur in the State of Madhya Pradesh where, according to journalist and activist Amiya Rao: '. . . the owners use the same technique as rich landowners do to keep their labour as bonded slaves — they advance them, even force upon them, large sums of money . . . ' (Rao 1980: 1883)[5]

Handloom Industry: Even the 1981 report of the Government-appointed Gurupadaswamy Committee recognized that

[5] See also Singh 1986: 159.

in Kanchipuram in Tamil Nadu, a large number of children in the age-group of seven to fourteen years were working on looms and had been pledged into work on a long-term basis (GOI 1981: 18).[6] Juyal, writing about the Varanasi silk industry, holds that it is a common practice for workers to take advances from the employers and in exchange put children to work (Juyal et al 1985: 84).

Recruited by Contractors

Brass Ware Industry: There are many methods of recruiting children. A very common way is through contractors or middlemen. In the brass ware industry of Moradabad, I was told by village officials that while adults go on their own in search of work, children are recruited by *dalals* (middlemen/brokers), who usually belong to the village and who are paid a commission for bringing child workers. *Thekedars* and workshop owners prefer children because they are easy to control. The middlemen look out for children. Their parents are offered an advance of Rs 100 or the equivalent of a month's wages. If a parent takes an advance, the child has to work whether he likes it or not. If he plays hookey, the wages of other children from the same village are cut: some control is maintained in this way. Parents of the children who belong to the town are induced into sending them to work by the lure of an advance of about Rs 500. This lump sum payment is a big incentive for parents and it is adjusted against a child's wages over a few months.

Pottery Industry: I asked several children working in the pottery industry of Khurja how they came to know that work was available in the potteries. Fazal, a ten-year old boy said:

> *Thekedars* come to the village and say they want children so we know that there is work. Often the *thekedars* don't want to give the work to adults. We are young, we can work fast and we don't get tired so easily (Burra 1987: 23).

Glass Industry: In industries where large numbers of

[6] See also *The Times of India*, 7 September 1981.

workers need to be recruited — sometimes on a daily basis —
a special role is assigned to workers entrusted with the task of
recruitment. Usually a former worker himself, the *jagaiya* (the
person whose responsibility it is to wake up workers on night
shifts. He is also the man who recruits labour for the factory
owner) of the glass industry is on the monthly pay-roll of the
factory-owner and, though he has a status superior to that of
the ordinary worker, he is not really part of the management
structure. The term *jagaiya* means the one who wakes others
up; he came to be so designated when the glass factories
functioned only at night and he had to go around waking up
the workers to report for duty. Today, he visits the local labour
markets in Firozabad to select those lucky ones who will have
work for the day. Familiar with the community, he ensures that
the same workers do not get continuous employment and thus
claim rights; on occasion, he can be bribed by those in dire
need of work (Burra 1988).

Match Industry: In the match industry of Sivakasi, village
contractors are employed and they transport children from their
homes to the factories. The contractors perform multiple functions: they wake up the children in time to board the buses,
they ensure repayment of advances given by match units to
workers and they act as the eyes and ears of the factory owners
to report new arrivals in the village who may have come to
create trouble for the entrepreneurs by organizing the labourers
(MIDS 1985: 59–60).

In the match industry,

> Inquiries showed that the factories engage agents to procure
> child labour. Often money is advanced to children rather than
> their parents — and this keeps them bound to the employer
> (Sarma 1979: 346).[7]

In a study conducted in the Sivakasi match factories in Tamil
Nadu, Kulkarni reported one woman as saying: '. . . the child
in the 'womb' is pledged to the factory, and consumption and

---

[7] See also Menon 1979; *The Indian Worker*, 17 September 1979: 4.

maternity loans are obtained on the undertaking that the child born, girl or boy, would work for the factory!' (Kulkarni 1983: 1855).

BONDED CHILD LABOUR IN AGRICULTURE

Where bonded labour is widely prevalent as in the States of Rajasthan, Uttar Pradesh, Bihar, Orissa and Andhra Pradesh, child bonded labour is an inter-generational phenomenon. The pattern that emerges is that usually a father or grandfather has taken a loan. After slaving for many years, when the man becomes too old to work, his master demands that the young son or sons be sent to replace the father and, around the age of ten, the young child is introduced into the system of bondage. Sadhu and Singh (1980: 42) quoting a National Labour Institute study on bonded labour showed that 21, 10.3 and 8.7 per cent children below fifteen years were bonded in Andhra Pradesh, Karnataka and Tamil Nadu respectively.

Most of the child bonded labourers in the rural areas are sons of bonded labourers. In most cases by having a male member of the family working as a bonded slave, the family becomes impoverished and for survival send younger sons into bondage. As Marla says:

> First, the boy has to tend cattle, and later he has to perform the complicated agricultural operations. As long as he is young and strong, once mortgaged by his family to the landlord, he becomes the private property of the master, a thing with human flesh and blood that can be easily manipulated according to the whims of the landlord's family (Marla 1977: 46-7).

In some areas of India, like Andhra Pradesh, Orissa and Bihar, child bonded labour is widespread. According to a study done in Andhra Pradesh by the Rural Wing of the National Labour Institute, child bonded labour known widely as *Jeeta Gadus* or *Jeeta* (a term used to refer to bonded labourers mainly in South India) was widely prevalent in the villages of Sidipet, Medak

and Gogipet *talukas* (an administrative unit of the district).
These children were tied to moneylenders and local landlords.
In some villages it was found that landlords were using primarily
child labour (NLI Rural Wing 1977: 539).

There are regional variations in the profile of bonded labour.
Thus, according to the National Survey on bonded labour conducted by Marla, in Andhra Pradesh 20 per cent of the bonded
labourers in the state were under the age of fifteen years (Marla
1981: 44). In Orissa children below the age of fifteen years
make up 20.5 per cent of the total bonded labourers in the
State (ibid.: 93). In Rajasthan, 17 per cent of the bonded labourers are twenty years old or younger (ibid.: 104). And in
Tamil Nadu 10.6 per cent of the bonded labourers belong to
the age group of eleven to fifteen years (ibid.: 113). It is only
with respect to Gujarat that it was found that no bonded
labourer identified was younger than twenty years (ibid.: 62).

Children become bonded for the smallest thing. In Bihar,
Ramlakhan Bhuiyan of Ramkanda village borrowed Rs 100 to
buy clothes and has been working since he was the height of
a man's thigh. He was about twenty years when this story
appeared (Mundle 1976: 725). A similar story is that of Ram
Lakhan who sold himself for Rs 10. That was eighteen years
ago when he was hardly five years. His parents had died and
he had nothing to eat or wear. So he asked the village moneylender to lend him Rs 10. The orphaned boy was given the loan
but on condition that the labour of his life belonged exclusively
to the moneylender till he paid his debt (Mundle 1976: 653).

In a study of a Karnataka village, Sudha Rao found that the
jeeta servants who belonged to the peasant, Harijan and ar-
tisanal castes were all under fourteen years and invariably from
families which had incurred debt. According to her, 8 per cent
of the total households in the village had *jeeta* servants (Rao
1984: 769).

A newspaper report documents how tribal children in
Raipur district in the State of Madhya Pradesh are mortgaged
to landlords at the age of seven years. For a sum of about Rs 200
given at the time of marriage, the young man becomes a full-

fledged bonded labourer since he will never be able to repay that sum. In course of time, his children are also mortgaged and the story repeats itself (*Indian Express*, 11 April 1984; *M.P. Chronicle*, 17 April 1984). A more recent report pointed out that there were about 2000 child bonded labourers in the Raipur district of Madhya Pradesh alone (Chanthanom 1989: 4).

It is a characteristic of feudal agrarian relations that families of agricultural labourers are bonded to their masters for several generations. The bonded child labourer is bonded not so much because he is a child as much as because he is a member of a bonded family. Commonly a family takes a loan, is charged interest at usurious rates and provides services to the landlord and his family in order to pay off the debt. The bonded family is hardly paid any wages but is given something in kind for its bare sustenance. When the father is old or dies, the young sons of the family step into their father's shoes and the cycle continues (Murthy et al 1985: 2). One estimate has it that nearly 7.5 million children below the age of fourteen years were in bondage (*The Times of India*, 1 July 1989).

While there are different estimates of child bondage in India, the then Minister of State for Labour announced in 1980 in Parliament that a random sample survey in a hundred villages in ten states estimated that the incidence of bonded labour was 22.4 lakhs (1 lakh = 100,000) and 66 per cent of the bonded labourers belonged to the Scheduled Castes and 18.3 to the Scheduled Tribes (*The Indian Worker*, 29 December 1980: 3). The states of Andhra Pradesh, Bihar, Orissa, Rajasthan and Uttar Pradesh are all known to harbour bonded child labour.

STREET CHILDREN

Street children constitute the third category of children who work for survival, and are largely found in semi-urban and urban metropolitan centres. These children find themselves on the street because they have either run away from their families, or been abandoned or kidnapped. They usually live in public places such as railway stations, bus stops and footpaths and are without the protection of their families. They may be self-employed such as shoeshine boys, newspaper vendors, rag-pickers, hawkers and vendors, or they may work in establishments like *dhabas* (small way-side eating places), as domestic servants and *coolies* (porters), or as casual labourers on construction sites, as helpers in shops, and so on. Not all children who work in urban metropolitan centres fall into the category of street children for there are many children who work as part of family labour, or return to the womb of the family in the evenings. It is estimated that in Delhi, 400,000 children are child workers and 100,000 are street children (UNICEF n.d.: 17). In the city of Hyderabad, it is estimated that there are 30,000 street children (Rao and Malik 1992: 2). A study undertaken by Ghosh in 1992 estimated that there would be between 75,000 to 100,000 street children on the streets of Calcutta (Ghosh 1992: 1). There are an estimated 25,000 street children in the city of Madras (Arimpoor 1992: 8) and in Bangalore city, Nandana Reddy estimates that there are about 45,000 street children of whom 25,000 are homeless (Reddy 1992: 3). It is their aloneness which makes street children particularly vulnerable to the anti-social elements of the city and places them into a special category for purposes of programme and policy (Prasad 1982; Ganguly 1984; Rai 1984; Anklesaria 1984; Mehta 1983; Shukla 1984).

There is very little authentic data about how many such children there are in different places. But the most significant fact about them is their physical separation from their families. In the town of Aligarh in Uttar Pradesh, I had an opportunity to interview a few children in the Children's Observation Home without any adult being present and over a period of a few days. A couple of stories will bring out the plight of such children.

Rasheed and Baheed are two brothers aged thirteen and eight years respectively. They were picked up under Section 3 of the U.P. Children's Act, 1951, which says that any child found alone in a public place can be caught by a policeman and taken in protective custody. Rasheed and Baheed were escaping from

he knows his father will never come for him. It is now some years since he left home. The memory of abject poverty is very vivid on his mind. His memory of his home is very hazy. Raju will remain in custody till he is eighteen or unless he runs away from the Home as many children do.

WORKING CHILDREN

Children who work as part of family labour make up the fourth and last category mentioned. They will be referred to as working children. These children are to be predominantly found in agriculture where they help their parents in a number of ways. Male children in rural areas begin helping parents at five or six years of age and are inducted full-time into agricultural work by the age of nine or so. Grazing cattle, collecting fuel and fodder, farm activity, household chores, looking after younger siblings and, accompanying parents to work-sites elsewhere are some of the tasks they have to perform (Kishwar and Horowitz 1984: 69–103).

A number of working children are also found in home-based work, helping their parents (Kulshreshta and Sharma 1980; Juyal et al 1985; Hasan 1978). Such home-based work could be for a number of industries such as the *agarbatti* (incense sticks) industry spread out in the States of Andhra Pradesh, Madhya Pradesh, Maharashtra and Gujarat (Jhabvala and Sebstadt 1980–1: 29; Krishnakumari 1985), the garment industry in West Bengal (*Shramshakti* 1988: xl), the coir industry in the State of Kerala (Gulati n.d.) and the *beedi* industry in the States of Tamil Nadu, Karnataka, Andhra Pradesh, Gujarat and Maharashtra. It is typical of home-based, piece-rate work that the rate payable to the adult per unit of output is so low that the parents are compelled to put their children to work in order to barely survive (Bhat 1987).

Working children are often to be found amongst migrant families at construction sites, sugar factories, brick-kilns, mines and plantations where circumstances do not permit the parents to leave the children behind in their homes. The children of migrants form a very large percentage of the non-domestic, non-monetary child labour force (Pichholiya 1980: 106; Sud 1985). Malabika Patnaik's study (1979: 674) reveals that 'as many as 80 per cent of the children of migrants are workers. This is four times higher than the rate among the settled population.' Similar accounts are given by Khandekar (1970: 53) and Sebastian (1979: 181–98). Ghanshyam Pardesi (1985) writes that children below the age of fourteen years work in the Udaipur marble mines. This is also the case in Madhya Pradesh where Arindam Sengupta tells us that in the unorganized kilns, quarries and mines, women and children form a majority of the work-force. In the limestone kilns and quarries in and around Katni in north-eastern Madhya Pradesh, 70 to 80 per cent of the workers are women and children. They are engaged in back-breaking work, carving out chunks of stone from the earth, breaking them up and then carrying them in baskets to the edge of the pit. They have to climb about 100 feet (Sengupta 1983: 80–1).

In the plantation sector, the then Minister of State for Labour, Mr J.B. Patnaik, told the Parliament that the proportion of child labour in all the tea plantations had risen from 4.9 per cent to 8.4 per cent (*The Indian Worker*, 31 March 1980: 10). He gave no explanation for this. A more recent study undertaken by Sharit Bhowmik, pointed out that under the Plantation Labour Act, children above the age of twelve years could be legally employed as permanent workers. Acccording to Bhowmik, 'the plantation industry thus enjoys the dubious distinction of being the only industry in the organized sector which legally permits the employment of child labour' (Bhowmik 1992: 2287). Bhowmik quotes from the Tea Board of India statistics according to which, the total number of child labourers were 54,899. The bulk of child labour lies in the plantations of Assam and West Bengal. In Assam there were 42,458 child labourers and in West Bengal there were 10,676 children employed. The tea growing states of South India, on the other hand employed very little child labour. Only 433 children were reported employed in the plantations of south India (ibid.).

Working children are also affected by the rigidity and in-flexibility of the schooling system. The schooling schedule does not allow children to take time off during sowing and harvesting seasons. Nor does it allow children to re-enter the school system at times convenient to them and their families. The subsistence economy of rural India forces poorer households to utilize the labour of their children whether it is for agricultural operations or for household chores, which releases adults for a more directly productive activity (Khatu et al 1983: 69). According to a report on child labour written by Patel and Alagh (n.d.: 17), about 52 per cent of the child workers from rural labour households worked as agricultural labourers. Another study reported that the proportion of child labour in agriculture to the total child labour force in the country has gone up from 80.35 per cent in 1961 to 87 per cent in 1971 (Murthy et al 1985: 15). The major part of the child labour force, therefore, is to be found in the agricultural sector. The figures were calculated from the 1961 and 1971 censuses. Murthy, Ramiah and Sudarshan point out that the capacity for child labour in non-agricultural sectors is very low.

Another sub-group falling into this category is made up of children, particularly girl children, who accompany their mothers working as part-time domestic servants. The vulnerability of the female child to sexual abuse in the setting of the urban slum pressurizes the parents to see that she is never alone.

It is necessary to point out that the categories employed are not water-tight compartments and many children could be classified as belonging to more than one category. For example, the children who work in certain industries like the glass industry of Firozabad and the carpet industry of Mirzapur-Bhadohi in the State of Uttar Pradesh, and the match industry in Sivakasi in the State of Tamil Nadu could be classified under the first category of child labour where children work in factories, workshops and mines. Equally, since some sections of the child population working in these industries have been pledged by their parents against loans taken by them (Kulkarni 1983: 1855;

MIDS 1985: 59–60; Burra 1988), they could also be considered as belonging to a sub-group of bonded child labour. Again, street children who operate in the urban environment without the shelter of their families can also be looked at as children who are working and necessarily a part of the labour force. However, a distinction here must be made: while all street children are part of the labour force, it is not as if all child labourers are street children, for many of the children in the cities live with their parents and work in a variety of contexts; at home and outside it as well. Despite these definitional problems, these categories are useful not only from an analytical point of view but also from the policy perspective. Programmes to deal with their specific disabilities and the contexts in which they are set will vary according to category.

3

Children in the Glass Industry

Vijay Pal, age sixteen or seventeen years: 'I started working at the age of six earning Rs 5 for a six-hour shift. Today I make Rs 19 a day in a twelve-hour shift blowing glass. A blow glass worker can only work for ten years. Working for twelve to fourteen hours a shift means that the life of a worker is shortened by half. By the time a glass blower has reached thirty years of age, he cannot work much. Soon I will not be able to work as a glass blower. If I manage to save money, I'll start a shop; otherwise, when I have children, I will send them to work.'

When I met Vijay Pal in 1986,[1] his scalp had been burnt when another worker carrying molten glass bumped into him. He could not go to work for one month and did not get wages for that period. He borrowed money from his co-workers to pay for medical treatment.

[1] I visited Firozabad in July 1986, to study the glass industry and the conditions of workers there. While the first part deals with the plight of workers in general, the second part addresses itself to child workers in particular. Visits to factories, interviews with factory owners and local government officials and lastly, discussions with some villagers of the area, built up a horrifying picture of the appalling conditions under which children and adults use up their lives in the glass factories of Firozabad. This experience of twentieth-century India does not appear to be significantly different from what industrial workers in nineteenth-century England must have gone through. As we shall see later, some of Marx's observations about the predicament of workers in his time appear to be remarkably apposite

THE ORGANIZATION OF THE GLASS INDUSTRY

Firozabad is a *tehsil* (an administrative unit of the district) in Agra district of Uttar Pradesh (U.P.). It is also the home of the glass bangle and glassware industry, which is a multi-crore business. Out of 289 registered units (of which 133 units are registered as glass-blowing factories), approximately 70 per cent are not in fact working. However, they get their coal quota at controlled rates and sell it at a 100 per cent premium. The Labour Department certifies that on the day of inspection a particular number of workers were working at a particular unit. The Excise Department gives a certificate of production on the basis of which the Director of Industries recommends a coal quota. On record, even the temperature in the furnace is mentioned to prove that the factory was actually working (Chatterji 1986: 12; Pal 1986; and Barse 1986a). People say that the owners of bogus units can earn as much as Rs 10 *lakhs* (Rs 1 *lakh* is equivalent to Rs 100,000) a year through the black-marketing of coal without lifting a finger (Awasthi 1986: 127). Workers cited the example of Som Glass Works where many of them were working. This unit had not functioned for five years but they had been getting a regular coal quota at the controlled rate. Many units which had permanent labourers have shut down their units in order to get rid of their permanent workers. Today, labourers are recruited on a daily basis in the labour markets at Kotla Mohalla and Ghantaghar. They are, therefore, totally at the mercy of the employers.

The black-marketing of coal allows factory owners to keep their units closed and yet make money. Since 1974, the Uttar Pradesh government has stopped the setting up of new industrial units which use coal as their main source of fuel. Bogus units established earlier can then sell their coal quota at a 100 per cent premium to units which are operating. In this way,

---

even in the context of the workers of Firozabad. The visit to Firozabad was part of a year-long initiative by the Indian Social Institute, New Delhi, to prepare a report on child labour.

they are able to earn money without the burden of running a factory.

Another common practice in Firozabad is that units close for part of the year, ostensibly for furnace repairs. Workers, however, have a different story to tell. According to them, a *taarkash* (the man who threads hot glass onto a rolling pin) and a *belanwala* (the man who rotates the rolling pin) make 400–500 *toras* (strings of 312 bangles) in one shift which goes on for at least twelve hours. (Officially, there are supposed to be three, eight-hour shifts). However, for purposes of tax, they show that only 200 *toras* are made. The profits made on the side allow the factory owners to shut down the factories for part of the year while they live off their illegal profits and their coal quotas (Pal 1986). This is also true of glassware production. Now that there is no excise verification on goods produced, the amount of black money made is even more and the effect on labour is obvious. The sum total of it all is that since factories remain closed for much of the time, where there should be a shortage of labour, there is in fact a surplus of labour.

Factory owners and government officials deny that there is any exploitation of workers in the glass industry. According to them: 'How can there be exploitation if workers come willingly to work?' Yet many factory owners admit that they have dispensed with their permanent staff. According to the proprietor of the Saraswati Glass Works, till 1965 they had only permanent workers. They were entitled to only three days leave with pay in a year. But in 1980–1, the rules changed and permanent workers were entitled to fourteen days leave with pay. It was therefore decided to do away with all permanent staff. In 1986, he gave forty workers about Rs 2.75 lakhs and asked them to leave. Talking about the advantages of daily wage workers, he said quite candidly: 'the temporary worker knows he can be removed. It is easier then to get work out of him.'

This was amply substantiated by what workers had to say. A *taarkash* said:

Everyone says that a *taarkash* gets Rs 150 a shift and a

belanwala gets Rs 80 for working in one shift. But no one ever asks how many days in a week we get to work. In peak season, a *taarkash* or a *belanwala* gets work for three days a week and never for more than four or five months in the year.

A *jagaiya* explained his helplessness and pointed out that he could not bring the same man for more than seven days to the factory. If he did so because he felt that the man needed the money, he would be in danger of losing his own job. In the same way, if the factory owner feels that a particular worker is indulging in *netagiri* (politicking) or *unionbaji* (unionizing), then the *jagaiya* has no choice but to abide by the wishes of the factory owner and not to recruit the man, however unfair the decision might be.

When work is scarce, workers are prepared to work on any terms. As one *belanwala* pointed out:

> I have been unemployed for two weeks. I finally went to the *jagai* and told him that I would give a percentage of my wages to him.

It was settled that the *jagaiya* would get Rs 80 from the factory but pay him only Rs 65. This apparently is the order of the day.

The local mafia (thugs and goons hired by factory owners) not only prevents labour trouble in Firozabad but also prevents highly skilled labourers from moving away from their factories. For example, if a man has mastered the art of blowing a particular type of fine glass for which the factory owner has got a big order, then it is virtually impossible for that worker to leave. It goes without saying that if the worker leaves, the order is lost. Many big companies like Air India, Oberois, ITDC (India Tourism Development Corporation) and Nestles order their glassware from Firozabad. It is not unknown for a worker to be killed if he threatens to take business away. Thus while thugs prevent highly skilled workers from taking business away, they also ensure that other workers do not create union trouble and do not insist upon their rights to minimum wages and better conditions of work. In Firozabad, workers are subject to severe exploitation and their circumstances are akin to those of the labourers of nineteenth-century England. They have no choice but to work twelve to fourteen hours a day. If they refuse, there are always unemployed people waiting to take over their jobs.

DANGEROUS WORKING CONDITIONS

Workers in the glass industry are intimidated for a variety of reasons. One important reason why factory owners need a mafia is to hush up the many industrial accidents that take place because the working conditions are notably unsafe. The industry is technologically very primitive and the pressure on the workers is tremendous. There are two types of furnaces used — the pot furnaces for making only bangles and the tank furnaces which make a variety of glassware as well as bangles. The pot furnace unit is smaller and can run only twelve hours and therefore there is only one shift. The temperature in these furnaces ranges between 700°–800° C. The tank furnace units are much bigger and the temperature goes upto 1800° C. In the summer months, the temperature is so high that only the most tenacious workers can manage to work in the excruciating heat. Combined with this heat, in factories where glasses are made in presses, the noise is deafening. The heat, noise and dust obviously have serious ill effects on the health of workers (Chatterji 1986; Barse 1986 b, c). The net effect is that tuberculosis (TB) is widespread and the life of a worker is cut short by ten to fifteen years. But since there is no dearth of labour, to the factory owner it makes no difference what happens to the worker.

Marx pointed out that this was a result of the demands of capitalism which puts a tremendous pressure on the worker and which consequently leads to ' . . . generations of stunted, short-lived and rapidly replaced human beings, plucked, so to speak, before they were ripe' (Marx [1867] 1982: 380). Writing about the over-worked labourer in 1833, he observed that they 'die off with strange rapidity; but the places of those who perish are instantly filled, and a frequent change of persons makes no alteration in the scene' (ibid.). This is also the case with glass workers in Firozabad. At a *pakai bhatti* (a unit where bangles are baked in layers on metal sheets covered with silica sand) in village Chandwar, a worker had fainted due to heat exhaustion. This worker is a *pakaiwala* (the person who places trays of bangles into the furnace and also stokes it) and is thirty-six years old. The heat in the *pakai bhatti* is unbearable and it was not possible to stand even ten feet away from the furnace. This man started working at the age of eight and this summer he has fainted three times due to dehydration. He told me that he has only one more month of working life left in him. If he faints once more, he will tell the *thekedar* (contractor) to find another *pakaiwala* to replace him. According to this *pakaiwala*, there is an unwritten rule that a worker, when he is about to collapse, warns the *thekedar*.

No factory owner wants a labourer to die on the premises as there would be an inquiry and compensation would have to be paid. Workers said that in summer 200–400 glucose drips were given daily to workers who faint with dehydration and heat exhaustion. Private practice is flourishing in Firozabad where there are almost 200,000 workers employed. Each glucose drip costs Rs 65. Depending on how urgently the work needs to be done and how indispensable the worker is, the factory owner pays for the treatment. Otherwise, the worker borrows from others. The greatest fear of a worker is to collapse with heat exhaustion. He not only loses his day's wages but also has to borrow for expensive treatment (Pal 1986). Factory owners, however, deny that serious industrial accidents take place. The proprietor of one of the biggest glass factories in Firozabad, in fact said that except for the occasional case of heat exhaustion, workers did not suffer from any adverse effect of intense heat. In his factory, cut *nimbu* (lemon) is freely available to workers if they feel the heat very acutely, he proudly added.

A noticeable feature in many factories is that workers in fact display few visible injuries and burn marks. The workers' explanation for this state of affairs is that factory owners do not employ anybody other than a very healthy person. They not only cannot afford to have a death on their premises but the work involved is so strenuous and the conditions so appalling that only the healthiest survive. A *mutha uthanewala* (the man who removes the spring of hot bangles from the rolling pin) said that factory owners and the supervisor decide how much a man can make in a day. If a worker produces less than the required quantity, he is dismissed without wages or with only half the wages. Since there are always plenty of desperate people who are unemployed, the *jagai* looks around for somebody in very good health.

Glass bangles are being made illegally in tank furnaces since 1982 because the capacity of tank furnaces is greater and they run round the clock. Owners of tank furnaces openly make glass bangles because there is no excise duty on them. These bangles are of slightly inferior quality as the colour is put on them after the molten glass comes out of the tank furnace. These factories also make laboratory equipment, bulbs, chimneys, glassware, etc. Out of sixty glass manufacturing units, only twenty-one units are registered for purposes of excise. From the 1986-7 budget onwards, production verification has stopped. Whatever the factory owners declare as their production is accepted for purpose of Central excise. In 1985-6, the excise revenue was to the tune of Rs one crore. In 1986-7 the estimated revenue was supposed to be not more than Rs 15 *lakhs*. On record the production of glassware has gone down by a third. There is absolutely no control now on what the factory makes and sells. 30 to 40 per cent of the total production of a tank furnace unit is in making bangles where the profit is as high as 50-60 per cent.

The story of Firozabad is one of power, corruption, blackmail and exploitation. The inhuman conditions of work take their toll upon the health of workers. A man by the time he is thirty-five years old is almost finished and has to rely upon his children to save him from starvation and imminent death. There are almost 50,000 children below the age of fourteen years working in the glass industry making it one of the highest concentration of child labour in the world. If a person starts working at the age of eight or nine, he is burnt out by the time he is thirty-five. Poverty and ill-health force him to use his children and the vicious cycle continues inexorably.

In these conditions, what is the future of the workers of Firozabad? Is there any hope that this vicious cycle will ever be broken? Workers in the glass industry have some suggestions which they feel will go a long way in improving their lives. They want that the Government of India institute a high-level investigation into the black marketing of coal. If the government was able to stop the coal allotment to bogus units which have closed down on the pretext of seasonal repairs, it would force factory owners currently living off black money to reactivate their factories. If all the registered units were actually working, there would be no shortage of work and the factory owners would not be able to exploit the workers so easily. If there is full employment, the economic condition of workers will automatically improve.

PLIGHT OF CHILD WORKERS

The plight of child workers is indeed painful. As mentioned earlier, the two boys working in the glass industry were both left behind by their parents to pay off loans. They were lonely, homesick and had to live by themselves at the *pakai bhatti*, cook their food on silica covered trays and work near furnaces whose temperatures went up to 800° C. The older boy was studying in school till a few months back, when his father had an accident working on a thresher and lost his arm and the boy was withdrawn from school and brought to Firozabad. His father had taken an advance from the *thekedar* and the boy was to pay off the loan from his wages.

The other boy comes from Tundla village in Agra district. His father also took an advance of Rs 500 from the *thekedar* and left his little boy behind. On being asked whether he had any brothers and sisters, the boy put his head down and began to cry. An old man sitting next to him explained that the boy was feeling homesick as his father had just come a few days previously to collect his wages and had gone back to the village without him.

Interviews with workers, factory owners and the local MLA revealed that there are almost 50,000 children below the age of fourteen years working in the glass industry at Firozabad: the total labour force is estimated at 200,000.

A visit to any glass unit shows at a glance that at least 25 per cent of the workers present are children. The official figures reported by the Labour Department estimate that there are 65,000–70,000 workers and that children constitute only 13 per cent of the total labour force. Official figures are considerably lower than what was reported in the field. Firozabad would then appear to have one of the largest concentrations of child labour in India.

PARTICIPATION OF CHILDREN IN THE WORKFORCE

Child labour is a touchy issue in the glass industry because of government's recent interest in the subject. In fact, according to factory owners and government officials, children are employed only to serve water to adult workers. But when faced with the facts, they present a complete *volte-face* and plead the case for the poor thus:

> What can we do when fathers bring their children to us and beg us to employ them? If we did not help out, these poor people would starve.

While factory owners make out that they are in fact helping the poor to survive by employing their children, the arithmetic of glass manufacture tells a different tale. Child labour is so important for the glass industry that if factory owners did not employ children, their production would go down by 25 per cent. The owner of a big glass factory went to the extent of saying that 'the glass industry cannot function without children. They run much faster than adults and therefore production goes up.'

Children perform a variety of jobs in the glass industry. Their work is not very different from that of children in nineteenth-century England. A tour of four of the largest glass-blowing units and one glass bangle unit (where only bangles are made) showed that children are involved in almost all the processes of bangle-making and glass-blowing and many of these processes are extremely hazardous for them.

Ashok, an eleven year-old glass factory worker, was interviewed by film maker Meera Dewan. He describes his first day at work when he did three shifts. He was new to the job and therefore made a small mistake and was beaten up for it.

> I was so tired, I didn't do the work correctly, I made a mistake. This man next to me, he gave me a slap . . . it was such a hard slap that I couldn't ever forget the work now! (*Target* 1986: 54).

Children do all manner of jobs in glass factories. They were seen carrying molten glass on a seven-foot iron rod called *labya* from the furnace to the adult worker and back to the furnace. Nearly 85 per cent of the total child labour force was engaged in this activity and these are Labour Department figures.

Children sit in front of furnaces where the temperature is said to be about 700° C. In many of the factories where the children were drawing molten glass from tank furnaces in which the temperature was between 1500° C and 1800° C, the face of the child was within six to eight inches from the opening of the furnace. Since he was small in size, he had to put his arm right inside in order to draw adequate quantities of molten glass. As a result, his body was almost touching the furnace.

Most visitors to Firozabad are taken on a conducted tour of some so-called model factories such as Advance Glass Works and Om Glass Works, who are makers of high-quality glassware for companies such as Air India. In these factories, child labour exists as well but one does not notice children so much because they are relatively spacious; after the factory owners have told the visitor their human interest stories of poverty and child labour, one can actually leave the factory premises believing that factory owners are in fact doing the poor a good turn by employing their children. If however, one manages to visit factories other than the ones highly recommended, the conditions are well and truly horrifying.

One such factory is the General Traders (GT) Glass Works where the bulk of the glassware is made in automatic presses. Like other factories, they also make bangles and blow glassware. It is frightening to enter this factory where obviously labour inspections have never taken place. The whole factory floor was strewn with broken glass and naked electric wires were to be seen everywhere. The noise in the factory was deafening and there was hardly any space to move without bumping into somebody or other. At least 30–40 per cent of the labour force in this factory seemed to be made up of children of the ages of eight to thirteen years (Barse 1986 a, b, c). They were carrying glasses made in presses on forks to the conveyor belt. They were sitting in front of small furnaces re-heating the *loam* (molten glass) on which colour had been applied. But mainly, they were engaged in carrying *loam* on *labyas* (the seven-foot iron rod used for carrying molten glass). There were children sitting on the ground in front of blow glass workers, closing the mould after the molten glass was put into it. Their job seemed to be to line the mould with paper and close it after the blow glass worker had put the blown glass into it. As soon as the child closed the mould, even before he had time to remove his hands, the mould would catch fire because of the paper inside it. The whole process takes a few seconds from the time the worker brings the molten glass on a *labya* to the glass blower and the blown glass is put into the mould. After that, children carry the product to another worker who cuts it and then it is taken away for further heating. While I was watching the children at work, about ten to fifteen young workers, including several children ran past me in a passage about three feet wide carrying molten glass. One worker bumped into another and part of the molten glass from his *labya* fell one inch away from my foot. There was no place to move because behind me were some loose wires and across this narrow passage, other children were sitting on the ground with their backs to the passage in front of small furnaces, re-heating the *loam*. If the molten glass (the temperature of which I was told was nearly 1200˚ C) had not fallen near my foot, it would have fallen on a child's back. Under these working conditions, it is not surprising that industrial accidents are frequent though government officials and factory owners deny it. People even went to the extent of saying that fatal and near-fatal accident victims are thrown into the furnaces to destroy evidence (Barse 1986 a, b, c).

Children are undoubtedly the most common victims of such industrial accidents because their bodies cannot take the trauma of such accidents easily. The interesting thing was that in spite of frequent burn injuries and accidents, I did not see any obviously injured worker in the factories. The reason for this was clear after a visit to neighbouring villages and conversations with workers.

Sriram, about nine years old, and a *thandibatiwala* (the person who carries the molten glass after it is beaten into shape, back to the furnace) could not open his left eye which was very sore. A piece of hot glass flew into his eyes. He was being looked after by co-workers as his parents had left him there.

Grace, aged sixteen years, was wounded when he took the spring of glass bangles to show the supervisors. The man tried to break a piece by hitting it. Part of this flew into Grace's face and when I interviewed him, his face looked as if a hive of bees had attacked him.

While workers, including child workers, are paid on a time-rate basis in the bigger factories, in the smaller units where bangles are joined in a process called *judai* (to join), all workers are paid on a piece-rate basis. In most of these units, particularly the *katai addas* (unregistered units where designs are cut on bangles), children can be seen everywhere. The bangles are brought by the *thekedar* who has a unit in or near his house.

He engages the labour and pays them according to the intricacy of the design. Breakage of bangles while cutting the design is adjusted against the wages of the workers. As it happens, children often end up by losing a whole day's earnings for breaking bangles accidentally. It takes a while before a child starts earning a reasonable wage.

The *judai addas* (unregistered small units where bangles are joined over acetylene flames), also have a very large number of child workers. At one *adda* (unregistered workshop), out of twenty workers, at least three or four were very small children who were not quite eight. The room was so dark that only their eyes could be seen staring out of the inky blackness. It was lunch-time and the acetylene lamps had been switched off. The room was full of soot and there was no ventilation as the acetylene flames could be extinguished by the breeze. The workers in this unit came from Hallapur village, which is about four kilometres from Firozabad town, on bicycles. The workers said that 50–60 per cent of this work was done by children and this led to tremendous eye-strain as the worker sat in front of the flames working continuously for twelve hours without removing his eyes from the flame. Many workers said that the high incidence of tuberculosis (T.B.) amongst *judai* workers was a result of inhaling kerosene fumes (Pal 1986; Champaka-lakshmi n.d: 12).

Minimum Wages

Surprisingly, there are no minimum wages fixed for the glass bangle workers. Minimum wages were first introduced in 1974 for glass bangle and blow glass workers. In 1981, a revision of wages took place by a government order. In 1982, a high-powered tripartite committee met and another government order was issued for revision of wages only for the bangle industry. The tripartite committee of labour leaders, union members, employers and government officials fixed the minimum wages and a government order (GO No. 4560 (ST) O/36-1-637/ST/81 Lucknow dated November 12, 1982) was passed.

However, after the 1981 government order, the Glass Industrial Syndicate, Firozabad, filed a writ petition in the Allahabad High Court against minimum wages for bangle workers. It is said that the High Court slapped a contempt of court order on the UP Labour Secretary for insisting upon minimum wages for glass bangle workers. The state government withdrew the GO of 1982 by GO No. 4195-36-3-55, dated 25-11-1983.

THE LABOUR DEPARTMENT AND ITS VIEWS ON CHILD LABOUR

Child labour is an indispensable part of the glass bangle and glass-blowing industry of Firozabad because it is cheap (Chatterji 1986: 10; Barse 1986 a,b,c). The Labour Department at Firozabad has recommended to the higher authorities that child labour should not be banned because unless a child starts working at a very young age, he will not get acclimatized to the intense heat. They have even suggested that hostels be constructed where children who have to work on the night shift can stay. The argument is that children, who have to work at night because factories have to run at night, cannot walk back to the village at that hour and therefore they must have a place to stay. Since the glass industry cannot function without children and they have to run at night because otherwise factory owners will face losses through the heat in the furnaces going waste, children must work at night.

Night-work for children is forbidden under the Factories Act (63 of 1948) which, under Section 70, prohibits the employment even of adolescents below the age of seventeen years. But night-work continues and children as young as seven and eight years work in the night shift. Factory owners today are not as honest as their counterparts in England in the nineteenth-century who admitted that:

> Great difficulty would be caused by preventing boys under eighteen from working at night. The chief would be the increase of cost from employing men instead of boys (Marx [1867] 1982: 372)

In fact, this is the main reason why children are employed in the glass industry. Marx sarcastically explains the rationale for exploiting children by factory owners. He said that factory owners were not interested in discontinuing night-work because in industries which use furnaces, not only is there a loss from machinery lying idle but there would be a waste of fuel as well. The argument in favour of night-work was also that otherwise, time would be lost in heating up the furnaces and the furnaces themselves would suffer from changes in temperature.

CHILD LABOUR BUT ADULT UNEMPLOYMENT

In India today, child labour is being justified on the grounds of poverty. If the children of the poor do not work they will starve, it is argued. Another common argument is that poor children should work; otherwise, it is asserted, they will become vagabonds and anti-social elements. These young persons need to be harnessed for productive work. But a fact that is not being recognized is that child labour cannot be justified in a country where there is rampant adult unemployment and under-employment. Ashok (referred to earlier) has an unemployed father. This man told Meera Dewan that he gets up at 4 a.m. to make morning tea for Ashok so that the boy can go to work. He feels bad about making his son go to work, so he helps out in his small way by making the morning tea and bringing Ashok's lunch to the factory (*Target* 1986: 53).

Ashok describes his working day thus:

> I pass on the iron rods with the melted glass on it to the blower, come back for a bite, and then go and give the next one (ibid.).

Marx's explanation for why glass manufacturers do not give regular meal-times to children is that it would be time lost or 'wasted' (Marx [1867] 1982: 374). Describing the lives of child labourers in the glass industry in England in 1865, he remarks:

> A certain amount of heat beyond what is usual at present

might also be going to waste, if meal-times were secured in these cases, but it seems likely not equal in money-value to the waste of animal power now going on in glass-houses throughout the kingdom from growing boys not having enough quiet time to eat their meals at ease, with a little rest afterwards for digestion (ibid.).

The exploitation of children in the glass industry is to be seen to be believed. Ashok's story is the story of every other boy in Firozabad, some of them even younger than Ashok.

. . . I leave the house at four in the morning, after having some breakfast. Then it takes an hour to reach the factory site. I go from one to another, to find out where they need a person to carry the hot iron rods. Sometimes, I sit in one factory waiting for the work. If I get it, that's fine. If not I have to go home without the work and money (*Target* 1986: 53–4).

Child labour is to be found everywhere in the glass factories and although children are engaged in the most dangerous of jobs described earlier, the Labour Department of the State Government in their recent report said that:

Compared to national standards, the above rates per thousand worker population are not alarming. Glass work is known to be less dangerous as compared to chemical works, power generation and basic metal industry (GOUP 1986 a: 6).

The Labour Department Committee was headed by the Deputy Labour Commissioner, Agra and the Assistant Director of Factories (Medical). The Committee, during the course of its inspection, found that:

Children as young as ten years of age were working but the processes in which they were engaged did not call for excessive strength or activity.

Labour laws are openly flouted in Firozabad with the complete connivance of the local bureaucracy. The Labour Committee Report of April, 1986, admits that while children under the age of fourteen years are prohibited from working under the Factories Act, yet they found that all the glass-blowing and glass bangle-making factories were employing children. Knowing that this was the case, when 125 factory inspections had taken place up to April 1986, only twelve employers had been prosecuted for violation of Section 67 of the Factories Act, which says that 'no child who has not completed his fourteenth year shall be required or allowed to work in any factory.'

Owners of glass factories are aware that children cannot be employed under the Factories Act. This is why when government teams come to inspect factories, children just disappear. This is what happened when the Labour Department Committee went on its inspection tours. According to its report, Shankar Novelties Glass Industries had violated Section 67; Emkay Glass Works had only four children working because most of the children were removed from the premises as soon as the management came to know about the visit of the Committee in a neighbouring factory. This was also the case with the Om Glass Works from where most of the children had been removed before the Committee visited the factory. In the Refugee Glass Works and in Ashok Glass Works, illegal child labour was found.

When every single glass factory in Firozabad employs children illegally, it is quite obvious from the figures given by the Committee on the number of prosecutions launched under Section 67 of the Factories Act that they have only touched the tip of the iceberg. Instead of condemning child labour and prosecuting employers of child labour, the Labour Department justifies child labour on the grounds that:

1. Child labour exists because of poverty.
2. The children of the poor are not interested in conventional education.
3. This is a hereditary occupation.
4. Children need to work at an early age to get acclimatized to the intense heat.
5. Most of the work that children do is non-hazardous.

It is undoubtedly true that the children in the glass factories of Firozabad — like children elsewhere in India — work because their families are poor. But the argument that child labour is therefore necessary must be rejected. To blandly blame the abstract notion of poverty is to ignore the particular economic and social circumstances that contribute to the persistence of child labour. Once these circumstances are analysed and understood, the possibility of changing them now arises rather than wait for that distant day when there is no more poverty. It is here that the exploitation of the worker by the glass factories of Firozabad must be viewed as a means of ensuring the privileged position of factory owners. The obnoxious conditions of work shorten the productive life of the worker forcing him then to depend upon the labour of his children. During his productive period, since he gets employment for only a few days in a week and for not more than four or five months in the year, he cannot afford to educate his children; his children, then, are denied the option of breaking away from the rigours of their lives. For small sums of money, parents pledge their children to life-times of bondage. The area MLA and others contended that 90 per cent of the children are bonded slaves.

In the absence of alternative employment opportunities, the workers are dependent for their livelihood on the glass manufacturers. With low and uncertain wages, it is difficult for them to feed their children; the option of sending their children to school is simply not real (Burra 1986 b, c). Not surprisingly, illiteracy is widespread amongst these children. Nevertheless, there are a few examples of parents who have put their all into educating their children despite their desperate economic straits. Said a worker in response to a question as to whether he would train his child in his avocation:

> My life is virtually over at thirty-six. Do you think I want my son to suffer like this? If I can somehow see him through school, I'll try and keep him out of this industry. I don't want my son to die at the age of forty years which is bound to happen to someone working twelve to fourteen hours a day

in this intense heat. But I know that I cannot work beyond another month; then how will I pay for his school clothes? If he doesn't have proper clothes, the teacher will not let him enter the class-room. Sooner or later, circumstances will force me to put him to work.

To justify child labour on the grounds that the children need to be acclimatized to the intense heat is only a reflection of our inhuman society which can even make such a suggestion. It has perhaps not even occurred to the Labour Department that such intense heat can in fact have very adverse effects upon the health of the child. Or does the department believe that with growing numbers, the children of the poor are an expendable commodity? And if this is the attitude of the bureaucracy to the plight of working children, then obviously for them the work that children do is in fact non-hazardous.

The premise of the Child Labour (Prohibition and Regulation) Act, 1986, is that there can be no doing away with child labour as it is a consequence of poverty. Such an attitude does not bode well either for the families who are poor or their children who labour. Both Article 24 of the Constitution and Section 67 of the Factories Act explicitly direct that children below the age of fourteen years are not to work in factories. Article 24 forbids the employment of children in hazardous occupations. Yet the Act does not make the glass industry out-of-bounds for children.

The Ministry of Labour has set up a Child Labour Technical Advisory Committee to draw a line between hazardous and non-hazardous processes in hazardous industries: children will be banned from working in the former and allowed to work in the latter. Any attempt to carve out an area of non-hazardous processes in a hazardous industry is fraught with risk for children. This writer believes there can be no non-hazardous process in a hazardous industry. To illustrate, children in the glass factories are always exposed to hot, flying pieces of glass, whatever particular activity they are engaged in. Also, once children are allowed to work in a hazardous industry, who is to police the factory and ensure that they are doing only safe jobs? The answer cannot be a bureaucracy that is corrupt and amenable to power and influence; even assuming it to be conscientious, which bureaucracy can monitor what 50,000 children in the glass industry are doing? More fundamentally, the Committee will not even be able to find children when it visits such factories for they are whisked away whenever an inspection team is around.

What is the future of the children of Firozabad?[2] They do not have much of a past, steeped as they are in poverty, malnutrition and illiteracy. Their future depends in large part, on governmental response. Today, the prospects for these children are not at all bright. They can look forward to lives very similar to that of their parents, trapped in a web not of their own making. Can we not implement the Constitution of India and provide conditions for universal primary education? Why should the State be so chary and coy in dealing with the vested interests of Firozabad?

---

[2] When it was discovered that children were working under very adverse conditions in the glass industry, the U.P. Labour Department, instead of banning child labour, made it mandatory for glass factory owners to make payments to child workers through the post-office savings bank. Under the Department's new regulations, glass factory owners will have to provide midday-meals to child workers. The meals are to be financed by the department. Needless to say that this is a gross violation of the Factories Act, being aided and abetted by the Labour Department itself! (See *Indian Express*, 18 January 1987)

4

Child Labour in the Lock Industry of Aligarh

INTERVIEWS WITH A DOCTOR IN ALIGARH

T *he patients were all workers in the lock industry em-*
ployed in paint workshops, polishing or electroplating
units. They complained of continuous coughs, blood in their
sputum and a feeling that their heads were about to burst.
The compounder was making up packets of multi-vitamin
tablets.

The doctor was very matter of fact when I asked him
why he was prescribing only multi-vitamins when the com-
plaints seemed so serious. His reply was: 'Most of these
people are already too far gone. You can't do anything to
save them. At least this medicine gives them a feeling that
they are being treated. The multi-vitamin capsule looks like
a strong medicine. It makes them feel good. When they reach
the last stages, I give them cortisone. But death is only a
matter of time.'

'How can you be so callous?' I asked.

He replied, 'It's not a question of being callous, but one
of being practical. How can you tell a lock-maker to stop
working if he wants to live? That is his whole life. There are
no other opportunities in Aligarh. The entire population is
dependent on lock making.'[1]

[1] The lock industry of Aligarh is over a hundred years old and is considered
to be the traditional occupation of the people of Aligarh district, in the State
of Uttar Pradesh. It is concentrated, however, in Aligarh city and its adjoining
areas.

ALIGARH CITY: THE BACKGROUND

Aligarh city is divided into two clear-cut halves by a railway line, which divides the city north/south. In the northern part

---

There are between 80,000–90,000 workers involved either directly or indirectly in the lock industry. Of the total workers, approximately 7000–10,000 are children below the age of fourteen years. However, these are only estimates and no one is sure of the actual figures. According to the factory owners and government officials, there are only 5000 children working out of 55,000 workers, comprising 9 per cent of the total labour force. The actual numbers are, however, much larger (Burra 1987a).

Field-work

During field-work I visited about fifty polishing units, fifty electroplating units, twenty painting units as well as thirty homes where either filing or assembling or packing was being done. I was able to visit ten factories in the industrial area and meet scores of workers who were working at home in the city and in the outlying villages. The villages I went to were Bhambola, Jaffarabad and Barola in Aligarh *tehsil*; however, these visits were not very useful as children were not engaged in hazardous work there. I also visited the inner city a couple of times between 8 p.m. and 11.30 p.m. to see whether children were working at night. I spent twenty-one days in the field on three separate occasions out of the project period of three months.

The Research Assistant, who was employed for a month, had two helpers to assist him. He was assigned the job of listing the number of units and assessing the number of child, adolescent and adult workers in each unit in thirty *mohallas* (localities) of the Upper Kote area, which boasts the highest concentration of the most hazardous processes in the lock industry. He went only to those units that were visible from the street but did not attempt to interview the employers or employees both for lack of time and because he did not want to arouse suspicion. In these thirty *mohallas*, he saw 683 units where the processes of electroplating, spray painting and polishing were being carried out. Apart from these processes, he also observed that the jobs of operating hand-presses, assembling and making keys were being performed in many of these units.

According to the information collected by the Research Assistant, out of 6936 workers in the 683 units visited, there were 2475 children below the age of fourteen years, accounting for 35.68 per cent of the total work force in the sample. Children accounted for more than 50 per cent of all workers only in two areas, Qazi Para and Tan Tan Para, out of the thirty *mohallas* studied. The data collected indicate the size of the problem even though formal sampling techniques were not employed.

of the city is the Civil Lines and in the southern portion, the old city. These two portions of the city display a striking contrast where the overspill from the old city, population growth and urban development have resulted in the formation of two distinct cultures and patterns of settlement.

The old city is the ecological centre of Aligarh. This has the tightly knit core of the central business district and fans out towards the eastern-southern suburbs. Most of the Muslim majority *mohallas* (residential localities), which house both businesses and homes, are located in the centre and are surrounded by Hindu localities. This area is communally sensitive because the residential areas are populated by Muslims but trading and commercial activities are in the hands of the Hindus. It is in this area, as also in the Jama Masjid and the major shopping centre of Upper Kote, that several small and medium-scale lock-making household industries are located. There is almost no contact between the two areas of the city, the civil lines and the old city.

According to a study on communal violence and its impact on development and national integration conducted by the Centre for Research in Rural and Industrial Development (CRRID), in Aligarh district of about 1575 registered manufacturing units, it was found that only 7 per cent of the manufacturers were Muslims. And of these 7 per cent, about a fourth of them were involved in the lock-making industry (CRRID n.d.: 28). Thus, a very large proportion of industries and manufacturing units in Aligarh are owned by Hindus.

This study also made the significant point that Muslim-majority *mohallas* have fewer educational facilities and the drop-out rate and non-attendance rate of Muslim children were much higher than those of children belonging to other religious communities. 'Around 80 per cent of the Muslim school children either drop-out or fall in the category of non-attendance' (ibid.: 29; IDS n.d.: 23).

Most of the traditional lock-makers — both Hindu and Muslim — are engaged in this work for part of the year as agriculture alone cannot support them. Since most producers are depend-

ent upon others for supply of components, there is a great deal
of inter-dependence amongst the castes/communities as certain
processes are the exclusive or near-exclusive preserve of certain
castes/communities. Thus, the Kohlis (a Scheduled Caste community) are mainly involved in casting activities. Muslims are
more or less exclusively doing polishing work and in the intermediate stage, like the manufacturing of levers, are involved
with the making of keys. The assembling of the final products
is done by Muslim Safis, Mathur Brahmins and Jatavs. The
suppliers are mainly Hindu Banias (Varshneys). The relationship
between the traders and the direct producer of locks is that of
superordination and subordination (CRRID: 47). With the coming in of merchant capital, the position of the direct producer
has been worsened. His working day has been lengthened and
his earning power reduced substantially (ibid.). With the influx
of outside capital into the lock industry, there have been structural changes in the industry which have brought about a shift
from the household to the factory system, especially in the
mode of producing locks (ibid.: 52).

The big lock industry, owned by Hindus, is located in the
outskirts of the city, while the smaller units, owned by Muslims,
are in the interior. While most of the manufacturing units are
owned by Hindus, the labourers are either Muslims or Scheduled Castes leading to tension between them for scarce jobs.

THE LOCK INDUSTRY: A HISTORICAL BACKGROUND

The lock industry of Aligarh was started in 1860 by the Postal
Department. In the early years, the making of locks was a village
industry and locks or components of locks were made by the
artisan in his home, with the help of his family labour. Many
families, who found it difficult to support themselves only by
agriculture, started making locks. There were also many castes
like the Maithili Brahmins and others, whose lands were
usurped by the Thakurs and big landlords of the area, who then
also joined the lock industry. Most of the padlocks were made
in the surrounding villages. As the demand for locks increased,

the lock-makers found it difficult to commute and many families sold their lands and shifted to the city. But these were essentially small village craftsmen.

After the Partition of India in 1947, there was a sudden shift in the social composition of lock-makers. Many of the traditional lock-makers in Aligarh city were Muslims who went away to Pakistan leaving a void. They were the real craftsmen and for a while there was a slump in the lock industry. While Muslim artisans or master-craftsmen who were the backbone of the lock industry went to Pakistan, there was a migration of Punjabi Hindus to Aligarh. These families were not engaged in lock-making traditionally. But realizing that the lock industry was a profitable venture, they set up small units by hiring labour and this led to the mass production of locks.

Thus, whereas the village craftsman or lock-maker was able to provide for the needs of fewer people, once the industrialist stepped in, locks began to be manufactured on the factory scale by people whose main contribution was their capital. The demand for locks has increased tremendously and the lock industry is seen as one with a very good future.

But inspite of mass-production of locks in factories, the village craftsman has not been wholly displaced. Locks are still being made in the adjoining villages of Pilakhana, Atrauli and Barola. The village artisan brings a model to the financier or well-known lock trader, gets his order, buys the raw material and components, finishes the product and gives it to the trader who then puts a brand name on it such as Parker, Plaza and so on. But the bulk production of locks is done by financiers and lock manufacturers in the big factories.

THE LOCK INDUSTRY TODAY

According to A.L. Anand, in 1982 there were about 3000 units both in the organized and the unorganized sector, manufacturing, assembling locks and their components. There were only five or six units in the large sector; the rest were in the small-scale sector. Out of the total units in the small-scale sector, about 150 units were registered and the remaining units were run by artisans as household and cottage industry (Anand 1982). Locks or parts of locks are made in almost every home in the old city. The practice of using children as part of family labour is very common. It is estimated that about 80 per cent of the country's locks are made in Aligarh district.

PROCESSES IN THE LOCK INDUSTRY

There are two methods of making padlocks. One is the traditional method where the lock-maker designs a lock and gets an order from the trader. The trader is usually also a financier who may give a loan to the lock-maker to buy raw material and other components. Once an order is placed, the lock-maker gives the raw material, namely brass or iron, to the *dhalai* (moulder, who usually belongs to a Scheduled Caste community) along with a model. The *dhalai* casts all the pieces according to specifications and returns them to the lock-maker who then files them. Those components like the handle, springs, keys, etc., which have not been cast by the *dhalai* are bought from the market, the lock assembled and then returned to the trader. The trader gets a final polish given to the locks and his brand name engraved on them and then markets them.

Most of the heavy brass and iron locks are made this way. The smaller and less expensive locks with names such as Link, Horseman and Mobaj as well as mortice and cycle locks are mass produced in factories. In this process, the lock manufacturers have their own production units where they cut scrap iron sheets called MSA sheets — which they get from the automobile industry — on power presses. Thus the outer cover of locks, the lid, flat keys and other parts are all cut from MSA sheets. Some parts of the lock like the handle are also cut and bent and grooves made in the big factories. Once this is done on power-presses, the work shifts to the hand-presses where the components are smoothened and holes pierced in keys or key-holes pierced in lock-cases. Hand-presses and power-presses are used for a variety of jobs. A die is fitted into the machine which will do a particular job. For every process, there is a separate die.

These rusted components of locks are either sent for *dhol* (drum) — this is a term used for drum polishing — or polishing on buffing machines. Those parts of a lock which are visible from outside such as the handle, cover or keys, which need to be electroplated, are first polished on buffing machines. Those parts which are not visible are sent for *dhol*. If visible parts are not electroplated, then they are spray painted.

Children do no work with *dhalais*, or in *dhol* polishing, *dhol* plating or on power-presses. But children are used in all other processes like working on hand-presses, polishing on buffing machines, in electroplating and spray painting units, for filing components, making springs and assembling and packing of locks.

It is important to note here that some of these processes like working on hand-presses, electroplating, buff polishing and spray painting are also done for the hardware industry in Aligarh. Children working in these units are therefore not exclusively working for the lock industry.

There is not even one factory where all the processes (of which there are approximately forty-five) are carried out in the same premises. Most of the factories get some parts made outside. The work is given on a contract basis and it is the responsibility of the contractor to get the work done. All workers are paid on a piece-rate basis and work anything upto forty-eight hours at a stretch when the work-load is heavy.

In the big factories, components are cut and then farmed out to artisans to do the filing, finishing, etc. There are different contractors for different jobs and varying systems for getting the work done. Some people are paid by the gross, others are given a weekly wage and still others are remunerated according to lots. Ninety-five per cent of the workers have no protection as they are piece-rate workers.

In some units, popularly known as *karkhanas* (literally means factory and legally they would come under the Factories Act, 1948) the premises and machines may belong to a man who directly hires labour and gets work done on a lot basis. In yet others, the man who owns the machines may rent them out to different sub-contractors who arrange for the labour. Sometimes a sub-contractor may himself work on the machines, but this is rare. By and large, those who own these machines do not work on them.

In the lock industry the 'putting-out' system prevails for a variety of reasons. Small firms are able to survive because they act as sub-contractors to the larger firms and supply special components and help out at certain stages of production during periods of peak demand. Secondly, legislation such as the Factories Act and various Labour Acts help perpetuate the 'putting-out' system, which is the best way of maintaining profits without any obligations to the workers. A third major reason which allows the 'putting-out' system to flourish is that there exists a large number of small peasants in the countryside around Aligarh city, whose lands do not provide a full livelihood; through the 'putting-out' system, they are able to save and then invest the capital in the financing of cottage industry rather than in the factory system.

The small entrepreneur is himself fairly poor and he survives primarily by exploiting those who are even poorer. The small entrepreneur is almost as uncertain about getting work as the labourer and therefore there is a high mortality rate with smaller units having to close down because of economic insecurity.

Wage Structure

There is no uniform wage structure in the lock industry. The method of payment is, by and large, the piece-rate system. In one assembling unit, the owner said he paid children Rs 25 a month for a ten-hour day! Workers in a polishing unit said that children, if they work twelve to fifteen hours, can earn up to Rs 15 a day and an adult Rs 25. In electroplating units, child workers can earn Rs 5 to Rs 10 a day depending upon the number of hours of work. Many children interviewed said they worked for more than twenty hours at a stretch. They would take a short nap or d nk tea if they were very sleepy and continue to work. I met two children who had worked thirty-six hours at a stretch and who were paid 60 paise an hour as over-time! Many children, I was told, worked for several months without wages, particularly in the polishing units. After that, they earned Rs 50 a month. Only after working ten to fifteen years was a man able to earn Rs 600 a month and that also for a fourteen-hour day!

The payment of low wages to workers have other ramifications as well. Poor parents are not able to afford the expenses of school-going children if the education is not subsidized. But more importantly, as pointed out earlier: 'The generally prevailing low wages/remuneration for work of the parents forces them to involve child labour in the traditional business of the family' (ibid.: 26-7).

There is no fixed wage rate and different jobs/processes are paid according to different rates. For example, for cutting a key-hole with a pointed chisel in the lock-case called *dibbi* (a term used to describe a flat and small box) and also fitting a key, a child earns Rs 3 per thousand and he can complete 1000–1500 holes in a whole working day! Sometimes, a child is paid 30–35 paise per gross. Likewise, in a electroplating unit, in an eight to ten hour working day a child could tie 1000–1500 locks/handles on copper wires. For this work, he is paid Rs 2 or Rs 3 per thousand! The rate was also fixed at 30 paise per gross.

While there is no uniform wage structure in the lock industry, my interviews revealed that on the average, a child earned nothing for the initial period of apprenticeship, after which he began to earn Rs 50 per month. This unpaid period for learning the skills varied from process to process but rarely exceeded one year. For the first couple of years, the child earned a monthly wage of Rs 50 a month but his working day normally lasted twelve to fourteen hours. He was paid no over-time. On the days that the unit was closed, he got no wages. All units are closed on Wednesdays and units owned by Muslims are also closed on Friday.

After a few years, the child earned between Rs 125–150 per

month for a nine-hour working day. He was also paid over-time depending on the urgency of the order and the mood of the contractor. These workers were considered permanent by *thekedars* (contractors) because they were regular employees but they were not entitled to any other benefits such as medical assistance, Provident Fund and so on. The salaries of these children were also cut for days they were absent due to ill-health or on Wednesdays, when units were closed.

Thus, a child earned Rs 50 a month or about Rs 1.60 paise per day for an average of a twelve-hour day! Any day he did not come, his wages were deducted. A child who earned Rs 125 a month for a nine-hour day got approximately Rs 4 per day and was not paid for the days he was absent or the factory was closed.

Many explanations were advanced for preferring the piece-rate system to a fixed-rate system. According to factory owners, the labourers employed in polishing, electroplating and painting units were prone to alcoholism: if workers were paid fixed wages, they would disappear for days at a time and not come to work. Another unit owner said that this system of payment was best for both labour and factory owners because the factory owner has assured output and the labourer, if he is hard-working and sincere, can earn a lot of money!

But the main reason, as another factory owner frankly pointed out, is that polishing, electroplating and spray painting are the three most hazardous processes in the lock industry and he felt that contract labour was not covered by any labour laws. The unit owner has no responsibility to the worker if he falls ill or gets seriously hurt when working and he does not have to provide medical assistance or compensation if the worker dies. This is the primary reason for getting work done on a 'put-out' system, where the wages are paid according to output and there is no job security.

Workers were interviewed randomly from the neighbouring areas. Most of the workers and unit owners were engaged in electroplating, polishing on buffing machines and spray painting. Most of the workers engaged in polishing work live near

Mehtab Ka Nakla near Shahja Marg. In this locality, almost 500 children go every day to work in the polishing units in the Upper Kote region. I interviewed six children and seven adults who had been working on buffing machines. They were covered in black emery powder. Although they had bathed after returning from work, the colour of their skin was black. I was told that children, when they start learning this work, do not get any money except for the occasional rupee or two to go to the cinema.

They worked twelve to fourteen hours and were paid monthly wages. The children were between the ages of seven and eleven years. One boy had come home at 2 a.m. when the work was over. He was eleven and had been working for three years. In the first year, he got paid nothing because he was learning the job. In the second year, he received Rs 50 a month. Now, he earns Rs 150 a month. His father is a rickshaw-puller and he has three unmarried sisters. He was never sent to school. He then went to work with another polisher. In the unit where he works now, there are almost twenty workers of whom fifteen are children of his age.

An old man pointed to two small children who were his grandchildren. They were both working as polishers. When I told him that *thekedars* said they paid children Rs 500 a month, the crowd of about fifteen adults and eight children laughed and said that the children were not even paid Rs 50. And if a person got ill, as was inevitable, he not only lost his day's wages, but also had to borrow money for treatment. On the weekly day off when the power supply was shut off, the worker loses the day's wages.

After working for six months, they start earning Rs 50–60 a month. A child starts working at the age of six or seven years. He usually goes to work along with his neighbours. An average working day is between twelve to fourteen hours. Since there is a shortage of power and most small units cannot afford generators, work continues through the night. The *thekedar* or unit owner decides what constitutes a working day. If units are not operating because of electricity breakdown, then the working day (that is the number of hours that constitutes a working day) stretches out way into the night.

After the third year, the child starts earning Rs 150–250 a month if he works diligently for twelve to fourteen hours a day. It is only when he is about twenty-five to twenty-six years of age that he may be able to earn as much as Rs 500–600. But, as the workers pointed out, after working under such conditions, very few are able to manage a twelve-hour shift. Within a matter of six to seven years, that is by the time a child is thirteen or fourteen years old, he is afflicted by tuberculosis, bronchitis, asthma and other diseases.

PROCESSES IN THE LOCK INDUSTRY AND PARTICIPATION OF CHILDREN

Children are employed to work on hand-presses which cut different components of locks. Of all the processes in which children are employed, the activities of polishing, electroplating, spray painting and working on hand-presses are the most hazardous for the health of workers, particularly child workers. The hand-presses become particularly dangerous because children are made to work very long hours — anything from twelve to fourteen hours a day. Carelessness caused by exhaustion is the main cause of accidents and often, children lose the tips of their fingers, which get caught in the machines.

Polishing on Buffing Machines

The work of polishing is perhaps the most hazardous job undertaken. Rusted pieces of metal are polished on buffing machines. The bobs on these machines are covered with emery powder. The piece is held by hand against the bob and the rusted portion is polished off. The face of the worker is within ten inches of rotating machines which run on power. The worker is bent over and directly inhales the emery powder and metal dust. Polishers can easily be identified because they look like coal-miners. They are covered from head to toe in this black powder. If a piece slips from the hand of the worker, it can severely injure another worker.

I visited about fifty such polishing units where more than 60 per cent of the workers were less than fourteen years of age. Children of eight and nine years could be seen working very late at night. I saw some children sleeping on the premises and some eating there as well. There were no exhaust fans in any of the units. Children who were too young to work on the machines could be seen gumming discs and then covering them with the black *masala* (as this mix is called. It is a term used to describe a mix of ingredients). This process generates a lot of dust and therefore factory owners keep buffing machines in a separate place.

Most factories in the industrial area had a separate place where buffing machines were kept. But factory owners felt that they were not responsible for the working conditions as the machines and the space were given on rent to the contractor, who hired the labour.

While large factories have their own buffing machines, most of the polishing work is done in the Upper Kote *mohallas*. This is where there is a maximum concentration of such unregulated units. Most of them are unregistered and there is no control over working conditions, hours of work or wages. In the lanes and by-lanes of Upper Kote, child labour is very visible. In many buffing units I visited, more than 70 per cent of the workers were children. Buffing units are also found in the Khirni Gate area and in the other parts of the city, but the highest concentration is in the Upper Kote area.

Electroplating

Electroplating is another extremely hazardous process in which more than 70 per cent of workers are children below the age of fourteen years. These children are engaged in tying polished metal pieces on copper wires, which are then strung on rods and submerged in acid and alkaline baths. In many of the units I visited (approximately fifty), it was not possible to enter the premises because of the noxious fumes which also made one's eyes water. Electroplating is hazardous for a variety of reasons. For one thing, the chemicals used such as potassium cyanide, trisodium phosphate, sodium silicate, hydrochloric acid, sulphuric acid, sodium hydroxide, chromic acid and barium hydroxide are extremely dangerous. The hands of children were in these solutions for the better part of a twelve-hour day, if not longer. Secondly, an electric current passes through these chemical tanks and children often get shocks. The floors of these units were wet and accidents were frequent.

Although most units had a convertor, which transformed AC current into DC current and though the current passed did not exceed ten volts, illegal electricity connections taken from street-lights made this extremely dangerous. There were cases of electrocution.

Electroplating units can be found in all parts of the city though they are concentrated in the Upper Kote area. In none of the units did workers wear gloves or aprons and there were no exhaust fans installed anywhere. Many of the smaller units were run by people who had worked in a supervisory capacity in larger factories, saved money or taken loans and then set up their own units. Every single unit owner interviewed said that he would not allow his own children to even go near the unit! Their children were all in local schools. But these very owners used child labour because they admitted that it was cheaper than employing adults!

Many units were working at night as well.

Spray Painting

At least 50 per cent of the total labour force in the spray painting units observed was made up of children below the age of fourteen years. They were engaged in placing pieces of metal on trays which they then carried to the painting table. They were also employed to pass on pieces to the man who held the spray gun. In this process, they inhaled substantial quantities of paint and paint thinners. Many children were found working beyond midnight.

HAZARDS TO HEALTH

Polishing

Fazal Ahmed is thirty-five years, and has been working on a buffing machine for ten years. Now his two sons have also started working. Ahmed said that almost all polishers suffer from chest disorders, particularly tuberculosis. Polishers inhale vast quantities of metal dust and emery powder in the course of their work and consequently find it very difficult to swallow. Another worker said that after a few years, polishers also find it difficult to breathe. I met two boys, eight and twelve respectively, both of whom were working as polishers and who already had TB!

Electroplating

One electroplating unit owner, Nabi Ahmed, had himself worked for twenty years in an electroplating plant. Although most workers were abjectly poor, some were able to set up small units but could not afford to hire labour. Now about forty-five to fifty years old, Nabi Ahmed had a severe asthmatic condition and could hardly breathe. He has stopped working and employs others. On being asked whether his children were working, his answer was: 'So long as I am alive, I will never let my children work. Look at my condition. I cannot even breathe easily. I do not let my children even enter the premises. Both my boys aged seven and nine years are studying.'

However, Nabi Ahmed has to employ other children if he wants to make enough money to avoid having his own children work. But that is described as *duniya dari!* (ways of the world).

Nabi Ahmed said that electroplating work is very dangerous. He recalled the case of a child who, by accident, put some potassium cyanide in his mouth thinking it was salt and died instantaneously. Ever so often a child tastes some of the liquid in the chemical tanks out of curiosity, as small children tend to do, and gets seriously ill or dies. But there is no one who can say exactly how many deaths, accidental or otherwise, take place!

Gyan Prakash, aged thirty-five years (though he looked older), worked for several years in the Tiger Lock Factory near Marris Road. They had a big electroplating plant in which he was a supervisor and was responsible for mixing chemicals in the tanks. He always wore gloves. One morning, he made a solution with potassium cyanide and dissolved it with his hands. At lunch time, he took a break and washed his hands before eating; the minute he put the food in his mouth, he started vomiting blood. He vomited four or five times and was rushed to the Employees State Insurance Corporation (ESIC) Hospital. He was ill for a long time and never went back to work. He thinks that perhaps the glove was slightly torn and some chemicals had stuck to his nails and these did not come off with washing.

Gyan Prakash has worked in several *karkhanas* but he finds it hard to work in electroplating units. The smell of acids gives him a headache and he is unable to eat. Now he works only in a supervisory capacity in this unit. He has three children who go to school. He does not want his children to work so long as he can work. According to him, electroplating work is very dangerous work and particularly so for children. As he said, 'Although every child who comes to work is warned not to put his fingers in his mouth, children are, after all, children. How can I keep such vigil? But we know that potash (potassium cyanide) is used and we have to be careful.'

This is not the end of the story. Liquids in these tanks are heated, and strong fumes are inhaled by adults and children alike. Many workers, both adults and children, work continuously for days on end, night and day. As another worker said: '*Malik ko to kaam se matlab hein. Admi mare ya jiye, usko kya farak padta hein?*' (the owner is only interested in the profit margin. What difference does it make to him if the worker lives or dies?)

In the electroplating plants, hazards to health arise not only from the acids and alkalies used but also from electricity. In Tan Tan Para, a *mohalla* in Upper Kote, an eleven-year old worker was recently electrocuted when his foot touched a naked wire. The poor wiring system, the presence of water and illegal connections from street-lights are the main reasons for people being electrocuted or receiving severe shocks. One adolescent youth complained of severe problems of breathlessness ever since he received an electric shock. Another electroplating unit worker said that in his work-place, a worker had been saved in the nick of time. Two wires got joined together and the nickel bath got electrified. The young worker of about fifteen or sixteen was arranging wires on the rods. He was unconscious for a long time.

Workers, whether polishers, painters or electroplaters, say that a lot depends on what a man can afford to eat. If he is able to get decent food, milk, butter and so on, he can ward off illness more easily. Otherwise it is a downhill path. Needless to say, those who work in these units cannot afford to eat well!

Spray Painting

A painter told me that he had worked in a spray painting unit for fifteen years. He started working at the age of ten years. After five or six years of working twenty hours at a stretch, he found that his body would get very hot and he felt like hitting someone. He said that this went on for five or six years. He was always close to losing his temper and many times he felt that he was close to murdering someone. According to him, this was a physiological condition and not just a psychological state. He could actually feel the blood rushing to his head. Finally, he left the job because he felt that he might not be able to control himself. He thinks that this was due to the combined impact of paint thinners, the bright lights, the heat of the ovens and the long hours of work. He was alright soon after he changed jobs. Now he has set up his own spray painting unit where he employs both children and adults! He plans to remove his own son to do some other work.

AN OVERVIEW

Doctors, workers and unit owners say that except for those

cases where a child gets electrocuted or dies by consuming acid or alkaline solution, there is no immediate health hazard to children! Or in other words, since no systematic medical survey has ever been done, the exact nature of the health problems children are affected by is not known. The common ailments reported are cough, cold, temperature and breathlessness. But these are not taken seriously. Signs of pneumoconiosis, tuberculosis and bronchitis are visible after a child has worked for five or six years. By that time, he is already an adolescent. When the child gets very ill and cannot continue working, only then does he go to the doctor.

Local doctors and hospitals do not even have a clue to the number of children afflicted. Figures of pneumoconiosis, which is an industrial occupational hazard, vary from 5 per cent to 40 per cent. Many doctors who say that a person suffers from pneumoconiosis do not even know what its exact symptoms are. All they can say is that it is an occupation-related lung disorder. Some doctors say that the capacity of the lungs of those working in polishing units get greatly reduced causing breathlessness but they cannot say to what extent this happens and what the mortality rate is. Everywhere I went in the Upper Kote area, people talked of death and disease stalking their *gali mohallas* (by-lanes in a residential locality) and this, they said, was directly related to the work people were doing. However, no one could give any exact numbers or percentages. But they said that the number of people, specially children, who got ill, was very high. Doctors say that almost all the workers — adults and children — who work in these units get tuberculosis.

While pneumoconiosis exists among workers in buff polishing units and electroplating units, no doctor knows what happens to these patients! According to a textbook on Preventive and Social Medicine (Parke 1974), pneumoconiosis is caused by dust particles within the size range of 0.5 to 0.3 microns. After a period of exposure to these dust particles, fibrosis is caused in the lungs which may cripple a man and reduce his working capacity.

Pneumoconiosis is definitely an occupational disease caused

by working conditions. There is also no cure for it. The only thing that can be done is to prevent secondary infection and to remove the person from the place of work. But doctors point out that workers are not in a position to take long-term treatment and leave their jobs. Children, since they are not legally workers, cannot avail of the facility of the Employees State Insurance Corporation (ESIC) hospital. As a worker's condition worsens, he goes from doctor to doctor looking for an instant cure. He is also deceived by local medical quacks who call themselves Registered Medical Practitioners (RMP). These people are not qualified doctors. Many of them have worked for a while as compounders and dispensers and promise the patient quick results. They pump the patient with cortisone tablets and powders which give the man some instant relief. What ultimately happens to patients, both adults and children, is difficult to tell. Not one doctor I interviewed in Aligarh could give any authentic information!

Other occupational diseases prevalent amongst lock-makers, particularly those working in electroplating and painting units, are occupational dermatitis, eczema and perhaps even cancer. Workers in electroplating plants are also exposed to lung cancer.

Not many studies have been done on the health status of lock workers. One important study is that of Mohammad Anees in 1978 (Anees 1978). Although he concentrated only on chest disorders amongst adult workers, nevertheless his findings are relevant for an understanding of the health conditions of working children in this industry.

Anees's study, which also reviews the work done by other doctors on occupational health, says that exposure to vapours of lead, copper, zinc, brass and iron, etc. may produce metal fume fever, an acute febrile illness that clinically may resemble bacterial infection of the lungs (ibid.: 7). His study shows that the inhalation of nickel in the form of carbonyl or dust, which is necessary when working in electroplating units, gives rise to broncho-pneumonia or cancer of the lungs and nasal sinuses. Likewise, Anees says that:

The air contaminated with chromic acid mist or with the dusts of chromates and bichromates is the principal source of exposure to this metal in this industry. Chronic bronchitis and cancer of the lungs are occupational risks in the chromate producing industry (ibid.: 8).

Anees's study also points out that in the lock industry, the worker is exposed to mineral dusts, specially that of iron and brass, while in polishing he may get an additional exposure to chrome mist, nickel and other inorganic and organic dusts. Since the majority of workers are employed in ill-ventilated and over-crowded premises, the likelihood of chest diseases is very high.

It was also noticed that the proportion of workers from small factories had a higher percentage of chest diseases (40 per cent) against 23.6 per cent from the bigger factories. Anees's research showed that pulmonary tuberculosis, chronic bronchitis and short respiratory illnesses were the common chest diseases suffered by lock workers.

According to the inter-disciplinary study undertaken by the Aligarh Muslim University and cited earlier, while the number of children below the age of fifteen years numbered 1560, the number of persons above sixty years of age were only sixty-two. It was observed that:

One serious feature noted . . . is the considerably small number of persons who have attained 60 years of age. In fact, in the age group of 41–60 years . . . the number of individuals [goes] on reducing as the age advances. The poor living and working conditions cause so much damage to the health that living beyond 50 years becomes difficult (IDS n.d.: 20).

LABOUR LAWS AND THEIR IMPLEMENTATION

Though the lock industry per se is not a forbidden occupation under the Child Labour (Prohibition and Regulation) Act, 1986, children are not allowed to work in processes which involve the use of certain chemicals. But since most lay persons do not know what these chemical compounds actually contain, it would be surprising if the staff of the Labour Department was able to identify these chemicals. Children are not allowed to work in hazardous employment, but the lock industry is certainly hazardous.

Though the lock industry is not a forbidden occupation either under the Employment of Children Act, 1938 (now repealed) or under the Child Labour (Prohibition and Regulation) Act, 1986, children may not work in factories or in hazardous employment according to the mandate of Article 24 of the Constitution. From what has gone before, it will be evident that the Constitutional directive is not being implemented.

When we examine the provisions of the Factories Act of 1948, it becomes apparent that they are being blatantly violated in the lock industry of Aligarh. The Act unambiguously lays down (Section 67) that children below the age of fourteen years are prohibited from working in a factory. The evidence collected in this study points to the fact that this provision is implemented largely in the breach.

Some factory owners evade the law by circumventing it. For example, any premise in which the manufacturing process is being carried on is considered a factory if there are ten or more workers and if power is used; if power is not used, there must be twenty or more workers involved (Section 2 (m)). By this definition, most electroplating, polishing and spray painting units would fall within the purview of the Act. Yet, factory owners seek a loop-hole by partitioning their premises and isolating the areas where work is being done with power. Workers then need not be paid according to law nor do they receive the benefits of paid leave, medical assistance, Provident Fund, etc. By this device, they also evade excise duty as their units are then considered to fall under the categories of small-scale or cottage sectors.

The Act also provides (Section 14 (1)) that effective measures shall be taken to prevent the inhalation and accumulation of dust or fumes or other impurities which are likely to be injurious or offensive to the workers. My observation as well as medical evidence clearly reveal that the activities of electro-plating, polishing or spray painting are manifestly injurious to the health of both child and adult worker. Not a single exhaust fan was found in any of the factories visited except for the spray painting units, where work could not have been done without it.

The Factories Act lists twenty-two notifiable diseases that are caused by direct contact with chemicals and paints and these are considered occupational diseases. The Act also casts a duty upon medical practitioners (Section 89 (2)) to report such cases without delay. This is not being done.

Another provision (Section 16 (1)) states that no room in any factory should be overcrowded to an extent injurious to the health of workers. Most of the smaller units in the Upper Kote region were overcrowded and the pavement outside used as an extended work-place. It was physically impossible for all the workers to fit into the cramped premises. I was told that in polishing units the most common type of injury that occurred was when a piece of metal slipped from the hands of a worker and hit another. It was also noticeable that buffing machines were far too closely arranged for safety.

The regulations under the Factories Act to protect the interests of children above the age of fourteen years are also not followed. All children above fourteen years are supposed to be registered (Section 73 (1)) but no one maintains any registers. Also, children are not supposed to work for more than 4½ hours and not at all during the night (Section 71 (1)). In fact, they commonly do.

In almost all cases observed, children worked for far more than 4½ hours and usually for even more than eight hours. Children and adults working late at night were a common sight as well. One justification for night-work was said to be the regular power-cuts (usually between 1 p.m. and 5 p.m.) during the day. Contractors were keen to finish the job at hand as even they were not assured of regular work; workers could not afford to refuse night work because employment was not available throughout the week or month and they needed the money.

The nine-hour day shift would normally continue well into the night, for the contractor counted only the hours the work was actually done, and not the hours the worker was present. As mentioned earlier, children came early and left very late; it was not practicable for those who lived far to go home and return and also, power could theoretically come on at any time.

State governments are given powers under the Factories Act to declare some processes or operations as dangerous and can also declare a unit to be a factory even if it has less than ten workers and does not use power. But Section 85 (1) exempts units where owners manufacture products only with the aid of their families. The State Government of Uttar Pradesh does not appear to have exercised the powers it has in this regard. The escape clause that unit owners may employ their own children has come in very handy for them. My interviews revealed that almost nobody engages his own children in hazardous processes: there was only one such case of a man who worked along with his sons on two rented buffing machines. Even he was aware of the dangers involved and though one son developed a severe chest problem, the father was too poor to keep his children at home. On being asked, unit owners would invariably say that the children working with them were their own: they knew this was permissible under the law. If one was to believe this story, a convincing explanation would be needed for the extraordinarily large size of the families of the lock-makers of Aligarh!

In conclusion, there is unmistakable evidence that the jobs of polishing on buffing machines, electroplating and spray painting are injurious to the health of workers, whether adults or children. Polishers inhale emery powder and metal dust and they work in such crammed spaces that workers frequently get injured because pieces of metal hit them. Working in electroplating units for children means that they have to keep their hands in solutions of dangerous chemicals like potassium cyanide for long periods and, die when the universal curiosity of children to taste anything new, in this case these foul liquids seizes them. Moreover, electric current taken illicitly also causes disability and death. Children in spray painting units inhale unacceptably large doses of paint and paint thinners leading to severe chest disorders. Breathlessness, fever, tuberculosis, bronchitis, asthma and pneumoconiosis are some of the symptoms and diseases that affect the children of the lock industry. Malnutrition and poverty combine to exacerbate the ill-effects of their working conditions and considerably shorten their lives. The most telling evidence of the hazards involved in polishing, electroplating and spray painting is found in the fact that no unit employer employs his own children in any of these processes. The other processes of the lock industry do not seem to be hazardous in themselves for the health of children. But children working on hand-presses do lose the tips of their fingers when fatigue blunts their senses.

The only course of action in the circumstances is to impose a ban on children working in this industry and enforce it strictly. Even if some of the processes in the industry are not hazardous in themselves, once a child enters the units, it is impracticable — to say the least — to try to confine his/her work in only non-hazardous processes. If it was feasible to physically isolate the hazardous processes by clear geographical demarcation, and possible to count on the co-operation of the owner, the question of children being permitted to work in non-hazardous processes could have been considered. Since all the operations are inextricably intertwined in the present arrangement of the lock industry, a ban appears to be the only solution.

5

The Child Gem Polishers of Jaipur

At least 50 per cent of all children working in the gem polishing industry are completely illiterate. Some of them have been educated up to the third standard and others dropped out even earlier. Since the education they had received was so meagre, whatever they learnt in the early years has been forgotten and today they are completely illiterate. Surprisingly, this is one industry where the need for education for upward mobility is seen as an absolute necessity by all those involved in the industry.

THE GEM POLISHING INDUSTRY OF JAIPUR, RAJASTHAN: PAST AND PRESENT

The gem industry of Jaipur is as old as the city itself. Jaipur is the capital of the State of Rajasthan and a few hours away from New Delhi by road. In AD 1727, when Jaipur was built, Maharaja Jai Singh invited a number of jewellers from Delhi, Agra and Benaras and gave them royal patronage to start the gem industry in Jaipur. The tradition of royal patronage was continued by Maharaja Ram Singh who ordered the principal market of Jaipur city to be named 'Johari Bazaar' or the market of jewellers and the main city square to be known as 'Manak Chowk' or Ruby Square.

Jaipur is well known for its coloured gem stone industry just as Surat in Gujarat is the main diamond-cutting centre in

India. Coloured gem stones can be either precious or semi-precious. The precious gems are sapphires, rubies and emeralds. The range of semi-precious stones is much larger and includes, amongst others, lapis lazuli, turquoise, corals, garnets, amethysts and topaz. Ninety-five per cent of all coloured gem stones in India are polished in Jaipur. The other centres of gem polishing are Cambay in Gujarat where agate is polished, Bombay, Hyderabad, Karwar, Trichur, Coimbatore, Nellore, Cuttack and Calcutta. While there are several processes in the coloured gem processing industry which will be explained later, the different processes are usually collectively referred to as gem polishing. Henceforth in this report, the term gem polishing will be used for the sake of consistency. It must also be mentioned here that the gems polished in Jaipur are not only made for use as jewellery but are also carved for decorative purposes. Carving is also done for jewellery though the processes are slightly different. The carving of gems is also considered to be a part of the gem polishing industry.

Under royal patronage, the jewellery business thrived and since Jaipur was strategically located on the imperial route between Delhi and the South, the traders were able to get raw material and unsold gems very easily. They reshaped, polished and set the gem stones in gold and silver ornaments which became famous in the courts. In earlier days, the gems cut and polished for the royal families were very large. Today, the gem industry caters to the international market. The easy availability of cheap labour here makes it lucrative business. The other main gem polishing centres in the world are Israel, West Germany, Thailand, Sri Lanka and Taiwan. According to Shekhar Vashisht, a gemologist based in Jaipur, the main buyers of Indian gem stones are the USA, France, Hong Kong, Italy, Japan, Kuwait, Saudi Arabia, Singapore, Switzerland, UK and West Germany. The USA is the biggest buyer of emeralds. India earns about Rs 1400 *crores* (1 *crore* is equal to 10,000,000) per annum from the export of gems.

Though the gem polishing industry is the single largest employer in Jaipur city, there has never been any census or survey of gem artisans and workers. Conversations with those in the gem trade suggested that there are at least 60,000 workers engaged in it. Of these, it was learnt, 51,000 (85 per cent) are Muslims and 9000 (15 per cent) are Hindus. Hindu workers are ethnically either Marwari or Gujarati. I was told that there are about 12,500 women and female children amongst the Muslim workers, accounting for about 25 per cent of the work-force of that community. The Gurupadaswamy Committee Report of 1979 (GOI 1981: 9) came to the conclusion that there were at least 10,000 children in the gem polishing industry. Investigations in Jaipur point to there being at least 13,000 Muslim children (over 25 per cent of the Muslim work-force) and over 600 Hindu children (about 7 per cent of the Hindu work-force). It can safely be assumed that over 13,000 children below the age of fourteen years (or over 20 per cent of all workers) are involved in the gem industry. If one were to include children between the ages of fifteen and eighteen years, the percentage share of children in the total work-force would probably go up to a figure of about forty. The estimates of working children given above are likely to be on the lower side. (Burra 1987b)

The gem polishing industry, as mentioned earlier, is as old as the city of Jaipur and to that extent it is a traditional occupation of most workers in Jaipur belonging to the Muslim community. Children learnt the craft from their fathers and both girls and women participated in the activity. *Bindai ka kaam* (the work of making holes in beads), was traditionally done by women and even today, is done by them. However, as the international demand for gems increased, the ultrasonic machine for drilling holes was introduced and now this work is done by unskilled adult males. As a result production, and consequently wages, have risen too. Women have been displaced from the gem industry as the technology of gem polishing improved. Girls work at home because of the tradition of *purdah* (the seclusion of women).

The great influx of child labour into the industry is a relatively recent phenomenon because the international demand for gems has risen sharply and parents see this industry as a

means of upward mobility for their children. Earlier, children
worked with their parents but they combined school with
learning the craft. In many families, the tradition of gem polishing has been kept alive through several generations. It required
a certain amount of knowledge about trade and the outside
world, for which some education was essential. Since the demand for gems was not very high, child labour was not very
widely prevalent. Today, the need for cheap child labour is
closely linked to the international demand for and competitive
prices of gems.

It was widely accepted in Jaipur that the official figures
regarding the export of polished gem stones do not account
for even a third of what is illegally exported out of the country.
It is therefore very difficult to assess the total production of
polished gem stones in Jaipur. The only available figure is that
90 per cent of the total production of gem stones is exported.
I visited more than 500 units where the work of gem polishing
was being carried out. I also visited about twenty homes where
the work of gem polishing was being done with the help of
family labour and a few *havelis* (mansions) where master craftsmen were getting work done on a lot basis, for traders, in their
own homes. I spent twenty days in the field and was able to
interview nearly a 100 children below the age of fourteen years
in their schools. Wide-ranging discussions were held with different segments of the gem polishing industry: fifty workers,
ten traders, three master craftsmen, three exporters and several
government officials.

PROCESSES IN THE GEM INDUSTRY

The cutting and polishing of gems in Jaipur is done by simple
machines which do not cost more than Rs 1000 or so. The
rough stones are imported from all over the world.

The first process is to sort out the raw material and then
cut them in required facets or sides. Gem stones are first slit
by means of a thin disc of relatively soft metal whose edges are
slightly indented. The cut stone or *ghat* (rough cut stone) is

then cemented to a wooden stick for rough shaping against an emery of carborundum wheel.

The artisan uses a stone lap; while sitting on the floor, he turns the *jindra* (lap) by means of a *kabana* (bow), the string of which is the driving device. By his side is a bowl containing emery, the consistency of which is adjusted by mixing it with water before it is used for grinding. In his left hand, he holds the stone that he is manipulating and in the other, the bow which makes the grinding stone rotate. After charging the lap with the appropriate abrasive, the lapidary first grinds the table facets. The other facets and angles are dependent on the design.

After the stone has been given a rough shape, the master craftsman takes over and corrects the slight irregularities left by the cutter. Once the shape and facets are cut and polished, the work is given to children to do the final polishing by using oxides which give the stones their lustre.

The chief forms of cutting stones are the 'brilliant cut' and 'the step cut'. Transparent stones like emeralds, rubies and sapphires are facet cut and translucent stones like turquoise, corals, opals and star stones are cut in cabochons and do not have sides. A simple cabochon has a carved top and a flat base.

The processes mentioned above are the most basic ones used in the gem polishing industry. The machines used vary according to the type of stone being polished. Thus, while ruby beads are made by hand because rubies are precious stones, garnet — a very cheap stone — is mechanically polished in drums. Precious stones are processed by hand and the semi-precious by machines to cut down the cost of production and increase supply.

Children are engaged in large numbers in the making of *ghats*, faceting and polishing of semi-precious stones but in the precious stone industry, children are largely engaged in the final polishing of the gems with oxides where there is absolutely no danger of any damage to the finished product. In the final polishing of gems with oxides, the entire labour force consists of children below the age of fourteen years.

STRUCTURE OF THE GEM INDUSTRY

The term commonly used for commission agents and brokers is *dalal* (middlemen/broker). These people are merely go-betweens between the workers and the trader.

Amongst artisans, there are two or three types of people. Most artisans are usually referred to as *ustads* (masters) because they impart training. But for greater clarity, a distinction is made here between the *ustad* and the master craftsman who gets work on a contract but who generally does not employ children below the age of fourteen either because the quality of work he does requires skills a child does not possess or because the child below the age of fourteen is likely to cause damage.

At the next level are people referred to later as *ustad* contractors. These are adults who have learnt the work from master craftsmen and who have set up their own workshops and mainly employ children below the age of fourteen. They use children because they are a source of cheap labour recruited under the guise of apprenticeship.

At the third level are the workers, who work either for master craftsmen, *ustad* contractors, traders and exporters or are self-employed. More than 80 per cent of all workers fall in this category.

The gem industry is a multi-tiered industry. At the top of the pyramid is the exporter/trader/manufacturer. The entire industry functions through *dalals*.

There is no uniformity in the structure of the gem polishing industry. In the big export houses and trading units, the work is supervised by supervisors who come in the category of management and are the trusted lieutenants of the exporter. There are different categories of employees; first is the person who grades the raw material. Once it is graded, each piece is marked with a pencil showing the place where the stone is to be cut. The person in charge of grading and marking the raw material is called a *marking karnewala* or *nishan laganewala*. After the pieces have been marked with a pencil, each stone is sliced and given a rough shape known as *ghat*. The person who makes this rough shape is called a *ghat bananewala*. Once the *ghat* is ready, then it is sent for various types of polishing.

Many different kinds of arrangements exist in the gem polishing industry. For instance, the *ghat* machines may belong to the worker but the premises to the exporter. Sometimes, both the premises and the machines belong to the exporter and all the workers are paid employees of the exporter or trader.

There is another kind of structure, where the master craftsman sets up his own workshop and the trader brings the raw material to the craftsman who employs twenty-five or thirty workers in his *haveli* (mansion) and uses children in the polishing of gems with oxides. If the work-load is too much, he may in turn pass on the work to other workers who have been trained by him and have their own workshops — the *ustad* contractors. These *ustad* contractors in turn employ both adults and children and also work themselves.

There is a third structure that exists where the worker may own a machine at home — usually to process semi-precious gems — and where the small-time trader, who does not want to be burdened with regular employees, gives the raw material and the worker uses his family labour, the women and children, and gives the finished goods back to the trader. This petty trader may be a wholesale dealer or even an exporter and he deals directly with the artisan at home and thus saves the commission he would otherwise have had to pay the *dalal*.

A fourth system is where the worker has his own machines, buys the raw material, processes the stones and then sells them directly to the dealer. These may be finished or semi-finished products. A common sight is the gathering of workers — both adults and children — at Ghat Gate every evening between 5.30 p.m. and 7.30 p.m. The workers carry small packets of gems to sell to *dalals* who buy the goods directly from the workers and sell to other brokers who in turn sell to exporters/manufacturers.

The *dalal* is crucial to the gem trade and acts as an intermediary between the worker and the dealer. He is paid a 4 per cent commission by the worker to sell the goods to the trader. He knows where and who is making what and it is his job to provide the goods to the trader on time. The worker is in no position to look for contract with the trader directly because this is too time consuming.

At Gopalji Ka Rasta in Johari Bazaar, the *dalals* meet every evening carrying shopping bags of precious and semi-precious gems which they bring from the workers and sell to the traders. The commission agent is vital for the worker, the small dealer and the artisan. He not only sells on behalf of the worker in the local market but also helps the small-time artisan-turned-dealer in exporting his goods.

The most common arrangement is one where the worker is employed on a monthly wage. He may be employed by the master craftsman, the exporter, the trader or the *ustad* contractor. The number of people who are self-employed is relatively small. However, since the gem polishing equipment is not very expensive, several workers try and save their money and invest in a machine so that they can buy raw material from their savings and sell the finished products to the *dalals*. This ensures an added income and is one of the ways by which, in a small way, the worker gets to make money.

Thus, at the very top is the exporter who may have his own manufacturing unit or may contract the work to a master craftsman, who has his own labour force. By and large, I was told, master craftsmen do not become traders themselves because traders would then entertain suspicions about whether the master craftsmen had misused or interchanged the raw stones given to them for their own purposes. Therefore, traders discourage master craftsmen from getting into business and are willing to pay very high prices for the work done.

Child labour is most widespread in the semi-precious stone industry where children are engaged in almost all the processes. In the precious stone industry, they are engaged in fewer processes such as cementing roughly-shaped stones on sticks and finally polishing the finished gems with oxides.

ADULTS AND THEIR WAGES

The Marwaris and Gujaratis comprise 15 per cent of the total labour force engaged in the processing of semi-precious and precious gem stones but control 95 per cent of the market. The Marwaris, who start working in the actual fashioning of gems, are usually adults in the age range of twenty to thirty years and have at least a BA degree. They start as workers only because their ambitions are either to get top management jobs or to start their own business. They get paid high salaries of at least Rs 2000 a month and work a few years in order to gain experience on the job. The Gujarati workers have less education, are usually within the age range of fifteen to twenty years and are paid between Rs 1000–1500. The Muslims who control less than 5 per cent of the business provide 85 per cent of the work-force. An average worker gets paid Rs 20–25 a day or Rs 500–650 a month. By and large, the workers are illiterate or semi-literate.

The methods of paying wages in the gem industry are varied and there is no uniformity in the wage structure. The highly-skilled *ghat bananewala* gets an average monthly salary ranging between Rs 1000 and Rs 5000 a month depending upon the value of the stones he is fashioning. Such are the wages paid to highly-skilled workers in the precious stone industry. The worker does not earn anything on days when he is ill or the workshop is closed.

Most master craftsmen, who also work as *ustad* contractors, get paid by gross weight for faceting and making beads. Thus the raw material is first weighed and labour charges given by carat weight to the master craftsman who shares it with the workers. If the weight of the raw material is reduced in the process of faceting or of making beads or if there is any breakage, it is not the responsibility of the labour.

In the case of cabochons and carving of gems into figures, payment is made according to the weight of the finished produce. The trader wants the carved piece to weigh less so that he can pay less and the craftsman wants the piece to weigh more because his payment is dependent on the weight of the finished stone. The rate of these jobs is higher so that the artisan is not tempted to make a bulky piece just to get more money.

At every level, the trader's/exporter's main attempt is to conceal from the worker — be it the master craftsman or the artisan or the low-level worker — where and for whom the product is being made. The higher the stakes, the greater the subterfuge. Thus for example, if the exporter has an order for a chess set in a precious stone, he will not give all the work to one artisan but pretend that he has only an order for two knights. Once those are complete, he may ask the artisan to make him two bishops and perhaps give another pair to another artisan. By the time the artisan realizes that he is in fact making a chess set for which the trader is probably going to make a thousand per cent profit, it is too late for him to raise his labour charges. A shrewd artisan, if he knows that the need of the trader is great, can command very good labour fees; but to do so he needs to be educated and to be able to understand the demands of market forces and the wily ways of the trader whose main aim is to make a quick buck and somehow keep the profits with himself. The role of education in upward mobility will be discussed later.

In Jaipur, the gem polishing industry is considered to be the best employer because the wages are relatively high and the prospects very good. All around, people see their contemporaries who have risen from being mere workers to dealers and show-room owners. Everywhere one goes, one finds people trying to make a fast buck by either buying cheaply and selling at a premium or starting a side business. Many low-level functionaries run small businesses in their spare time and involve other members of the family.

People talked in awe and envy of those who had made a lot of money in the business. The big exporters had their own show-rooms in New York and owned cinema houses and real estate. Those who were not in the same league hoped to reach it in another generation. Jewellers were always referred to as 'crore-patis' (multi-millionaires). There were many exporters who had recently reached the top and made their millions. At every level, the person aimed and aspired to reach the next. Thus the worker wanted to become an *ustad* contractor and the *ustad* contractor wanted to become a dealer. A dealer hoped to set up a show-room on Mirza Ismail Road, the main business area. And everyone wanted to become an exporter.

But while there were examples of upward mobility amongst those who had gone into business, there was not much evidence of this process amongst workers. The bulk of the workforce remained artisans, dependent upon their wages. Every now and then, a worker would save a little money, buy raw material, finish the goods and sell to a *dalal* and, if he was lucky, make a neat profit. But examples of such success stories amongst workers were rare. This fact, however, did not prevent people from trying.

The chances of upward mobility are also very real so it is not inconceivable that a person raises his economic status within a few years. The main thing was to assess the situation and to play one's cards well. There were people who were not gem polishers but were trying to enter the industry by sending their own children to work at a young age. The gem industry of Jaipur is seen as the main avenue for upward mobility.

WORK, APPRENTICESHIP AND THE EXPLOITATION OF CHILDREN

There are two categories of working children in the gem polishing industry. The first category is made up of those who work full-time from 8 a.m. to 6 p.m. and belong to families of manual labourers: they are lowest in the economic hierarchy. These children are in the age-range of six to ten and are completely illiterate.

In the second category are children of families who have a fairly steady income: some parents are involved in gem polishing but others hold occupations as government servants, tailors, barbers, etc. Their children go to schools — mainly government schools — and work for about four hours a day after school. Their age-range is ten to fourteen years.

The children of master craftsmen or good artisans who earn more than Rs 1000 a month do not work even though gem polishing is done at home. They also enter the gem polishing industry but usually after they have completed their schooling and certainly not before the age of fifteen years. The reasons for this state of affairs will be explained later.

While an attempt has been made to distinguish between different categories of children involved in the gem polishing industry, some children do not fall within this scheme. Some children of artisans may be working full-time and some children of manual labourers may be going to school. But by and large, the categories described earlier would hold good for the bulk of the child labour force in the Muslim community.

Child labour is recruited under the guise of apprenticeship training by master craftsmen, *ustad* contractors, exporters and traders. While child labour is very visible in the walled city of Jaipur and particularly in workshops run by *ustad* contractors, children also work in *havelis* in Johari Bazaar, but they are fewer in number and less visible. It is also very difficult to link a worker to his employer and therefore to say which big exporters are exploiting children is not easy. This statement is clarified elsewhere. In what follows, the exploitation of children by *ustad* contractors will be described.

Children in the gem polishing industry are engaged ostensibly as apprentices, but in fact provide cheap labour. The learning process takes anything up to five or even seven years and the child begins work usually at the age of six or seven. During this period, the child does not get paid regular wages, but is occasionally given a few rupees so that he continues to be interested in the work.

The general pattern for children who work from 8 a.m. to 6 p.m. is that in the first one and a half years, the child gets no wages — not even in kind — and he works for at least ten hours a day. During the first year, he learns to attach unpolished gems on sticks for polishing, fetches and carries for his master, does domestic work, cleans the premises and so on. By getting a child to do this work, the *ustad* contractor saves on a domestic servant and the wages of an adult worker. By engaging a child to do all the running around, and some unskilled work, he saves around Rs 150–200 a month.

In the second stage, when the child has worked for a year and a half or so, he is shown how to grind one facet on a stone besides continuing to do domestic work. This goes on for three or four months and sometimes, the *ustad* contractor stretches this period to a year without wages. After two years, the *ustad* contractor starts paying the child Rs 50 a month and occasionally gives him some old clothes, tea and sometimes even food. In the second stage, the child does work worth Rs 250–300 a month, at the very least. Every now and then, when the child becomes restless and wants to learn more and there is danger that the child may leave, the *ustad* contractor increases the wages and as the wages increase, the child is given more directly productive work and less domestic work. The *ustad* contractor does not want to pay wages and make the child do domestic work when there is a ready supply of younger children who can be engaged without wages.

Once the child has spent three or four years and has started learning to make more facets, he is worth at least Rs 300–400 to the *ustad* contractor. By this time, he may get Rs 100 a month and old clothes, tea and food. By the time the child is fourteen or fifteen years old, he has learnt most of the finer polishing techniques and would be earning about Rs 150–200 a month whereas an adult would get Rs 500–600 for the same job.

It is at this stage that the *ustad* contractor finds it difficult to hold on to the child on the pretext of training. At the age of fifteen or sixteen, a child who has learnt some skills can do about 30 per cent more work than adults, I was told, and it is at this stage, that the *ustad* contractor is really interested in hanging on to the child. He may marginally increase the wages of the child and promise to teach him some more, thereby retaining him for a couple of years more. Beyond five or six years, it is impossible to keep the child because by then there is also community pressure to release him. The parents of the child are also interested in shifting the child to another contractor so that the child can bring in a regular wage.

It must be mentioned that this system of exploitation under the guise of apprenticeship training is not confined to *ustad* contractors but it is not as visible elsewhere. While this category of high-visibility children, who work full-time, is made up of the off-spring of casual labourers, one finds that often artisans also bring their children to master craftsmen with the hope that if the child pleases the master craftsmen, his future will be assured. These children work almost the same hours but may not be as young. The children I had an opportunity to see were in the twelve to fourteen age-group. But I did not get an opportunity to talk to those, who were either very young or did not wish to speak in front of their master.

The children who went to school in the morning and worked later were more accessible and I was able to interview sixty-four children in five different schools, all below the age of fourteen years. Out of these sixty-four children, only five said they got a holiday on Sundays as well as a half-day on Fridays for prayers. All the others got time off from work only on Fridays and worked the full day on Sundays. The children said that they got no wages although they worked four to five hours a day, six days a week. All of them said that they got money on festival days from the *ustad*. Only three boys had got Rs 15 on festival occasions. The others got Rs 10 or less.

This money they gave their parents. Sometimes, the parents gave the child half the money and sometimes only a rupee or two. Only one child who drilled holes in beads on his father's machine got paid Rs 2.50 for drilling holes in a hundred beads. He said that the market rate was Rs 5.00 for this work. He had opened an account with the State Bank of Bikaner and Jaipur. Five boys saved the money with their mothers. The others liked to spend the money on eating out. I asked the children whether they knew how the money they earned was spent. Shamim, a twelve-year old said: *'Hamare upar he kharach ho jata hein'*(The money gets spent on us.)

It is difficult to make an accurate assessment about the number of children in these two categories and their proportions in the labour force. At Galta Gate, on one occasion in the afternoon, I had counted fifty-seven children below the age of fourteen years in thirty units. But on a morning visit, I could count only ten children in the same workshops. This gave me the impression that a large number of children were in fact going to school and working later.

In Zia-ud-din Ka Mohalla at Char Darwaza, I countered eighty children below the age of fourteen years. The *ustad* contractors for whom the children were working said that these children were full-time workers and did not go to school. At Baba ka Tibba in Ramganj Bazaar also, I counted twenty children who were working full-time. On Kalyan Ji Ka Rasta, all the twenty-five children were full-time workers.

In many of the units I visited, the children were not sitting at the machines but were engaged outside the unit, either carrying a jug of water or fanning a coal *chulha* or stove or just standing around. I was told by Aminbhai that all the children gathered around were working full-time. In Ramganj Bazaar, child labour is widely used. One dealer in gems has an album with coloured photographs of children working. He said that his foreign clients were very impressed that small children could be made to work and this fact was used to profit in his sales strategy. The myth of a traditional occupation coming down from father to son was also repeatedly used to good effect!

How Exporters Exploit Child Labour

It is not just the *ustad* contractor who exploits child labour but owing to the way in which the industry is organized, it is very difficult to link the exporter with his workers. The really big exporters dealing with precious stones often get workers to work in their *havelis*. Behind the locked doors of Johari Bazaar in Gopal Ji Ka Rasta and in Haldion Ka Rasta, workers are cutting, faceting and polishing gems for exports and do not come under any kind of labour legislation. And child labour is engaged here as well. In the evenings, it is possible to see young boys of ten and twelve years wearing *thehmats/lungis* (a long cloth worn by men) with their faces, hands and clothes streaked with green colour — chromium oxide — the agent used for polishing emeralds which are largely exported to the United States.

When asked, government officials, traders, brokers, contractors, local people and tourist taxi drivers, all deny that the work of gem polishing is done anywhere other than in the walled city where the Muslims live. This is factually incorrect. Exporters and big-time traders directly engage workers including children but it is very difficult to assess the number of children employed in the precious stone industry. According to the Labour Commissioner of Rajasthan, there are approximately 2000 children employed in the precious stone industry but this figure is based more upon speculation than hard data. In fact, any attempt to research the gem industry is fraught with difficulty. The standard reply if one asks to see how gems are cut and polished is that exporters do not want people to come and visit their units because they are afraid that trade secrets will be stolen. This explanation, however, is blatantly untrue and only a means of preventing any kind of inspection from taking place. The atmosphere here is uncanny. No one knows who is doing what behind closed doors. A veil of secrecy covers the entire place. It is impossible to get what might seem to be even a simple piece of information. One is deliberately misled. Even structurally, the layout is like a maze and it is quite impossible for someone to go back to the same place unaided. I however, was fortunate to be able to see the manufacturing process organized by one of the major gem exporters in Jaipur.

Through a local contact, I was asked to come to Johari Bazaar and then taken to a *haveli*, which was like a maze. We went through various narrow corridors and everywhere four or five workers were either cutting or making *ghats* under the strict supervision of the management. In several rooms, a *munim* (accountant) could be seen sitting by the hour and his main job was to shield his master. If any official came to enquire too closely about the activities of the exporter or wanted to meet him, the standard reply was: *Party ko milne gaye hein* (He has gone to meet buyers). In fact behind most of these rooms, precious gems are being polished but no one knows who is doing what. From the second floor of the Delhiwale Ki Haveli, I could look into several other *havelis* and everywhere there were workers polishing gems. In many places I could see children but it was difficult to count them as I was accompanied by the work supervisor of the export agency. All the *havelis* seemed to be connected for we entered from one side street and came out through another, and I had lost track of direction.

I was then taken to Badi Chaupar, where we stopped in front of a wholesale grain market in which poor-quality wheat was being stored. The man took me inside. It was a horizontally layered building. In the first quadrangle, there were some flour-grinding machines. In the second quadrangle, there were just some gunny bags stacked up in piles. In the third quadrangle, on the second floor, emeralds of very high quality were being polished. There were deep niches in the walls which opened into a courtyard so that natural light was available and in every niche, there were four or five workers directly employed by the exporter on a monthly salary but without any protection under labour legislation. It so happened that I had visited the area previously. But when I asked the local shopkeepers if there was any gem polishing going on, I was categorically told that I was in the wrong locality! People are generally afraid to give any information about the gem polishing industry because of the clout of the exporter/trader/manufacturer. The stakes are so high that no one wants to unnecessarily part with any information.

The same work supervisor took me to their semi-precious stones units in Char Darwaza. I asked whether the machines and the premises belonged to the *ustad* contractor but was told that both belonged to the exporter. This was a cutting unit where children were working. The arrangement was very neat. The work supervisor engaged a labourer whom he trusted and who was paid the same wages as other workers. But this labourer was also given an *inam* (gift) because it was his responsibility to see that nothing was pilfered and also because he paid the wages of the other workers, who were paid a monthly wage. Since children were also working here, I was told quite openly: 'Why engage an adult for Rs 500 to do a job that a child is willing to do for Rs 50?'

Big-time exporters do not pay or have any direct dealing with the lower category of workers but engage manufacturing supervisors to do the dirty job. This arrangement persists in most units where the work of carving, faceting, grinding and polishing is being done for a particular exporter and where the labour is not doing work in their spare time for other exporters. The child can be made to work for Rs 5 a day while an adult will demand at least Rs 25 for the same job. The man who recruits the labour is given an incentive to recruit cheap labour for his employers to boost their profits and the cheapest labour is child labour. Behind closed doors and veils of secrecy, children toil and exporters prosper!

WHY PARENTS SEND THEIR CHILDREN TO WORK

It is quite clear from what has gone before that all employers — whether exporters, master craftsmen or *ustad* contractor — are interested in child labour because it is the cheapest form of labour available. The only redeeming feature of the situation, if it can be called that, is that the children live with their parents in the same neighbourhood and, therefore, at least they have a home to go to. As one master craftsman said:

> It makes me mad to see how little children are being exploited both by the parents and the employers. The employers are like blood-suckers, draining the man and taking advantage of his helplessness. It would have been better if these children had never been born for the life these children lead is one of sheer misery.

To a question as to whether the child was actually learning on the job, his answer was:

A child of six or seven has neither the physical nor the mental ability to absorb the work. The child who starts working at the age of six or seven years can never become an artisan; he will only be a worker and he will end up by sending his own children to work at an early age. A child of fifteen is another matter, particularly if he is educated. He can learn in a year or two what a child of seven cannot in five years. Apprenticeship training should start at fifteen years and not before. These children are not being trained, they are being used.

If it is easy to see why employers employ children, the parents also have a point of view. Employers of children felt that it was the irresponsibility of the parents that resulted in their children working. Rashidbhai, an *ustad* contractor said:

80 per cent of the parents live off the earnings of their children and sit around gambling and drinking. There is nothing the government can do for such useless people. Their greed and laziness is their main problem.

But conversations with working children told a different tale of exploitation. Hameedbhai is fifty years old. After working for forty years, he was able to save Rs 10,000. He decided to buy raw material — uncut emeralds — and worked for fifteen days with the help of his family members. Once the emeralds were processed, he took them to the *dalal* to sell directly thinking that thereby he would be able to keep the commission he would normally have to pay to an intermediary. On his first day in the market, he asked for Rs 15,000 for the goods but the *dalal* bargained for a lower figure. The day I met Hamidbhai, he had been beaten down to Rs 11,000. Hamidbhai could not wait any longer and said to me:

The *dalal* knows how little staying power the worker has and how to apply pressure. They know our desperation and from just looking at our faces wait patiently like vultures. The *dalal* knows that I can't wait any longer and tomorrow I may not even recover the money I spent on the raw material. I used my whole family to finish the goods and we will not be able to get even the minimum labour charges.

Hamidbhai's story is not unique in the gem polishing industry. Other adult workers said that *dalals* would not pay them for days on end. I witnessed an interesting tableau at Ghat Gate one evening where I was told that workers, both adults and children, come to sell what they have produced. The dealer who had taken me there said that if one wanted to make a quick buck on a deal, Ghat Gate was the place to do so. I was besieged by workers with little *pudias* (packets containing gems). The dealers were waiting across the road on the other side. One by one, they would cross the road and wait. While the labourers start gathering from about 5.30 p.m. onwards, the dealers move in for the kill around 6.30 p.m. The negotiations start only around 7 p.m. By that time, the worker is desperate. If he does not sell his goods that evening, there may not be an evening meal. The dealer or the *dalal* knows his plight so he waits. The smaller dealers buy from Ghat Gate and sell to big-time dealers at Gopal Ji Ka Rasta in Johari Bazaar. The big-time dealers supply to agents of exporters and the product that was bought in one evening for Rs 25 from the worker may ultimately end up selling for Rs 250 at the very least.

A *dalal*, who is also a small-time exporter, told me that the only way to make money was to be *'chatur and chaukan'* ('clever and alert'). The *dalal* waits to see how he can get: *'Ek rupaiye ka maal, aath anne mein* (To be able to buy goods worth one rupee for eight annas). *Dalals* proudly say that the time to buy is just before Id and Muharram, important religious occasions for Muslims, when the worker needs money. At that time, if you are shrewd, you can buy gems for a pittance: *'Ek rupaiye ka maal, char anne mein* (Goods worth one rupee for four annas). Shrewd *dalals* stock up at that time and it is also then that workers get indebted. It is not for nothing as Sajuddin Mian said: 'The rich are becoming richer and the poor are becoming poorer.'

While initially one gets the impression that working children are children primarily of artisans, on deeper investigation, I found that this was not so. In fact, there is a clear-cut hierarchy and the status of a man can be judged from whether he sends his child to work or to school. There is also a distinction between those who send their children to private schools and those who send them to government schools. There are three categories of parents. In the first category are master craftsmen and some less-skilled artisans who can earn up to Rs 100 a day. They generally send their children to private schools. Even artisans who earn less often prefer to send their children to private schools. Bade Mian is one of the most talented master craftsmen in Jaipur. He earns staggering sums because he is one of the few craftsmen who can copy antiques, particularly in jade. He has two sons, ten and twelve, who go to school. Bade Mian said:

Even during the summer vacation, I do not let the boys come to the workshop. Once a child starts making money or hearing conversation about money, he is tempted to work and his mind gets distracted from his studies.

Jabbarbhai, another master craftsman, said the same thing:

There is plenty of time for a child to pick up the job. If he wants to succeed in this competitive world, he must be educated.

I was told that the children who work full-time from 8 a.m. to 6 p.m. are children of *paldaras* (casual labourers). Bade Mian was of the view that 80 per cent of working children were children of rickshaw-pullers, bakery workers, barbers and the like. This was also confirmed by Jabbarbhai. The explanation proffered was that manual work is very hard and parents of these children do not want their children to end up doing the same job. They much prefer to send their children to the *ustad* contractor even without wages in the hope that the child will eventually be trained in an occupation which is more remunerative. This was confirmed to me by several other people like an auto-rickshaw owner-cum-driver, an adult worker-cum-supervisor who worked for Bade Mian, a cycle-repairer and several casual labourers I had the opportunity to interview.

I asked a school teacher why some parents, though keen to send their children to school, do not do so and was told:

> Primary education is virtually free and the school fees are Rs 5 for the whole year for classes III to V and Rs 30 a year for classes VI to VIII.

There are also special concessions for Scheduled Castes and Scheduled Tribes but the parents still have to spend at least Rs 150–200 a year on books and uniforms. It is those people who cannot even bear this additional expense who send their children to work.

Quraishi, a young contractor who is about twenty-five years old said:

> Of course, a child who gets education is smarter, he can grasp things more easily and will learn much faster. He will also earn a lot of money. But in this trade, even an illiterate fellow, after a few years of training, can earn Rs 20 a day, and earn it with dignity. If your father has been pulling rickshaws or hauling sacks on his back, this is clearly better.

I was told that no-one whose *khandani pesha* (traditional occupation) was gem polishing sent their children to work at a very young age. If an artisan was good at his job, the chances would be that his children would be at school. Most people said that more than 80 per cent of children who worked full-time had loans taken by their parents against the security of their labour but the loans did not generally exceed Rs 500.

It seems that about 50 per cent of the total child labour force in the gem polishing industry consists of children whose parents have either an uncertain income or a very hard life or both. These parents send their children to work in the fond hope that the child, if he is able to get into the gem industry, will be saved from working as a *coolie* (porter), cycle-rickshaw puller, *hathgadi* (hand-cart) puller, etc.

Behind Indira Market is Kalyan Ji ka Rasta. It is an area, I was told, where most of the working children belonging to families of casual labourers work. I saw eighteen workshops where gems were being polished. In most of them, two or three very little children below the age of eight were working. Some people had set up a makeshift arrangement on the road-side where a *charpai* (bed) was being used to give shelter from the sun. Three children were sitting under the shade of the bed, polishing gems. The children in this area were much younger than children I had seen elsewhere and I was told that all these children's fathers were manual labourers. Inside the *mohalla* in an open space, ten children were playing. They looked as if they had been working from the state of their hands and clothes. In one workshop three children, who could not have been more than six years old, were bent over a small coal *sigri* (stove). Their faces were not even six inches from the coal which they were blowing upon to keep the embers alive. They would blow into the embers, warm it and then fix the uncut gem stone on it. They had to do this repeatedly so that the stone was firmly stuck in the right position: it could then be sent for further grinding and polishing. These three boys were being supervised by an adolescent. I tried to talk to these children but they refused to respond and in fact did not even look up while I was talking. A crowd of about seven or eight people gathered around. The contractor, whose workshop it was, looked slightly aggressive and did not like my asking so many questions. He told me that in this area all the working children belonged to labourers' families. Their parents were in no position to send their children to school because they could not afford the expense of books and uniforms. I asked the adolescent boy if he had been educated. He could apparently only sign his name and do some simple accounts. He had started working at the age of six. An elderly man came up and said that he was the father of the adolescent boy and worked as a *khula mazdoor* (casual labourer) himself. He had two sons and three daughters and he had put them to work on gem polishing when they were six or seven. He said:

I am a *khula mazdoor*, working in shops loading and unloading goods. I sent this boy to school for a year or two but then decided that it was better to get the boys to learn a decent craft. So I brought them to the *ustad*. Even if they don't earn anything in the initial years, they will earn enough later to make a decent living after five or six years. My son has been spared the indignity of manual labour.

Three or four people who were also *mazdoors* said the same thing. It was the ambition of every *mazdoor* to get his child to become a *nagine ka karigar* (a gem stone artisan). Hafizbhai, father of one of the working children, said:

> If a man like me only lives on tea because I can't really afford too much food, what do you expect will happen? Most of us get T.B. and we can't afford to get any treatment. How can I afford to send my child to school? Even if my child gets no wages today, in a few years he will start earning a decent living.

I interviewed a cycle-repair man who had worked for twenty-five years on the footpath. He belonged to the caste of roof-thatchers. He had four daughters and two sons. He had four brothers who were carrying on their traditional occupations but all the children in the next generation were gem polishers. He took me to the unit where his eight-year old son worked. He said:

> I drop him off to work at 8 a.m. before I set up shop under this tree. The first thing I ask my wife when I get home is whether Bablu has come home. All the time I am worried. I want him to learn the trade but such a small child away from home can easily get into bad company. This is the greatest danger faced by young children.

Mohammad Ali had sent his boy to school for a couple of years but withdrew him in favour of the gem industry. He said:

> My wife was keen that the child learn to work rather than study. She would point to all the other families where children were working and not going to school. So I agreed to send

him to work. After all, Bablu is never going to become an
officer. If he can be spared taking up our traditional occupation, that's good enough.

I interviewed a rickshaw-puller at the bus stand who had
three daughters and four sons. All the boys were engaged in
the gem industry. The younger ones, at twelve and thirteen
years, went to school and also worked in the afternoon. He
said:

> Life as a cycle-rickshaw-puller is rough. I started as a mill-
> worker but the mill closed down and so for the last fifteen
> years, I have been pulling rickshaws. This work is very hard
> and although I can earn Rs 25 or Rs 30 a day, it is exhausting
> and uncertain. At least in the gem polishing industry, one can
> sit in a quiet, cool corner and work rather than sweat and toil
> in the heat.

In the last category are some parents who send their
children to work even when they can afford to send their
children to school. Rafiqbhai is in his mid-thirties and is an
auto-rickshaw owner-cum-driver. His whole family is involved
in the gem industry. His wife and daughters drill holes in the
beads and string them into necklaces. His two boys work for
the *ustad*. Although he earns about Rs 50 a day on the average
and can afford to send his children to school, he said:

> Why send the child to school when you can get him to learn
> a trade? After all, educated or uneducated, he will be in this
> line. There are no great advantages in education. But if the
> child starts learning young, he will start earning young.

EDUCATIONAL STATUS OF WORKING CHILDREN

Surprisingly even though education is seen as a must for upward
mobility in this industry 50 per cent of all children working in
the gem polishing industry are completely illiterate. As mentioned earlier, even those who were educated up to the third
standard learned so little that whatever they had picked up had

been totally forgotten. *Dalals*, contractors, master craftsmen, workers and artisans felt strongly that education was an absolute must for all children. I met and had the opportunity of talking to several adults involved in the industry and everyone of them felt that education was a must for all children below the age of fifteen years. Some cases are recounted below which indicate the depth of feeling about the role of education in the struggle for upward mobility.

Bade Mian as mentioned earlier is one of the most talented master craftsmen in Jaipur. He earns *lakhs* (Rs 1 lakh is equivalent to Rs 100,000) of rupees a year as an artisan because he is one of the few craftsmen who can copy antiques. He showed me a Chinese jade bowl, which he was working on, for which he was going to get Rs 30,000. He said:

> Let me tell you the story (showing me a half-carved jade bowl) of this Chinese jade bowl for which I am going to get Rs 30,000. A dealer came to me with a catalogue and asked me to carve the bowl from the design. One look at the design and I realized that the man had got an unsuspecting American to buy the bowl saying it was of the Shah Jahan period. I knew what the game was because not only am I educated but I have also gone to art school and I know that leaves turned this way on jade are only found in antiques of that period. This man knows that I can carve an exact duplicate. I know that antiques or goods that can be passed off as antiques sell at a premium abroad and therefore I could demand this price. I know that the dealer will make at least a *lakh* of rupees on this transaction; otherwise, he would not be willing to pay such a high labour fee.

Bade Mian is totally against the use of child labour. He himself only trains children above the age of fifteen years. He had only one young boy working for him but he insists that children first go to school and then come to him. Rehman is a twelve-year old boy who goes to the local school from 7 a.m. to 12 noon. He gets home, has lunch and then goes to Bade Mian's to work till 5 p.m. He was asked by Bade Mian to show me the units where children were working. I asked him whether children liked to go to school or to work. He whispered to me that children of his age hated to work all day because it was tiring and boring and their eyes hurt because they were glued to the gem. He himself did not mind learning from Bade Mian because he wanted to become a craftsman. He also did not go regularly. He took me to his father's unit. His father, Samirbhai, is a self-styled *ustad* contractor who told me that his *ustad* was also Bade Mian. In his unit, where there were seven children, the youngest — he proudly told me — was not quite five years of age! They were polishing cut gem stones. The workshop was absolutely dark and running exclusively on child labour. All the children were illiterate.

Bade Mian is a staunch believer in education for all children. He sometimes has a couple of children who come to learn from him but he insists that the child continue his education for part of the day or at least complete the fifth standard. His own four children are all at school but he wants them to get a higher education. He will only teach them after their education is over. Said Bade Mian:

> Without education, you are finished. You can easily be cheated by the trader. You can never hope to expand your business because you won't be able to speak or understand the language you need. You will never be able to communicate with the foreigners who are the real buyers.

This master craftsman went on to say that education develops the mind and the ability to grasp ideas increases. He said:

> Let me give you an example. When I started working there were fifty others with me, but I was one of the few educated boys. After five years of training, I left and started my own business and many of my former colleagues came to work for me. They were uneducated and till this day work merely as wage workers. There has been no change in their economic status. In my thirty years of experience, I can say one thing and that is: an illiterate child can never become an artisan.

In Zia-ud-din ki Gali I counted seventy children at work, all between the ages of six and ten years. I talked at length to the *ustad* contractor who was running his whole unit using child labour. He told me that his own children, including two daughters, were at school. He pointed to one of the older children working for him, who was about fourteen years and his own son and said:

> My father was a constable turned *dalal*. When I finished my matriculation exam, my father put me to work to learn the job of polishing gems. All my five children are studying. This boy (pointing to his fourteen-year old son), was in school till very recently but now I have withdrawn him from school because he does not really have an aptitude for studies. I want my children to be educated so that they can keep accounts, deal with traders and, if later we expand our business, they will be able to deal with foreign buyers.

Jalaluddin employs six children in a small room for polishing gems. He works along with them and also supervises the work. Three of the six children had had no education at all. One child had only been educated up to the first standard and the other up to the third standard. He said that more than 80 per cent of working children had no education at all. He blamed the short-sightedness of the parents for this state of affairs. He said:

> I am slightly better off than the parents of some of these children but I had made up my mind that I would starve and, if necessary, even let my children starve but I would not put them to work at an early age. I would educate them. In any case, just because a child is going to school, it doesn't mean that he can't learn to work for a few hours. But if a parent wants to make money on the child, then education is out of the question.

Jalaluddin, of course, offers loans to the parents of these children and effectively binds them to him while his own children go to school!

I interviewed sixty-four school-going children in government schools between the age of ten and fourteen years. The idea was to find out what their socio-economic background was. Interestingly, more than 85 per cent of children who worked after school were not children of artisans. Their fathers were either in government service or employed as barbers, tailors, bakers, masons and a few even as casual labourers. In some homes, the mothers were doing *bindai ka kaam* and in others, ultra-sonic drilling machines for piercing holes in beads had been installed; but these were not families of traditional craftsmen.

In a private school, I interviewed thirty-four children and more than 50 per cent of them came from families of gem artisans, though less than 10 per cent worked after school. But the children said that while they themselves did not work, other children did. My interviews with *ustad* contractors had also revealed the same trend. *Ustads* normally did not allow their own children to work but employed other children to do the work.

Children who work full-time are obviously the most deprived. But those who go to school and work afterwards as well also have a very tough schedule. In the gem polishing industry, the child does not need to work at a young age because everyone recognizes the need for education. Yet a large number of children do work. Part of the problem has to do, as sixteen year-old Jamal explained, with how parents feel: 'If we have too much time on our hands, we are likely to get into bad company and start abusing out sisters and mothers.' Or as Zakir, ten years old, said: 'Our parents think that if we play we will become vagabonds and get into bad company. They therefore want us to work.'

But studying and working places a tremendous strain on the child as interviews with school teachers revealed.

INTERVIEWS WITH SCHOOL TEACHERS

I interviewed six school teachers. They said that the strain on children who studied and went to work was enormous but, in spite of everything, they did not falter in their home-work. One

teacher said that despite their best efforts, these children did
not do well academically and then the parents would blame
the government schools for the child's poor performance. This
was one of the reasons why children dropped out without
finishing their education:

> 'How can a child study and work day in and day out for twelve
> hours without it having some adverse effect? After all, a child
> too is human!'

Another teacher said that sometimes the children did not
find time and had to do their home-work during the P.T. or
games period. Working children were considered to be very
conscientious but their ability to grasp was not as good as those
children who did not have to work. The teachers started discussing the relative intelligence of working and non-working
children. They were of the opinion that working children were
not as intelligent though out of six teachers present, one admitted that the problem was not that they were less intelligent
but that the stresses and strains of going to school and then
working took their toll and the working child was usually
exhausted even after a night of sleep. Another teacher then
said:

> There has to be a difference in the academic standard of
> children who can devote time to their studies and those who
> go straight to work. If a child comes to school at 7 a.m. and
> after a brief lunch, works till six in the evening and then does
> home-work at night, what can you expect? But one thing must
> be said of working children, they try very hard.

LABOUR LAWS AND THEIR IMPLEMENTATION

Surprisingly, while the gem polishing industry is the largest
single employer in Jaipur and polished coloured gem stones net
the Government of India foreign exchange to the tune of Rs
1400 *crores* a year, no labour laws apply to this industry.
Informed sources in the industry say that one of the main
reasons why India is able to compete in the international market

inspite of not getting the best quality raw material is that India has cheap labour. In the international gem market, India holds the fourth position with respect to the export of emeralds, which are mainly sent to the United States of America. In the export of rubies and sapphires, India holds the fifth position. India supplies the world market with the cheapest emeralds. The main competitors for India are Switzerland, Israel and Hong Kong where the labour charges are much higher.

The idea that the Factories Act should be made applicable to the gem industry was considered ridiculous when mooted. Informed sources said that the political clout of gem traders was such that attempts to bring this industry under the Factories Act had been abandoned. Some said that while the government was interested in the welfare of workers at one level, the need for earning foreign exchange was paramount and so production would therefore always have an edge over labour welfare.

My visits to several manufacturing units of exporters, described earlier, suggested that inspections would be impossible and it would be very hard to prove that a particular exporter is employing a particular number of workers. It is only when one is not a government official that exporters tell you proudly that they have fifty workers under them or 500 employed directly by them on salaries. Since the workers are working in verandas, sheds and places difficult of access and there are no name-plates anywhere, it is difficult to say who is working for whom. In fact, most of the big traders/exporters/manufacturers have their own permanent employees who are permanent only in the sense that they have been working for several years; they are not permanent according to the provisions of the Factories Act and do not get paid for days they may be ill or when there is no work. They are not entitled to any benefits under the Factories Act because these units do not fall within the definition of what constitutes a factory: in one *haveli*, while there may be forty workers employed, they would be working in several rooms and verandas.

6

The Child Potters of Khurja

William Wood, 9 years old, 'was 7 years 10 months old when he began to work.' He 'ran moulds' (carried ready-moulded articles into the drying-room, afterwards bringing back the empty mould) from the very beginning. He came to work every day in the week at 6 a.m., and left off at about 9 p.m. 'I work till 9 o'clock at night six days in the week. I have done so for the last seven or eight weeks.' Fifteen hours of labour for a child of 7! J. Murray, 12 years of age, says: 'I turn jigger and run moulds. I come at 6. Sometimes I come at 4. I worked all night last night, till 6 o'clock this morning. I have not been in bed since the night before last. There were eight or nine other boys working last night. All but one have come this morning. I get 3 shillings and six pence. I do not get any more for working at night. I worked two nights last week.' Fernyhough, a boy of 10: 'I have not always an hour (for dinner). I have only half an hour sometimes: on Thursday, Friday, and Saturday.'

(Karl Marx quoting from the Children's Employment Commission, First Report of 1863 describing the conditions of children working in the pottery industry of England).

THE POTTERY INDUSTRY OF KHURJA

Children in the pottery industry of Khurja today do exactly the same work as children did in nineteenth-century England. Their work is described locally as *uthai rakhai* (pick up and put down). They carry empty moulds to the worker who works on the jigger jolly and carry the filled moulds out in the sun to dry. The boys who do this work are called *phantiwalas* (the boys who carry the *phanti* which is a piece of wood on which five or six moulds are kept). About 95 per cent of all working children in Khurja are *phantiwalas*. The only difference in the conditions of children in the pottery industry today and in nineteenth-century England is that they work not more than nine or ten hours a day and rarely do night-work.

The pottery industry of Khurja is over 600 hundred years old and is considered to be the traditional occupation of the people of Khurja in Bulandshahr district of Uttar Pradesh. It may be clarified here that when people speak of pottery being a traditional industry of Khurja, they are really referring to the few families of Multani *kumbhars* (potters) who came with the Mughal armies. The local village potter, part and parcel of Indian rural society, is not included in this description. (Burra 1987c)

There are almost 20,000 workers engaged either directly or indirectly in the pottery industry. Of the total workers, approximately 5000 or 25 per cent are children below the age of fourteen years. However, these are only estimates and no-one is sure of the actual figures. But factory owners say that the total work-force within the factories is 6000 adults and a few hundred women and children. They arrive at these figures by calculating at the rate of nine workers in each factory and there are officially about 500 pottery units. But a study of about 25 per cent of the units revealed that except for a handful of units where there were less than ten workers, 90 per cent of them had more than twenty-five workers each with about 25 per cent of the work-force being made up of children below the age of fourteen years. Some units had almost eighty to ninety workers employed.

The pottery industry of Khurja makes a variety of ceramic goods such as flower vases, objets d'art, crockery, industrial ceramics like chemical porcelain, ball mill linings and balls, electrical and electronic ceramics like low tension (L.T.) and

high tension (H.T.) insulators, spark plugs, sanitary ware, stoneware jars, etc. Crockery and insulators account for the major
share of what is produced.

The annual turn-over of the Khurja pottery industry is Rs 8
crores (Bhattacharya 1982). If these are the official figures, I
was told in Khurja that actual production is three times what
is declared and the estimate is deliberately kept low in order
to evade excise. Individual units purposely show turn-over
figures of less than Rs 7.5 lakhs to claim exemption from excise
and retain their classification in the small-scale sector.

Other important pottery centres in Uttar Pradesh are located
at Chinhat, Chuna, Basti and Ghaziabad.

I visited more than forty-nine units where pottery was being
made in factories, ten units where work was being done exclusively with the help of family labour, ten units where, in
addition to family labour, some hired help was also used and
eight families of rural potters who did not make the famous
Khurja pottery but were exclusively involved with supplying
pots for the local market. I spent nineteen days in Khurja. I was
able to interview people from different segments of the pottery
industry: hundred workers — men, women and children —
twenty factory owners, eight *thekedars* (contractors), five
master craftsmen, five traders, two doctors and a few government officials.

THE KHURJA POTTERY INDUSTRY:
GENESIS AND DEVELOPMENT

Khurja is a small town located in the Bulandshahr district of
western Uttar Pradesh. It is hemmed in on both sides by the
rivers Ganga and Yamuna, which flow at a distance of forty-five
kilometres. It is approximately eighty-three kilometres by road
from Delhi. Khurja junction is well connected by rail, situated
as it is on the main Delhi-Howrah railway line. Thus it is very
conveniently connected with some of the major towns and
cities of India both by road and by rail.

The Khurja pottery industry has a long history. It is believed that Timur Lang, who sacked Delhi in 1398, had a band of soldiers amongst whom were also skilled potters. These potters stayed back and settled down in Multan (now in Pakistan) and near Delhi. They were adept at making blue pottery with Persian designs and colours. About 600 years ago, in the reign of Mohammad Bin Tughlak, some of the potters' families moved from Delhi to Khurja (Bhattacharya 1982: 8; Sharma 1978: 208). They started with red clay pottery and then went on to introduce blue glazes on red clay articles with an englobe or coating of white clay, painting floral designs with cupric oxide and applying a soft glaze containing glass, red lead, quartz and borax. The basic raw material was the locally available red clay.

At first the traditional potters made *hookahs* (pipes), *surahis* (water-containers) and vessels as well as decorated wares. They attracted the attention of the outside world when two of the master potters from Khurja were invited to the Coronation Exhibition in London in 1911 to demonstrate their skill on the potter's wheel. The grandson of one of the master potters, Rasheed Ahmed, is one of the leading master potters of Khurja and has recently won the master craftsman's award.

Until the 1930s, the pottery industry of Khurja was the preserve of two families of Multani *kumbhars*. In 1934, in order to develop the pottery industry the Government of Uttar Pradesh took the initiative and sent Professor H.N. Ray of the Benaras Hindu University to investigate the feasibility of making white-ware goods using modern technology and newer raw materials such as china clay, feldspar and quartz. The local potters were quite receptive to the new methods. But their activities did not make much headway till World War II.

The Second World War was largely instrumental in giving a boost to the ceramic industry because there was a ban on the use of various metals for making household utensils. During the war, import of ceramic goods was drastically curtailed and to meet the demand of ceramic wares for the war hospitals, the Uttar Pradesh government set up a factory in Khurja in 1942 for making such articles under the supervision of H.N. Ray. When the war was over, the factory had to be closed down in

1946 due to lack of demand for the products. It was decided then to convert the factory which had three small kilns, two chimneys and three ball mills into the Pottery Development Centre. The workers of the now defunct factory were provided with alternative employment. They were given the processed body and other raw materials from the Centre and were also allowed the facility of firing their green wares or unbaked goods in government kilns on payment of a nominal rent. This Centre is the first Common Facility Centre in the country and the main cause for the development of the Khurja pottery industry.

The Centre started in 1946 with only eight potters. Initially, it was purely a cottage industry producing cheap quality products which had a limited market. In 1953, Dr T.N. Sharma, a ceramic expert, was sent to Japan for training. On his return in 1955, he demonstrated the use of better technology using local raw materials. He also improved the jigger jolly machines and the shape of *saggars* (fire resistant containers in which unbaked pots are baked) and was primarily responsible for a number of schemes for the development of the pottery industry under the Second Five-Year Plan.

The Khurja pottery industry today has three types of entrepreneurs. The oldest are the master craftsmen, also known as traditional potters, who have adapted to the new technology and now make their art-ware largely with the help of the new technology using the terracotta moulds rather than the potter's wheel. But they have not given up their old methods of decoration, painting and glazes.

The second type of entrepreneur is the one who learnt the skills offered by the Pottery Development Centre and set up his own unit. And the third type of entrepreneur is the person who had the finance to set up his units but has not actually learnt the job himself.

Interestingly, the traditional village potter has not entered the industry. He continues his traditional work for a totally different market and is not included in the list of Khurja potters. By definition, the Khurja potter makes his wares for an outside market, while the local village potter produces to meet local needs.

The pottery industry in Khurja was set up because it was felt that there was a tradition of pottery in the area and a market for the goods. The people who were pioneers in this industry, like Dr Sharma, had envisaged that by setting up an industry and providing facilities, many people would get employment here. In fact, in the early years, the training was very rigorous and those who wanted to set up independent units had to prove their knowledge and ability, for the facilities provided by the government were crucial for their economic upliftment. But in later years the pottery industry developed independently: many people seeing the potential of the industry set up units without actually knowing the work just because it was a good business proposition. Today, therefore, there is not much similarity amongst the different types of entrepreneurs.

A common complaint of traders or financiers-turned-entrepreneurs is that the skilled worker-turned-entrepreneur has ruined the market because of his lack of knowledge, illiteracy and absence of financial staying power. Many of the smaller entrepreneurs are heavily indebted to local dealers who are making all the profits. The worker-turned-entrepreneur knows so little about the business side of pottery that he has no idea of the true value of his goods and because of his precarious condition sells his goods at a low price. Since the goods produced in all the factories are, quality-wise, almost on par with each other, the financier-turned-entrepreneur is not able to make as large a profit as he would like to. The result has been that a cartel of them has started marketing their own goods in order to bypass the local dealers. So great is the resentment against the skilled worker-turned-entrepreneur that these educated entrepreneurs, some years ago, tried to force the government to pass a resolution that coal quotas would only be given to those units which had a certain area of factory, size of kiln and quantum of capital. The idea was to displace the small entrepreneur but it did not succeed.

THE POTTERY INDUSTRY TODAY:
STRUCTURE AND MARKET

There are four types of pottery units in Khurja not including the local potter who produces red clay goods for the local market. Most of the other pottery units produce for the outside market. Out of a total of almost 500 units, less than 50 per cent actually function. The reason is the large-scale black-marketing of coal, which is the primary raw material needed in this industry. Workers told this researcher that a small unit owner could easily earn Rs 10,000 a month by just black-marketing coal and was also saved the problems of actually running a unit. Out of the 500 units that are registered with the Government Pottery Centre, approximately 300 are run by traders, twenty-five by traditional potters and seventy-five units belong to skilled workers who have saved money and set up on their own. About hundred units belong to people who have received training in the manufacture of pottery but who no longer use their own hands.

Looked at from another point of view, the units in the industry could be classified differently. The first and largest category is made up of independent pottery units, which are equipped with their own machinery and manufacture their own processed clay called body and glazes and have their own forming and firing facilities. Some of them also do decoration work on their products. There are 398 such units.

The second category consists of dependent units which have no processing and firing facilities of their own. They obtain the processed body, glazes and other raw materials from outside, make the green wares at their units and after applying the glazes, get the wares fired at the kilns provided by the Uttar Pradesh Small Industries Corporation Potteries Ltd. and pay a nominal rent. There are 126 registered dependent potters in Khurja.

There are twenty units which only manufacture the processed body and glazes and sell them to the dependent units which do not have these facilities. While the Government

Centre is supposed to do this, dependent potters require credit which the Centre cannot provide and therefore private manufacturers are able to do good business.

There are also units which only undertake the decoration of pottery articles on a piece-rate or job work basis. There are twenty such registered units.

Another category of potter who makes clay goods in Khurja is formed by the local potters who do not make goods for the outside market, but only for the local market. There are colonies of the local *kumbhar* in the city and in the surrounding villages who make large containers for water and grain, *kulhads* (clay cups) which are sold to *halwais* (sweetmeat sellers) and *sakuras* (small plates) bought for feasts and weddings. These traditional potters also make plates which are no longer in demand because of plastic and paper goods.

In a recent report on the development of the ceramic industry in India, it was estimated that there would be a crockery demand of 33 million sets during the Seventh Five-Year plan period. It is estimated that the demand for clay-based crockery from the urban sector would be 1,28,500 tonnes. According to the 1985 figures, 10,700 tonnes were produced in the organized sector and 71,000 in the small-scale sector. Of these all-India figures, the contribution of the Khurja units was 15,000 tonnes or more than 20 per cent of all the crockery produced in the small-scale sector in India. The small-scale sector, under which the Khurja pottery industry falls, supplies mostly stoneware items to people with little purchasing power. The middle-class purchaser is fed by both the small-scale and the organized sector manufacturer of quality stoneware, earthenware, etc., and the higher economic strata buy superior bone china products. Khurja makes about 50 per cent of low tension insulators in the country and about 10 per cent of the kit-kats. The only sanitary goods made in Khurja are foot-rests for Indian-style toilets.

While the demand for pottery is very high and growing, the goods produced by the local village potter have less demand than before. The village potter in Khurja is facing competition

from plastic, paper and dried leaf plates and bowls. As one
potter said:

> There is at least a 25 per cent fall in the demand for our goods
> even in the local villages because of the paper and plastic
> plates and saucers. Even though our goods are cheaper, there
> is more prestige in using plastic goods and these have become
> status symbols.

The local potter who uses the red clay locally available has
not made any advances in technology nor has he received any
facilities by way of improved technology from the government.
The Khadi and Village Industries Commission, which was
set up to help village artisans, introduced white-ware pottery
in the villages instead of promoting local methods. This venture
failed miserably for a host of reasons: there was no market in
the villages for these goods, the village potter did not have
resources for raw material or fuel and, in any case, could not
find avenues for selling the goods produced.

PROCESSES IN THE POTTERY INDUSTRY

In most of the big ceramic units, the raw material is processed
on the premises with the help of machines called jaw crushers,
edge runners, clay blungers, etc. The processes in the pottery
industry of Khurja are many depending upon the goods made.
One commonly used method is by throwing clay on the potter's
wheel. This is the traditional method of making red clay potteries throughout India. In Khurja, the traditional potters even
now use the kick-wheels for making decorated potteries. The
potter uses his hand pressure to shape the body. This process
is wholly manual.

Another method is known as the beating or patting method.
This consists of formation of clay-ware by beating a roughly
thrown piece of leather-hard clay with a wooden beater to the
required shape and thickness. This process reduces the porosity
of the clay body and makes it homogeneous and strong. In
Khurja, this process is used only for making the *saggars* or

containers in which the unbaked clay goods are put before firing in the kilns. The *saggar* body is put on the outside of a wooden frame and beaten into the required shape and thickness by a wooden beater.

Most of the crockery, plates, cups and saucers, etc., are shaped on the jigger and jolly machines. The jigger and jolly process is used to produce hollow single shapes on a mass scale. A jigger consists of a vertical shaft having a cup-shaped wheel-head which receives the mould made by plaster of paris. It is mostly power-driven and is provided with a foot-brake. Some units produce jiggered items without using power, by pedalling. A jolly consists of an inclined arm mounted on a pivot with a balancing counterpoise on one arm. The opposite arm carries a profile which is an iron tool to give shape to the article. Depending upon the goods being made, a quantity of clay is put into the mould fitted to the head and pressed to shape by the profile by lowering the arm of the jolly. For every article, a separate mould is fixed to the jigger head.

All the ceramic units at Khurja making crockery use this process. This technique, however, cannot make the complete product. Handles for teapots, jugs, etc. are made by slip casting and then joined to these articles.

For slip casting, a plaster of paris mould is made and the slip which consists of a semi-viscous slurry of the ceramic body is poured into it. The excess liquid is poured out after some time. The inside of the mould becomes covered with a thin layer of the body after the water is soaked by the plaster mould. After some time, the layer becomes hard and is removed from the mould. It is then finished by scraping off the extra clay, smoothened with fine sandpaper and, finally, with a soft wet sponge. This method is also used for making complicated shapes such as soup spoons. In Khurja, this method is widely used for making both chemical porcelain as well as crockery and tableware.

The slip is made from finely ground plastic body by adding small amounts of sodium silicate or sodium carbonate to act as deflocculent.

For both the slip method and the jigger jolly method, units make their own moulds of plaster of paris. But not more than three or four castings can be done from one mould efficiently. Making articles of complicated shapes or large sizes requires the use of several moulds for making the component parts which are subsequently joined.

Pressing in steel dies using hydraulic presses is used for making tiles and high-tension electro-porcelain. One tile manufacturing unit and a few high-tension insulator units (up to 11 KVA) at Khurja are using this technique. The technique is also being used by other units for making electrical kit-kats, technical ceramics and other products of simple shapes. Small articles are being made by handpresses.

In the organized sector, the green-wares are dried in rooms using a hot blast of air. But by and large, drying is done in the shade by keeping the green-wares on the floor outside or by stacking them in shelves for a few days.

Once the goods are dried they are scraped for any rough edges and smoothened with water. If they are hand-painted or decorated otherwise, they are given over to the painter and decorators. The dried goods not painted are sent for direct glazing.

The earliest potters of Khurja used indigenous red clay for their goods. But today all the raw material comes from outside. The china clay comes from Rajmahal in Bihar, Ahmedabad in Gujarat, Chandia in Madhya Pradesh and Bikaner in Rajasthan. The ball clay is available only in Rajasthan, Andhra Pradesh, Gujarat and Kerala. The feldspar comes from Rajasthan and quartz comes from Rajasthan, Andhra Pradesh, Gujarat and Madhya Pradesh. The main source of fuel, coal, comes from the collieries of the eastern coalfields situated in Bihar and West Bengal. The independent units get their coal against allotment directly from the mines. The dependent units are allotted the requisite quantity of coal from the coal dump of the Pottery Development Centre for firing in the rented kilns.

Glazes are homogeneous mixtures of silicate minerals and chemicals which melt to form glass and are used to provide a lustrous coating to the porous fired products to render them impervious. They fit the body intimately as the materials are mostly the same in both the bodies and the glazes. A ball mill is used to powder the glaze to the desired fineness.

The basic raw materials for the unglazed pot are quartz, feldspar, plastic clay and china clay. The basic composition of glazes is feldspar, quartz, china clay, marble or calcite, zinc oxide, barium carbonate, etc. In Khurja, mostly raw and opaque glazes are used which mature at medium temperatures. Different colouring oxides are used by Khurja potters for colouring glazes. Cobalt or copper oxide is used for all shades of blue and black. Copper and chrome oxide is used for the green colour. Iron oxide is used for giving the brown colour and manganese oxide is used for pink or violet colour. The traditional Khurja potters who have about twenty units now use commercially available glazes but some of them still prepare their own blue glazes and jealously guard the secret of their blue pottery.

The Khurja ceramic industry follows an intermediate level of technology. The wares are all single fired. Raw glazes insoluble in water are generally used. Barium glazes containing zirconia and/or titania as the opacifying agents are commonly used by the potters. The glaze is generally applied by dipping the dried green wares in the glaze slip. In some decorative wares, glazing is done by spraying. For various artistic designs, the colours are generally applied by hand painting by artists.

Once the goods are painted and glazed, they are baked in coal-fired, down-draught kilns. The kilns are of various sizes ranging from 2.4 metres (8 feet) to 7.3 metres (24 feet) in diameter. The wares are packed in *saggars* which are stacked inside the furnace for firing. *Saggars* prevent direct contact of the wares with the flames and fumes of the fuel which would otherwise spoil the colour and glaze of the products. They also help to keep the glazed articles in position without sticking to each other. The temperature of the kiln is highest at the top, around 1250–1280° C for insulators and 1200–1250° C for crockery.

Participation of Children in the Pottery Industry

The first job for the young child is to carry lumps of clay to the *kataiwala* (the worker who makes pots on the jigger jolly machine). Each *kataiwala* has one or two helpers, the *phantiwalas,* who are always children. Since this work is always done through a *thekedar* because the employer wants faster production, the work is done at a fantastic speed with both adults and children working at break-neck speed. An average *kataiwala* cuts 4000 pieces in an eight-hour shift and the *phantiwala* has to carry 4000 moulds outside in the open to dry and carry back 4000 empty moulds to the *kataiwala*. In one factory, I noticed young children of nine and ten carrying six moulds on a *phanti*. The moulds contained three-inch mugs, each of which contained 100 grams of clay. The mould itself weighed 300 grams. The combined weight of the moulds, the clay and the wood was about eight kilograms which the child carried on every trip. In an eight-hour day, he ran five kilometres a day at the very minimum with this load.

At another factory I saw children carry weights up to eleven kilograms on the *phanti*. I was told that on an average, the children made a thousand return trips in an eight-hour working day and covered a distance of six or seven kilometres. This was the work that children were mainly engaged in and their work was described as that of helpers!

This was not the only work that children did. Once the pots were partially dry, these children took out the half-dry pots and carried them to the workers who were engaged in finishing the work. In several factories, I noticed children stacking ninety mugs on a wooden platform and then carrying them on their heads to the adult workers. The weight of this burden, I was told by adult workers and factory owners, was more than ten kilograms. The children doing this work were so young that their hands and legs would tremble after they had put down the weight.

In one factory, I saw children unloading *saggars*, six at a time. Each *saggar* weighed half a kilogram. In one factory, a child of thirteen was carrying three *saggars*, each weighing eight kilograms. His body was bent double with the strain.

Another job that children are engaged in is removing handles from the moulds and carrying them to adults who finish them. Some children were engaged in just cutting handles to the required size. On the average, they had to cut at least 3000–4000 pieces in an eight-hour shift.

Some children were engaged in the scraping of the rough edges from the mugs and other crockery pieces. Others helped with the final water finishing.

The children who have had a little experience work on the jigger jolly machines, clean out the blunger machines and remove the pebbles from the processed clay. I saw children of ten, knee-deep in cold liquid clay, removing the large pebbles from the processed clay while the employer was standing outside the pit and giving instructions. Children are also sent into slip pits to get liquid clay for the moulds because adults do not like the work. It is taken for granted that children will clean the premises and do all the other menial tasks for which adults would be reluctant — such as running errands.

From village Bavanpur, approximately thirty to thirty-five workers come daily to work in the potteries and these include eight or ten boys of the ages of ten to twelve years. Most of these children come from families of *khet mazdoors* (agricultural labourers). Some of them own two or three *bighas* (a unit for measuring land) of land. The fathers of three boys also work in the pottery industry. Most of the children from this village belong to the caste of *dhimar* or *thakur*.

Sondha village is about fourteen kilometres from Khurja town and about hundred workers including thirty to forty boys and adolescents leave home daily at 7 a.m. to work in the potteries. Most of the parents of working children have less than five *bighas* of land. Most of the families own one or two milch animals which the parents tend, while the children labour in the potteries. The parents of ten to fifteen boys also work in the potteries of Khurja.

Interestingly, when I asked why children were being sent

to work when there was so much adult unemployment, the answer that twenty-six-year old Manohar Ram gave was: 'Many adults don't know how to cycle and even if they know, they don't own one. Children don't have that problem. They sit behind us and hitch a ride.'

Some of the children working in the potteries whom I had the opportunity to interview in depth seemed to be the sole earning members of their families. Kalu Ram is twelve years old and comes daily from village Dharaon. He has no father and his mother keeps poor health. He has been working for the past five or six years and supports three younger brothers and two sisters. Vijay Pal and Hira Singh are thirteen years old. They are orphans and also come from Dharaon. Vijay Pal lives with his grandmother. He has no brothers and sisters. He started working in the potteries recently, and grazed the landlord's cattle before this. He said: 'In the villages, there is no work for children. We are expected to work without wages only for a little grain. My grandmother thought that it was about time I started bringing in a regular wage.'

Hira Singh has a brother who is the local quack. They have fifteen *bighas* of land. He studied up to the fifth standard and then his brother told him to start working.

Laxman Das is twelve years old and is a local Khurja boy. He and his younger brother, aged nine years, are the only earning members of their family. Laxman Das was embarrassed at being asked what his father did and said: 'He has retired.' He and his brother support a seven-member family. The contractor, who was standing nearby when I was interviewing Laxman Das, said: 'The man's a drunkard. The mother is lazy. They do not work because they have children to support them.'

Ompal is fourteen years old. He started working a year back when he failed his sixth standard exam. It was also the time when his sister was getting married. He said:

> My parents needed money for my sister's marriage so my
> brother and I started working in the potteries. I thought that
> after a while I would go back to school but once you leave

school, there is no going back. We still have sisters to settle.
My parents have very little land.

I asked several children how they heard that work was
available in the potteries. Fazal said:

Thekedars come to the villages and say they want children
so we know that there is work. Often the *thekedars* don't
want to give the work to adults. We are young, we can work
fast and we don't get tired so easily.

Adults working in the pottery industry who took their
children to work said: 'Our wages are so low that often we
have no choice but to take our children to work to supplement
the family income.'

Sometimes, as Karimbhai pointed out, a child has no aptitude for studying:

My boy is working in the factory with me. He is thirteen years
old. When he failed his exams, I decided to put him to work.
My other children are at school. If the boy is not studying,
he might as well earn and pay for his own expenses.

But not all parents have this attitude. Savita, who has been
working in the potteries for the last ten years, said:

My husband and I feel that we should not put our children
to work at a young age. This is the age to play and run about,
not to work in factories inhaling clay dust the whole day. We
have decided that as long as we can manage, we won't send
our children to work.

There are roughly speaking, three categories of children
working in the pottery industry. The children of master craftsmen all have to learn the work of moulding clay on the traditional potter's wheel. But they do this work for a couple of
hours in a day after school only because the parents feel that
the child should know the technique even if he is later going
to be managing the business and not doing the actual work.
These children probably help out occasionally when the pressure of work is high but they are not regular workers. The

number of children in this category is negligible since there are only two families of traditional potters who are master craftsmen today.

In the second category are children of skilled workers, mainly Biharis, who have set up their own units and run these exclusively using family labour. Here the children do not go to school but work full-time with their parents. This category of entrepreneur rarely employs hired labour and works solely with the help of his family. Such working children as described above probably account for about 5 per cent of the total child labour force.

In the third category are children who work full-time in factories doing the jobs described earlier. Occasionally, a whole family is employed because there are small children who can help out with the work. But usually, children work alone. This type of working child accounts for more than 90 per cent of all children in the industry.

Children working in the potteries of Khurja were by and large illiterate. Many of them had studied up to the fourth standard but could barely read and write. While some children had left school because their parents wanted them to work, many children had failed their examination and the parents had felt that the child did not have an aptitude for studying and had withdrawn him from school.

One noticeable factor was that units producing quality goods did not employ child labour. Or only one or two children were present out of a total labour force of forty or fifty workers. Most of these units had tall racks next to the jigger jolly machines and the same adult worker would stack the *phanti* with the moulds on it. There was no need for a worker to run with the *phanti*. These units also came under the Factories Act and the owners said it was not worth their while to employ children when child labour was illegal in factories. Nor were children employed in units making insulators which require certain kind of skills. By and large, children are employed in units making crockery for bulk production.

While adult workers belong to almost all castes and communities, the children were either from *Koli, Dhimar* or *Jatav* families — Scheduled Castes or Muslims. I did not come across any children from high-caste families.

Most of the work that children do in the pottery industry can be done by adults as well. In fact in many factories, where children were not being employed, the same work was done by either adolescent boys or adults. But adult workers said:

> We don't like this work because it is tiring. The body of the child is supple and he can run fast, bend down and get up quickly without any problem. When you are older, it is difficult to do this work.

Factory owners and *thekedars* also said the same thing: 'If an adult is asked to do this work of fetching and carrying, he would take too long. Adults can't move with the speed that children can. It is not work meant for adults.'

WAGE STRUCTURE AND THE ORGANIZATION OF WORK

The wage structure is very flexible in the pottery industry. According to the Status Report on the ceramic industry at Khurja:

> In the beginning very cheap labour was available at 50–75 paise per day for the skilled workers and 25–50 paise per day for unskilled ones. The present wage of a skilled worker ranges from Rs 300–600 per month while an unskilled worker gets only Rs 150–300 per month. Jobs are generally done on piece rate basis but the pattern of income remains more or less the same. Cheap child labour is also abundantly available and utilized. Because of the low wages, ceramic industry has found a favourable labour pulled location at Khurja (Bhattacharya 1982: 9).

As has been mentioned earlier, there are three types of pottery units. The traditional potters, who largely make art ware goods, supply them to boutiques in the major cities of India and to the five-star hotels. Their goods are quality goods and all the skilled work is done by members of their families but

now that business has expanded, they do employ other workers
— mainly painters — who get paid on a job basis and earn upto
Rs 1500 a month. Many of them are art students who have got
a BA degree as well. Their other workers earn about Rs 500 to
Rs 600 a month and children earn on the average Rs 150–200
a month. Most of the work in these units is not done on contract
because here it is important to maintain quality rather than
increase quantity.

In the second category are those run mainly by Biharis using
family labour and a few hired workers. Here the wages normally
do not exceed Rs 300–350 a month for adults and less than Rs
200 for children.

The bulk of the labour force is employed in independent
units where they work on piece-rate wages. In every factory,
there are a few workers who are employed on *amani* (monthly
wages). But the majority of the workers are engaged by *thekedars* on piece-rate wages. Even those workers who are working
on *amani* for many years are not considered permanent
workers and as such not entitled to any leave. On days the
worker does not come, his wages are cut. In some factories
where the workers have been able to fight for better conditions
of work, the factory owner gives two paid holidays in a month.
But in most factories this is not the practice and workers work
seven days a week without a break.

Since most of the workers are employed by the *thekedars*,
the factory owner does not consider himself responsible for
the workers. Many workers said that *thekedars* sometimes did
not pay wages on time because they said the factory owner had
not paid them or for some other reason. The *thekedars* sometimes cut the wages of the workers as commission. In most
factories, a skilled worker earned not more than Rs 400 a month
and unskilled workers less than Rs 200 a month.

Many workers interviewed said that wages in the pottery
industry were low because of the large influx of Bihari migrant
labour. One worker said:

Most of these people belong to Gaya or Navada districts of

Bihar. For them, it is impossible to earn even Rs 200 a month at home. When they are happy with their wages, then who is going to raise our wages?

Another adult worker, Mahabir Ram, said:

The factory owners know how to exploit these Biharis. They offer them space in the factories to stay and coal to cook their food on. The Biharis are quite happy even though they get paid almost a hundred rupees less than the local adult workers for the same job.

Shafeeq, age forty, said:

'These people even work overtime without wages as a sign of gratitude to their employers. That is why they are employed.'

Different categories of workers were paid different wages. Some firemen said they were paid Rs 600; others said they were earning Rs 1100. Those earning monthly salaries earned more than those workers who were engaged by *thekedars*. Hardly any of the children interviewed earned more than Rs 150 a month for an eight-hour day.

Kalu Ram, all of twelve, commutes daily from Dharaon, a village near Khurja. He started working five or six years ago at a daily wage of Rs 5 a day. Today, he earns Rs 8 a day as a *phantiwala*. He is the sole supporter of his family of five brothers and sisters and an ailing mother. If he works thirty days in a month, he earns Rs 150 a month.

Vijay Pal and Hira Singh, mentioned earlier, earn Rs. 180 a month if they work thirty days in a month and don't take any time off. They also work as *phantiwalas*. Laxmi Das and his eight-year old brother earn Rs 150 a month and between the two of them support a seven-member family.

In one unit I visited, one woman with three children between the ages of eight and ten was able to earn Rs 12 in an eight-hour day after finishing 1000 mugs.

By and large, the wages were as follows: the *amani* workers doing *katai* (work on the jigger jolly machine) got Rs 500 a month, *phantiwalas*, if children, earned approximately Rs 150 a month but if they were older, they earned up to Rs 300 a month; those who fixed handles earned up to Rs 500; those who did finishing got Rs 300 a month. The workers who did glazing received Rs 400 a month. While workers on *theka* (contract) could earn as much in a month, they had to work twice as hard. Even the monthly wage workers had to complete a certain amount of work every day; otherwise, their salaries were cut but their work-load was not as heavy as that of contract labour.

In one factory, the workers told me that for scraping and water finishing the mugs, they got paid Rs 11 for 1000 pieces. Two people together could finish 2000 pieces in a day. Usually an adult would team up with a child and together they would do the work. It seemed that even individual workers tried to exploit children by making them work hard and then keeping a part of their wages for themselves as commission. This way, the adult worker could take it a little easy because the child would work harder. On contract labour, those who cut the handles earned approximately Rs 200 a month and those who joined the handles earned Rs 400 a month. To earn this much, the man had to work at break-neck speed and cut and fix 4000 pieces in eight hours.

Factory owners justified the use of contract labour thus:

> Workers on salaries become very lazy. An *amani* worker will cut only 2000 pieces on the jigger whereas the contract worker will cut 4000 pieces in eight hours. If you want production and increased profits, you cannot have salaried employees.

Ramesh, a work supervisor, said:

> These *maliks* (owners) are clever people. They want profit without responsibility for the workers. That is why 90 per cent of the work is done through *thekedars*. The factory owner then does not feel any responsibility for the labour.

He fixes a rate with the *thekedars* and it is the responsibility of the *thekedars* to pay the labour.

The bulk of the work is done through sub-contracting though the work is all done in the factory premises. The general pattern is that the factory owner has a few adult workers on what is called *amani* or a monthly wage. They supervise the work of the *thekedar* and maintain quality. In some of the larger factories, there are as many as five contractors who had a group of workers working under them. Sometimes, the *thekedar* also helped out and thus saved on one adult's wage. It was the dream of every adult worker to become a *thekedar*. All the workers working under the *thekedar* were paid piece-rate wages. Since they were daily wage workers, no labour laws applied to them.

An interesting fact I observed was that workers who had started very young and worked for fifteen or twenty years earned exactly the same amount as the new adult entrants. The reason for this state of affairs, I was told was:

> If you start working young, your mentality changes and you lose all purpose in life except to carry on with whatever you get. There is no fight left in you so you don't ask for your just dues. That's why employers prefer children. Also, you have to be really desperate in the first place to start work so young and the spirit is beaten out of you by the time you are an adult. Those who start working as adults earn more than those who started off as children.

HEALTH HAZARDS

In England in the nineteenth-century, writes Karl Marx, the pottery industries were amongst the most hazardous for the health of the workers. The Children's Employment Commission Report of 1863 drew attention to the kinds of health hazards faced by workers in the potteries of Stoke-on-Trent and Wolstanton. Marx, using the reports of the public health committees, has this to say:

> Dr Greenhow states that the average life-expectancy in the

pottery districts of Stoke-on-Trent and Wolstanton is extraordinarily low. Although only 36.6 per cent of the male population over the age of 20 are employed in the potteries in the district of Stoke, and 30.4 per cent in Wolstanton, more than half the deaths among men of that age in the first district, and nearly two-fifths in the second district, are the result of pulmonary diseases among the potters. Dr Boothroyd, a medical practitioner at Hanley, says: 'Each successive generation of potters is more dwarfed and less robust than the preceding one.' Similarly another doctor, Mr McBean states: 'Since I began to practise among the potters 25 years ago, I have observed a marked degeneration, especially shown in diminutions of stature and breadth.' These statements are taken from Dr Greenhow's Report of 1860 (Marx [1867] 1982: 354–5).

Further he writes:

Dr J.T. Arledge, senior physician of the North Staffordshire Infirmary, says: 'The potters as a class, both men and women, represent a degenerated population, both physically and morally. They are, as a rule, stunted in growth, ill-shaped, and frequently ill-formed in the chest; they become prematurely old, and are certainly short-lived; they are phlegmatic and bloodless, and exhibit their debility of constitution by obstinate attacks of dyspepsia, and disorders of the liver and kidneys, and by rheumatism. But of all diseases they are especially prone to chest-disease, to pneumonia, phthisis, bronchitis, and asthma. One form would appear peculiar to them, and is known as potter's asthma, or potter's consumption' (ibid.: 355).

While it may seem as if the work of *uthai rakhai* is not apparently hazardous because it is merely carrying pots from one place to another it is the total environment which makes the industry hazardous. According to Dr N.C. Saxena, the Hospital Superintendent at the local Khurja hospital, most potters who come to the hospital had asthmatic bronchitis, which then became tuberculosis. Out of 300 tuberculosis patients registered at the hospital for regular care, 70 per cent were potters. In his own experience of two years, there have been four or five patients with silicosis. According to Dr Saxena:

> If we have got 300 patients in our hospital, there would be another 700 patients being treated outside by private practitioners and quacks. But most of the patients must be going undiagnosed. There are at least two or three patients with asthmatic bronchitis in every pottery. The children working in potteries suffer from extra pulmonary tuberculosis and out of every ten, one has pulmonary tuberculosis.

Dr Saxena has been trained to identify silicosis but most of the local doctors treat it as tuberculosis. Silicosis is a pulmonary fibrosis caused by the inhalation of dust containing free silica. It is the most common and severe of all pneumoconiosis. It is basically a nodular fibrosis of the lungs. The lungs' vital capacity is reduced and the patient dies. There is no cure for silicosis which has now been identified as an occupational disease.

Dr Masood Ahmed runs a clinic in the centre of the town. Most of his patients are potters. He gets on the average twenty-five or thirty adult potters a day and an equal number of children. The most common complaint of his patients is asthmatic bronchitis and pulmonary tuberculosis. Out of 200 patients he had recently examined, 75 per cent were potters and 87.5 per cent of them had pulmonary tuberculosis, bronchitis and asthma. According to him:

> By the time the potter is thirty to thirty-five years old, the upper respiratory infection has gone into the third stage. By the age of forty or forty-five, the man dies. Most of the workers are too poor to take treatment. Many of them do not get paid regularly. We advise rest but that is impossible for them.

According to the International Labour Organization Encyclopedia on Occupational Health and Safety (Parmeggiani 1983: 2039), the silicosis hazard is encountered in a wide variety of occupations including the manufacture of pottery, porcelain, refractory materials, etc. 'Cough with sputum, is an indication of bronchitis, and chronic bronchitis is frequently associated with advanced silicosis.' The three main complications of silicosis are also the most frequent causes of death and those are pulmonary tuberculosis, respiratory insufficiency and acute pulmonary infection. According to the above-mentioned encyclopedia:

> Pulmonary tuberculosis is, even today, still the cause of death in a quarter of cases, and is the most frequent complication. It has recently been proved that tubercle bacilli grow and multiply far more actively in macroplages that have phagocytised silica particles than in those that have not done so, perhaps because the former have suffered a loss of vitality and are no longer capable of destroying the tubercle bacilli (ibid.).

There are specific hazards in the pottery industry. According to the same encyclopedia: 'Ball clay contains up to 50% free silica and so presents a potential hazard to sliphouse workers handling raw clay' (ibid.:1176).

Further, it is stated:

> The major health hazard is pneumoconiosis, which results from the prolonged inhalation of siliceous dust within the respirable size range, that is, particles up to about 7 μm in diameter. The risk arises from the combination of materials and methods and is proportional to the percentage of free silica in the inhaled dust; in general, it is confined to the pre-firing processes (ibid.).

These are not the only health hazards faced by workers but these are the most common ones. Workers who work as firemen at the kiln, lose their eyesight, I was told, by the age of about forty-five or so. Their main job is to stoke the fire and to periodically remove samples of pottery to check whether they have been properly baked. As workers said: *'Ankhon ko aanch lag jati hai'* (the eyes get affected by the heat). Those who work on the ball machines become deaf after some time. Children complained of frequent coughs and colds. The main reason, as one child told me, was: *'Selkhari se nazla ho jata hai'* (Soap stone dust causes colds.) Most of the workers who were affected by silicosis were those working on disintegrators. These were machines used to powder the broken *saggars* for re-use. In fact, most factories had this process not in their main area but outside because of the dust that flew out. But operators of the machines were affected.

When workers were interviewed in the factories, they said that the work was not hazardous. Part of the reason for this is that colds and coughs are not considered illnesses and no one wants to admit that they have tuberculosis. In fact, local doctors said they had no idea what happened to many of their patients as the minute a person heard that he had T.B., he would rarely come back to them. Most doctors, therefore, in order to keep their custom did not tell the patient that he suffered from T.B. but gave him whatever relief they could give.

Workers in Sondha village said that it was not uncommon to hear about accidental deaths in potteries. The main explanation offered was bad house-keeping on the part of the factory owners. A young adolescent, Birpal, recently died in a factory because the belts which rotate the grinding machines broke and he was trapped. Birpal's family was of course not compensated. Some workers said: *'Bachaon ko slip ke tank me bhej dete hein. Kai bacche thandi se behosh ho jate hein'* (They put children into the slip tanks and some children become unconscious because of the extreme cold).

This was verified by Dr Ahmed as well who told me that one of his patients had even gone into a coma because of this experience. Other workers in the village said that often working for some years in the potteries: *'Dum ghut jaata hai'* (One starts suffocating).

While there is substantial documentary evidence that pottery is hazardous work because of the large-scale use of silica which is one of the essential raw materials used, most workers interviewed at the factories did not complain of any health problems. Cold and cough and slight breathing difficulties were common but were not taken seriously by the workers themselves. It seems that not all workers in the pottery industry are exposed to health hazards because many are working with wet clay so there is a minimum of dust in the air. However, those workers directly grinding the raw material would be the most affected. This is also a relatively new industry and the impact of the working conditions on the health of workers may only manifest itself at a later stage.

LABOUR LAWS AND THEIR IMPLEMENTATION

Under the Factories Act of 1948, which also applies to Uttar Pradesh, a factory means any premises where ten or more workers are working, or were working on any day of the preceding twelve months, and where in any part of which a manufacturing process is being carried out with the aid of power. If any manufacturing unit has more than ten workers, they are supposed to provide certain facilities to their employees such as rest-rooms, drinking water facilities, toilets, etc. Workers are not supposed to be employed beyond a certain number of hours a week without being paid overtime. There is a strict ban on the employment of children in factories under the age of fourteen years.

In order to evade the Factories Act, 90 per cent of the units show that they have less than nine workers. In some factories I visited, I noticed around fifty workers. But when I asked the employer, he said there were only eight people working there! In every single factory I visited, there were over twenty workers employed and the factory owners made no bones about the fact that they were breaking the law. As one factory owner said:

> If there are more than nine workers, then we come under the purview of the Factory Act. This is a nuisance because we have to give bonus and provide employees' medical insurance, etc. That is why we show fewer workers.

But this was not an isolated response. Every single factory owner in Khurja I interviewed told me the same thing. Workers felt bitterly about it and said: 'Factory inspectors come. Labour inspectors come. They take money and go away. Who cares about labour?

Everywhere I talked to workers, the story was the same. Some workers said that one of the reasons why the industry was listed as a cottage and small-scale industry was because this sector was exempt from excise duty. One worker said:

> The factory owners make twice as much as they show in the books. All of them have two books. This way they have double benefit. They claim that there are only nine workers so that they do not come under the purview of the Factories Act. But you must have seen that this is a lie. There is no job security here and that is why there is so much child labour.

Everyone in Khurja — workers, employers, contractors and traders — were aware that under the Factories Act, child labour is expressly forbidden. When I first visited Khurja and talked to people, everyone denied that child labour existed. But when I showed them photographs of working children, then they said that the reason for their denial was because there was a ban on the employment of children under the Factories Act.

Many factory owners expressed the view that the main reason that there was no progress in the country was that there were labour laws. One factory owner said: 'You can either have production or you can look after the welfare of workers. Isn't it enough that we people are giving the poor employment? Why do we need laws to protect them as well?'

Soon after this study was published in a local newspaper, there were questions in Parliament. The reply of the then Minister for Labour was that it was the State Government's responsibility to enforce the Factories Act and the Child Labour (Prohibition and Regulation) Act, 1986. He admitted in Parliament that although the Labour Ministry had received an unofficial report (mine) about child labour in the pottery industry of Khurja, the State Government maintained there was not a single case of child labour to be found in this industry! (*Times of India*, 26 March 1988). When the author took up the matter in the press, the Minister admitted that the Central Government was surprised at the report they had received from the State Government that although forty-one inspections had been carried out and twenty-four people prosecuted, there was not a single case of child labour in the pottery industry (*Times of India*, 12 April 1988).

What seems clear from this brief study is that child labour is a fairly new phenomenon in the pottery industry of Khurja largely because of the need to mass-produce goods at low cost. The traditional Khurja potter did not have a very large market and therefore did not need children. Children only worked as part of apprenticeship training and along with getting regular education.

But with changing technology and the use of moulds, it became possible for such people to enter the pottery industry as had no background of pottery. It was also possible then to hire unskilled labour to do jobs which hitherto required specialized skills — e.g. the technique of moulding clay on the potter's wheel. Once the new technology came in, the demand for the goods grew along with an easy availability of cheap labour and this made Khurja a well-known pottery centre. The changes in the pottery industry also came at a time when in the rural areas mechanization of agriculture, the introduction of electricity and better technology created a class of rural unemployed youth who could not find sustenance in the villages. They flocked to the town for work and the only employment available was in the potteries. The local towns people found that the wages were so low that most of them tried to seek work outside. It was only when they found it impossible to get other work that they continued in the potteries.

Thus amongst the adults, the local people try to find work outside Khurja, preferably in big cities while Bihari and eastern Uttar Pradesh migrants leave their homes in large numbers in search of work and a livelihood and some end up here. It is because of a combination of factors that wages and conditions of work in the pottery industry are so bad. Low wages has meant in turn that families have to send their children out to work in order to sustain the family.

Obviously, the children who need help are economically and socially from the lowest strata of society. They are the most vulnerable to exploitation and are in fact working like machines for the profit of others. None of the work they do is of the type that leads to the acquiring of skills which may lead to better prospects and can thus be justified. If anything, the wages paid to adults who had started working as children are a little less than those who do the same work but entered the work-force at a later stage.

The conditions of most factories in Khurja are not so different from those described by Marx obtaining in the potteries of nineteenth-century England. In fact, Marx has been frequently cited in this study in order to draw attention to what is likely to happen to potters in Khurja in another one or two generations. The pottery industry of Khurja that employs child labour is relatively new and some of its ill-effects may not be noticed except in a later generation. But the reports from England in the nineteenth-century need to be taken seriously in order to prevent the same kind of consequences!

The pottery industry does not need child labour except as a source of cheap labour. Compulsory education and strict child labour laws will go a long way to remove child labour from the pottery industry in India as has been the case in England and Japan. There is nothing a child can do that cannot be done by an adult. But the children who come to work do so because of abject poverty. The only solution is to provide them with free, stipendiary primary education and find alternative employment opportunities for their unemployed or under-employed parents. There are laws against employing children in factories which need to be strictly implemented and employers employing children strictly penalized. The industry will not collapse if children are withdrawn from the work-force. It will only provide more work opportunities for adults.

7

Why Children Work in the Brass Ware Industry

The job of the moulder is a very delicate operation and if there is a slight mistake or accident the boy can get very badly injured and can even lose his limbs. He wears no protective gear and stands barefoot on top of the furnace to either put in the crucible or to remove it. The temperature in the furnace is about 1100° C. As one exporter/manufacturer, explaining the processes in his factory, said: 'See how dextrous this young child is. He has to be. Because even if a drop of molten brass falls on his foot there will be a hole in it.'

THE BRASS WARE INDUSTRY OF MORADABAD, UTTAR PRADESH

Moradabad is one of the most important centres of production of art metalwares in the country. It is the district headquarters of the district of the same name in the State of Uttar Pradesh and is situated about a hundred miles from Delhi on the right bank of the river Ramganga. Flower vases, planters, plates, dinner services, tea sets and various decorative objets d' art are all made here.

The history of the brass ware industry of Moradabad is lost in antiquity. According to the Moradabad Gazetteer, the original method of moulding was the *para* method by which earthen moulds were used to give shape to molten metal. After 1920, the *darja* (box moulding) system was adopted but only for small articles like handles and spouts. Cutlery began to be manufactured around 1925 and power began to be used towards the end of 1930. Imported brass sheets were used as raw material in the manufacture of utensils but as they were in short supply around 1940, the production of sheets from scrap, virgin copper and zinc was taken up locally.

In 1947, there were only three big exporters in Moradabad: Lala Bhukan Saran, Mousin Yaar Khan and Haji Kallan. After 1947, when there was large-scale migration from Punjab to Moradabad and other cities, the Punjabi Hindus saw the industry as a good investment and began sending samples abroad for orders.

As the industry developed, many outsiders came to settle down in Moradabad. They would get things made by the multi-process unit manufacturers who were known as *karkhanedars* (owner of a *karkhana* or factory). Many of the local Muslim elite also realized the potential of this business and began exporting goods. Haji Mohammad Jan Mohammad Dawood, who now have almost eight firms, and Haji Mohammad Jikaria Mohammad Yahiya, who also have several firms of exporters, are amongst the earliest ones.

After 1970, a new process of sheet work was introduced and this was done on lathes. Goods like planters began to be manufactured in this fashion which did not require a high level of skill. These goods were made in factories and a large number of the unemployed rural poor came to the city to work there.

The term 'art metalware', though not very precisely defined, is generally used to denote metal articles which have a higher input of 'artistic skill' as compared to functional household metalwares. More than 90 per cent of the goods produced in Moradabad are exported.

There are almost 150,000 workers engaged directly in the metalware industry. This figure would include manufacturers, suppliers, exporters and administrative staff. Of the total workers, approximately 40,000–45,000 are children below the age of fourteen years. The basis of the figures of the number of workers, both adults and children, has been discussed in detail later.

While the figure of 150,000 workers is an estimate for the metalware industry, this study was primarily of the brass ware industry. It is, however, very difficult to differentiate between the two as many of the goods made in a particular unit may be for both metalware and art-metalware. For the sake of consistency, the industry will henceforth be referred to as the brass ware industry.

Common items produced are flower vases, planters, wall-plates, candle-stands, dinner services, cutlery and so on. The estimated turn-over of the Moradabad brass ware industry for 1986-7 has been Rs 90 *crores* (Rs 1 *crore* is equivalent to Rs 10,000,000) and was likely to cross Rs 100 *crores* (U.P. State Brass Ware Corporation: Personal Communication). Other important art metalware centres in Uttar Pradesh are located in Varanasi, Jalesar and Almora.

There are several categories of manufacturing units in Moradabad. Some of the largest units — both in terms of size and in the number of workers employed — will be referred to as factories. At the next level are smaller manufacturing units, where more than one process is carried out — and these are known as *karkhanas*, the literal translation of which is factory. The owner of a *karkhana* is known as a *karkhanedar*. The term *karkhanedar* is also used to describe a contractor because many owners of multi-process or double-process units also act as middlemen for procuring items not made by them, from others. At the bottom level are the single-process workshops referred to as artisan units. While there are a large number of factories, most of the business is in the hands of the middle-level entrepreneur who both employs artisans directly in his multi-process unit, gets work done by them and supplies the goods to exporters (IDS 1983: 11). In some cases, factories do not get all the processes done in their own premises but place orders directly with multi-process unit owners, the *karkhanedars*. For the sake of simplicity, the term factory or factory owner will be used for those units or owners of units which are very large both in size and in numbers of workers employed on the same premises. The term multi-process unit will be used to refer to *karkhanas* and the term workshop for single-process units.

It is difficult to give authentic information about the number of establishments working in Moradabad. If a particular unit wishes to avail itself of concessions and facilities given by the government, it has to be registered with the District Industries Centre (DIC). According to the DIC, there were 3000 units registered with them as small-scale units with a capital of less than Rs 35,00,000. But many people this researcher spoke to said there were at least another 3000 units which were unregistered. According to the Factories Act, any unit employing more than twenty workers and not using power or more than nine workers using power is considered a factory. Once the unit is registered as a factory, its workers become entitled to certain rights under the Act. These rights include Employees State Insurance, Provident Fund, leave with pay and so on. Only 381 units were registered as factories and everybody agreed that this was a gross underestimation because employers were chary of becoming legally liable to provide statutory benefits to workers. It will be seen, therefore, that the statistics regarding the number of establishments and factories are quite misleading.

More than 90 per cent of the goods produced in Moradabad are meant for export and this explains the dominant role of the exporter in the industry. Exporters are of two types: manufacturing exporters are few in number and are those who have very large businesses.

Exporters who have entered the field of manufacturing have done so in order to maintain quality control and to preserve the secrecy of their designs. They directly employ few workers themselves and these are either supervisory staff or artisans with a high degree of skills. Their modus operandi is to have a number of captive multi-process units, who use their building space and machinery on the payment of rent. By this means, the manufacturer exporter is sure that his work will be done according to schedule but he has no direct responsibility for or relationship with the workers in these captive units. These workers are the employees of the multi-process unit owner, who usually works on the machines himself as well. Though the building and machinery belong to the manufacturing exporter, it is for the multi-process unit owner to organize his supplies of raw materials like black powder, chemicals and coal and with the help of hired labour, complete the job contracted out to him. In this type of arrangement, it was also found that many of the units in the premises of the manufacturer exporter were single-process units specializing in particular activities like moulding, scraping, welding, polishing and electroplating.

The non-manufacturing exporter is the more representative figure and accounts for a larger share of the business. His way of working is to ask a multi-process unit owner to give a sample and then place an order after tendering that sample to a number of possible competitors. Scraping, welding, and grinding (fine scraping) are activities commonly carried out in these multi-process units. It is rare for the processes of moulding, polishing and electroplating to be carried out in these multi-process units for these jobs require separate space as they generate a great deal of heat and pollution. The multi-process unit owner is charged with the responsibility not only of completing the processes which he himself carries out in his unit but usually also of getting the goods finished in other respects through different single-process units or workshops.

It will be seen from the above description that the multi-process unit owners, who are given orders by the non-manufacturing exporters differ significantly from the multi-process unit owners who are tied to the manufacturing exporters. The former have their own buildings and machinery and are not necessarily linked to a particular exporter. Besides, they operate on a wider canvas and normally get the wares readied in all respects for the exporter. While the multi-process unit owner is an artisan-turned-entrepreneur, the single-process unit owner attached to the manufacturing exporter is more commonly a worker, with a high degree of initiative but who does not perform full-blown entrepreneurial functions.

It was found that of the exporters, 75 per cent were Hindus and 25 per cent were Muslims. The Hindus were either Punjabis who went to Moradabad after Partition or Banias, local trading castes. Punjabi Mussalmans, Ansaris and members of the Khan clan made up the Muslim exporters. As regards the multi-process unit manufacturers, about 65 per cent of them are Muslims (Ansaris, Mansooris, Ghosis, etc.) and 35 per cent are Hindus (mainly Punjabis). Most Hindu labourers belong to lower castes like Bagvans, Balmikis, Lodhas and Ahirs. Amongst the Muslims, the poorer Ansari and Quraishi families work as labourers. While the bulk of the Muslim workforce is to be found in small workshops, the majority of Hindu workers are engaged in the large factories.

METHODOLOGY AND FIELDWORK

Data for this study were collected over a period of nineteen days on two separate field trips to Moradabad and its surrounding villages. During these visits, opportunity was taken to hold frank and participatory discussions (where possible) with workers, entrepreneurs, exporters, contractors, and others connected with the trade. In addition, there were interviews with government officials, doctors, social activists and others. During the period of fieldwork, I spoke to about 300 people belonging to different categories for varying lengths of time.

I visited fifteen large factories. They were large in terms of size of premises and by number of workers employed, who ranged between more than twenty and up to about seventy-five. Visits to the first few factories helped me understand processes of manufacture and, later, I began discussing issues with the factory owner or his representative. Access was made possible since a helpful government official accompanied me. But it was evident that the absence of a questionnaire created suspicion amongst some factory owners; in particular, those who were exporters or their employees were most reluctant to part with information. However, several factory owners — who were not exporters but supplied them with goods — spoke freely to me for they felt that government gave undue concessions to exporters and did not treat simple manufacturers with the same solicitude. Though the number of large factories visited was relatively small, they took up a disproportionate share of my time as they were dispersed in different parts of the town and had a large number of processes in operation.

I was able to visit some thirty medium-size multi-process units in which the number of processes were limited and less sophisticated as compared to those in the larger factories referred to above. Here I received cordial treatment almost uniformly. These units fell under the jurisdiction of the official accompanying me which was of great advantage for my work. Except for the odd child, children were not found working either in the larger factories or in the medium-sized ones. In many of the units I went to, I could see with the evidence of my own eyes that there were usually more workers than were reported to be employed by the owner or supervisor. When I asked about the difference, I was told disarmingly that a lower number of workers is reported in order to evade the provisions under the Factories Act that call for certain facilities to be given to workers if the unit is deemed to be a factory.

I saw about a thousand single-process workshops in the by-lanes of Moradabad, away from the main road. This statement needs clarification. These workshops are involved with the processes of moulding, polishing, scraping, welding, engraving and colouring. Of all these small workshops I saw, more than half were moulding units. Most of the workshops I saw had three or four workers, adults and children. Usually, these small workshops were closed off on three sides and faced the streets for the natural light and ventilation they offered. Commonly, these spaces were part or extensions of the residential complex but clearly demarcated. However, there were also some larger sheds where several adults and children were working in separate units with their own equipment but sharing common space.

Out of nineteen days of fieldwork, twelve days were spent walking through these densely populated Muslim localities, observing what was going on, spending a few minutes and sometimes engaging there in long conversations with the local people. The purpose of this exercise was to gain a representative understanding of what could be considered the most common form of industrial activity in Moradabad in which the largest number of people are employed, particularly children. One question that I invariably asked was whether the children working in these workshops were part of the families of the adults working there. And this I did by asking the children present what their fathers did and the adults about where their children were and what they did. Invariably, the children working here were hired labourers. I shall return later to this theme of children working as hired labour rather than as part of family labour — for it is my contention that official policy rests importantly upon the belief that children in the brass ware industry work along with their families and learn traditional skills.

Since I was there for many days and visited the same localities again and again, sometimes people would offer to take me to their workshops which were in their own homes. I then got the opportunity to see what kinds of units people were running at home. These visits also gave me the chance to talk to people at length — particularly women and girls — who were otherwise invisible. I learnt about the history and development of the industry and the situation of the labour force from older people and others who were not currently employed and involved directly in the industry. Very rarely did the children speak in the presence of adults and it was not possible to get to know what they felt about their work. The children would either listen to what the adults were saying or, if they were asked a direct question, would answer in monosyllables and then lapse into silence. Invariably when a question was asked of a child, an adult would answer. In units where the largest

number of children were working — the moulding units — it
was risky to ask children questions because of the hazardous
nature of the work. Concentration interrupted might have led
to accidents!

One day, leaving early in the morning, I visited six villages
within the radius of ten kilometres from Moradabad town.
Inspite of the fact that it was so early in the morning, both
adults and children were getting ready to leave for the day's
work. I had an opportunity to discuss with many mothers and
their neighbours the social and economic conditions they lived
in and was able to get information about the castes and communities they belonged to.

PROCESSES IN THE MANUFACTURE OF BRASS WARE

There are several processes involved in the manufacture of brass
ware. The basic raw materials used are copper and zinc. The
making of ingots and sheets is the first stage of the production
process. Ingots can be of two types: *silli* (oblong) and *gulli*
(round). Oblong or round ingots or brass sheets are used depending upon the type of article to be produced.

There are very few factories where ingots are made and
these factories supply the other manufacturing units. Copper,
zinc and scrap material are put into large graphite crucibles and
heated to high temperatures. The resultant molten metal (brass)
is then poured into smaller earthenware moulds to make the
ingots. The shape of the mould is either oblong or round
depending on whether oblong or round ingots are being made.
Only adults are involved in the manufacture of ingots.

The oblong ingots are sold directly to the *darja bhattis* (box
mould furnaces) in which the worker moulds the various parts
of the final product — for example, handles, spouts and lids —
as well as small bowls, plates and so on. He breaks off as much
of the oblong ingot as necessary, melts it and fashions his goods.

In the box mould furnaces, the following operations are
undertaken continuously. The mould or die is put into the box
and packed with a black powder made up of sand, clay, oil,

molasses and borax and sprinkled with a mixture of ammonium chloride. A piece of the oblong ingot is put into the graphite crucible and when heated, the molten metal is poured through a spout into the box. The metal solidifies almost immediately into the required shape and the box is then opened to remove the article with a pair of tongs. The mixture of black powder falls out and is then beaten up by hand in preparation for further use. This process is then repeated. Children are used here to rotate the cycle wheel that fans the furnace, to put the ingot into the crucible and heat it, to remove the crucible containing molten brass and hand it to the adult worker and to grind the black powder for re-use.

Round ingots are not sold in that form. In the factories where they are made, they are put onto rolling machines and pressed into sheets of the required specifications. Both round ingots and the sheets that they are fashioned into are manufactured according to the requirements of the indentor. Bowls and plates are examples of the type of goods which have a circular or spherical shape that are made from round ingots.

Apart from oblong and round ingots, the third possible starting point in the production chain is brass sheets. Here, children are not employed. These sheets are mainly manufactured by the Uttar Pradesh State Brass Ware Corporation and then supplied to the manufacturers of brass ware. The goods that are to be made from these sheets are not moulded. The most important item made from these sheets is the planter. The sheets are pressed in factories and given shape and design on electrically operated machines which have dies in them. These planters or pots are moved several times between the press and the furnace before they are given a final shape. They are then scraped by adults on power-operated lathes. In this semi-finished form the goods are normally sent to other multi-process manufacturing units, which specialize in the processes of polishing, soldering, electroplating and so on. Goods like planters, which are one of the most important export items, sometimes need ancillary parts like handles and chains, which are manufactured in box mould furnaces and later joined.

When the article in question reaches the stage of being given a shape — whether the starting point be oblong or round ingot or brass sheet — the processes to follow are by and large common, for example, all semi-finished goods are scraped, welded, polished and electroplated or silver-plated. Some wares are engraved and coloured as well.

Semi-finished articles are to be scraped in order to make them smooth and iron out the rough edges. Scraping can be done either by hand or by machine. When it is manual, this activity is usually undertaken by women and young girls and involves the use of chisel and hammer. Mechanical scraping, which involves the fixing of the articles on moving rods, is done only by adults in the case of larger wares but young boys can also be found doing this work for smaller pieces.

Welding can be done in three ways: using small furnaces stoves or gas cylinders. Children are engaged in large numbers in welding workshops and their main job is to hold the pieces together which are to be welded. Young women and girls tie metal wires around the parts to be welded in their homes and send them to the workshops for welding.

Once the semi-processed goods are scraped and welded, they are then to be washed and polished to give them the requisite gloss. Washing is done in a mixture which has hydro-chloric acid and this work is usually done by children. The article is first cleaned, polishing paint applied and then rubbed with a cloth or woollen pad. Polishing by machine involves mounting the piece on a spindle or lathe with polishing paint applied to a linen mop. The mop is held against the surface of the revolving article as a result of which it gets the required finish. If the goods are coloured, the lathe moves relatively slowly; if they are plain, they are polished on machines rotating faster and using discs covered with emery powder. Polishing machines are also called buffing machines.

Engraving is the cutting of a design into the surface of a metal. The engraver cuts the required design on the ware with the help of engraving tools and a light weight hammer. In the case of ordinary work, the design can be carved by the engraver

More than 50 per cent of children in
gem polishing are wholly illiterate.

Pottery Industry of Khurja

'Each succeeding generation of potters is more dwarfed and less robust than the preceding one' says Karl Marx about potters in nineteenth-century England. Will this be true of Khurja?

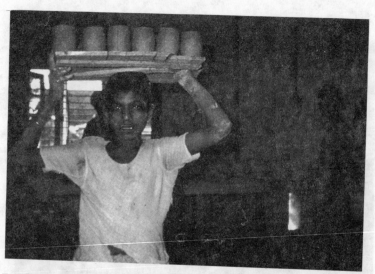

Fetch and Carry: Children of 8 years or 9 years carry weights of 10 kilograms or more, running upto 5 kilometres a day.

Brass-Ware industry of Moradabad

Lifting crucibles from the furnace.

If a child drops the crucible he will have no feet left!

Carpet industry of Rajasthan

On their toes from 8 a.m. to 6 p.m., 6 days a week! Working in this position stunts their growth, and deforms them!

Glass Industry of Firozabad

Children work in dangerous proximity to fire under temperatures which soar to 800° C, without gloves or any other form of protection. Accidents which are a common occurence under the circumstances are of course treated casually

Lock Industry of Aligarh

Child workers covered with metal dust. It is hardly surprizing that diseases such as tuberculosis are rampant among these children. Over 60 per cent of them are below the age of 14 years

Young polishers at work. If the piece slips it will ricochet off the wall and hit the child.

Safety and health hazards? Buffing lock components without gloves, goggles or a mask.

Dipping locks in acid baths, for electroplating. Chemicals used include potassium cyanide!

Gem polishing industry of Jaipur

Learning without earning: polishing cut gem stones with the aid of pulleys drawn by a motor.

Children toil behind closed doors
— a young gem polisher at work.

from memory. If the designs are intricate, the designs are first drawn on paper and outlined on the ware. After engraving, the resultant depressions are filled with shellac by heating the articles and applying shellac sticks. The articles are then glazed by rubbing with wood ash. Children and women are also engaged in this work. The main raw materials used are shellac, lacquer, colours, thinners, soft coke and zinc oxide. Frequently, goods are polished both before and after engraving.

Though not all wares are electroplated or silver-plated, when they are, it is the last stage in the production process. The purpose of this activity is to prevent or postpone the tarnishing of wares. It involves tying the goods on metal wires and then immersing them in baths of a solution containing potassium cyanide and silver nitrate while an electric current is passed. The next step is to cover them in ammonium chloride powder, which absorbs moisture and hastens drying. Children are to be found both in the activities of tying these articles to the wires and covering them with ammonium chloride powder.

It has been reported that till the late 1950s or early 60s, 89 per cent of all establishments in Moradabad worked without power with only 11 per cent using power. The establishments using power were engaged mainly in scraping, electroplating and polishing. Today, many items, particularly those made from brass sheets, are made by using mechanized methods. The large units have facilities for mechanical rolling, cutting and fabricating pressed sheet articles. There is still no mechanization in sheet beating, casting, engraving and enamelling, but more and more units are introducing a low level of mechanization in the processes of sheet work, soldering and scraping.

CHANGES IN DEMAND: IMPACT UPON TECHNOLOGY,
LABOUR AND STRUCTURE

There was a time about twenty-five or thirty years ago when the brass ware industry was entirely a cottage industry in which the artisan worked with the help of his family labour and virtually no hired help. I was told that the goods produced at that time were vases, decanters, wine glasses, decorative plates and the like. Though there was a small export market in the Middle East, most of the goods made were sold in India. The designs that were carved, the colours that were used and the wares that were thus made — all bore the unmistakable stamp of Moradabad and made that town famous for its particular type of brass ware. The skilled craftsman was in control of the industry to the extent that he purchased the raw materials himself, fashioned the goods and then sold them. Since there was a specialization in different types of skills, processes that could not be done at home were got done by other artisans.

The self-employed artisan of yore, who was the representative figure in the production system until a few years ago, is now conspicuous by his substantially reduced presence. In 1959–60, it was estimated that 66 per cent of workers were self-employed. By 1974, the proportion of self-employed workers was estimated at less than 1 per cent (IDS 1983: 29). This was not an isolated development.

The kinds of changes that have taken place in the organization of production of the brass ware industry of Moradabad have been well analysed in a study on the subject undertaken by the Industrial Development Services (IDS). It will be useful to quote here at length from that report:

> There has been an organizational change in terms of (i) an increase in the average number of workers per establishment . . . (ii) an increase in the number of multi-process establishments (karkhanas) (iii) decline in the category of workers described as 'self-employed' (iv) an increase in the number of manufacturers, suppliers and exporters who co-ordinate the completion of a number of operations through different sets of artisans. This is reflected in the shift in the ownership of working capital. In 1979–80 exporters accounted for 67 per cent of the working capital employed, while the other 33 per cent was accounted for by suppliers and manufacturers. Even allowing for a margin of error or a definitional discrepancy, it supports the decline in the self-employed

category and an increase in the proportion of wage earners among the craftsmen (ibid.: 5–6).

What accounts for these changes? Earlier, even though artwares were always earmarked for export, there was an important domestic market for brass utensils. Rises in the prices of raw material, the difficulty of keeping brass utensils from tarnishing and the growing popularity of stainless steel gradually eroded the domestic market. At the same time, there were significant changes in the nature and scale of demand from international markets in the USA and Europe.

Planters, dinner plates, tea services and other items of tableware were sought for in international markets. These were not the traditional brass ware items made in Moradabad like flower vases, decanters, wine glasses, decorative table tops and so on. The traditional methods of manufacture of the traditional items of brass ware which I have described earlier in Chapter 1 consisted of a series of operations being performed by a particular manufacturer such as, moulding in box moulds, welding, scraping, polishing, engraving and colouring. The technology thus employed was not suitable for mass production and mass production was called for by the new, enormous scale of international demand. Moreover, the kinds of goods that found a market abroad were such that they lent themselves to the technologies of mass production.

Planters, dinner services, bowls and so on could be manufactured by machines on which there were dies containing designs which were impressed upon large numbers of pieces simultaneously. Factories manufacturing sheets of different specifications sprang up in response to the new climate of demand and such sheets could now be ordered by other entrepreneurs according to their needs. The introduction of mechanization in the production of brass sheets made the procurement of this raw material much easier for the entrepreneur. It can thus be seen how the change in the quality and scale of demand was importantly responsible for the changes in technology that followed.

I have earlier drawn attention to the fact that the traditional methods of manufacture required artisans who had skills in particular areas such as moulding, engraving, scraping and polishing. With the advent of mechanization, certain skills became redundant. Scraping and polishing which were traditional female preserves were now done by machine. As a result, female workers were displaced in large number. In a later section, the situation of the female worker will be discussed in greater detail. Moulders still have an important role to play because they mould all the small attachments like handles, spouts, lids and decorations that are required even for goods made by the new technology. Engravers, on the other hand, have suffered a substantial set-back for they have no role in the new technological processes and there is little demand for traditional carvings.

The growth of the industry created a demand for a larger work-force and this demand was met by workers from the rural areas of Moradabad and from Bihar and eastern Uttar Pradesh. The level of mechanization is not particularly advanced: unskilled and semi-skilled workers are quite capable of handling the machines currently used. This is an additional reason for the changed profile of the brass ware worker as he becomes transformed from being a skilled artisan to a wage labourer.

The children of artisans, it would be safe to say, were always involved with the work of their fathers and mothers whether on a part-time or full-time basis. But such a situation obtained when the industry had a primarily cottage character. A combination of factors resulted in significant change. The prices of raw materials rose, there was a change in the nature and scale of demand, mechanization was introduced and women were displaced. Together, these events resulted in a substantial increase in the share of children in the workforce though this did not occur in a uniform way. For example, in the larger factories of Moradabad, it was observed that there were virtually no children at all. When I asked factory-owners why this was so, they offered two reasons. The first and more important one, which seemed convincing to me when I saw the machines involved, was that the new technology was not suitable for the height and strength of children. The size of the machine and the nature of the process involved such as, removing the round ingots from the furnace, pressing them into shape, re-heating and pressing the unfinished wares several times, seemed to be beyond the physical capacity of children. The other reason proffered by factory owners was that child labour was banned under the Factories Act and they would not want to risk prosecution or harassment on that account. Of course, it was easier for labour inspectors to inspect the comparatively fewer factories there are than the innumerable workshops. Yet, I felt that what the factory owner was doing was rational from his point of view in that it was not worth his while to employ children when the new technology was conducive to the use of adults rather than children, and the use of children would not yield economic advantage. Furthermore, factory owners would sub-contract the jobs of moulding, polishing and electroplating to workshops in which child labour was freely used and abused without attracting any legal liability for doing so.

Even if it is true that children are hardly employed in factories, nevertheless they are employed in most multi-process units and workshops and are engaged in a variety of processes such as moulding, welding, polishing, scraping and electroplating. The main explanation for the use of children in these processes lies in the fact that, apart from it being feasible to do so, children are paid less than adults and hence production costs are kept relatively low.

I shall now look at how the changed demand for brass ware has affected the structure of the industry. The relatively self-contained skilled artisan of yesteryear is no longer an important factor in the production process. The IDS study, referred to earlier in this section, points out how between 1959–60 and 1974 the proportion of self-employed persons dropped from 66 per cent to less than 1 per cent. The export market has increased the importance of entrepreneurial functions. There has been thus a shift in the pattern of ownership and control from the self-employed artisan to the entrepreneur or multi-process unit owner and middleman. In the late 1950s, the general pattern was that either the artisan worked in his own house, or in a room attached to his house but clearly for work purposes, or several artisans jointly rented a common shed. But today, there has been a shift in the pattern of ownership in the sense that those working in common sheds are more likely to be wage earners under one establishment or *karkhana* rather than several individuals sharing the common space (ibid.: 21).

It is clear, therefore that the category of self-employed artisans, who work for themselves with an investment in fixed and working capital, has virtually disappeared. Most artisans have been reduced to wage labourers even though outwardly the industry may retain the nature and structure of cottage industry.

It will be evident from the above that the most important factors in the changes that have taken place with respect to technology, the labour force and the structure of the industry has been the qualitative and quantitative change in the international demand for the products of Moradabad.

EMPLOYMENT, WAGES AND CONDITIONS OF WORK

I have referred earlier to the importance of the brass ware industry from the point of view of employment in Moradabad. Both governmental and non-governmental sources estimated that at least three-fourths of the population of the city was dependent for their livelihood on the industry. At least 150,000 people could be said to be engaged in the metalware industry and many more are employed indirectly. Though most workers were employed on a full-time basis, about 20 per cent of them are from the rural areas. The latter work during the slack periods of agricultural activity and are usually not available during the sowing and harvesting seasons.

In 1980, there were communal riots in Moradabad that claimed several lives and much property. The aftermath of the riots was a climate of distrust and uncertainty and long-lasting tension. Export orders could not be met in time and there was a slump in the industry leading to high levels of unemployment. Other countries stepped in when India failed to supply its goods. And the impact of the riots could still be felt till as late as 1985. The long period of economic insecurity has conditioned the way in which workers look upon the industry: today they are grateful for the work that they have and concentrate their energies upon earning a living. The absence of other employment opportunities makes the workers wholly dependent upon the metalware industry. Militancy and a trade union movement are both conspicuous by their absence.

When we look at the religious composition of the workers, it is apparent that those who work in big factories and large multi-process units are mainly Hindus and those who are employed in the smaller units are almost entirely Muslim. This is partly to do with the fact that the smaller units are located in the city centre which are Muslim dominated areas and where Hindu men are not encouraged because of the tradition of *purdah* (the seclusion of women). Moradabad is one of the few cities in India where Muslims outnumber Hindus.

Today, when business is thriving, there is hardly any unemployment for male workers in Moradabad. I was told that most people — excluding women — were assured of at least 200–250 days of work in a year. Most workers interviewed said that they could earn about Rs 400 to Rs 500 a month and nobody even referred to the minimum wages fixed for the industry as these were fixed many years ago and were much less than the prevailing wage rates.

In the last twenty years or so with the increasing demand for labour, there has been a large and growing component of migratory labour from the adjoining villages. Every morning, workers come from villages like Macheria, Hartala, Menather, Uchangaon, Langada, Betiyan, Majola, Khadakpur, Mulak, Kalyanpur, Dhakka, Jayantipur, etc. Those who own cycles, cycle to work. Early in the morning, the streets of Moradabad are packed with workers going to factories. Double Phatak is the area where workers can be seen at 7.45 in the morning either walking or cycling to work. The Amroha passenger train mainly carries workers from the more distant villages to work in the brass ware industry of Moradabad. These are, by and large, landless labourers or people with a little land and belonging to the Scheduled Caste communities or they are Muslims. There is also now a very large component of Bihari labour.

Local workers complain that their situation has worsened as a result of the entry of labourers from the rural areas and, in particular, because of those who have migrated from Bihar. For the Bihari workers and those coming from parts of eastern Uttar Pradesh, the brass ware industry has been a boon. The wages paid to them, even though lower than those paid to local people, are more than what they would have got in their own areas. Both these categories of workers, they felt, depressed the wages in the market as they were prepared to work for less. It was interesting to find in Moradabad that the wages paid to workers depended at least in part on whether they were city people, rural labour or migrant Biharis, the latter two categories being willing to settle for less. Conversations with factory owners revealed their preference: Bihari labourers were most in demand because they were the cheapest and always available. People coming from the adjoining villages were considered unreliable because they would stay away from work during peak agricultural seasons and city labourers were thought to be arrogant.

Three modes of payment are to be found in the industry: salaries, daily wages and piece-rate. The number of salaried employees is negligible both in absolute terms and as proportion of the work-force. Wherever it is possible to quantify the work to be done, wages are paid according to the piece-rate system. And where it is not feasible, people are on daily wages. For example, the moulder in a box mould furnace workshop was paid according to the amount of brass moulded. Polishers and electroplating workers were paid daily wages. Engravers and those who coloured the designs were paid piece-rate wages. Other workers who did miscellaneous jobs like fetching and carrying and are helpers were all on daily wages.

Most workers I spoke to had to work at least ten to eleven hours a day. When large export orders had to be met by deadlines, people would work through the night as well. Over-time would be paid for the extra hours of work put in and workers had no complaint about their long hours of work or about working at nights; they did not consider themselves to be exploited. The power supply in Moradabad being erratic and uncertain, workers would often spend hours just waiting for it and then work into the night as well in order to earn a minimum amount of money. In this respect, workers in the bigger factories were better off since there would be generators installed in them. Workers were not paid on days they did not report for duty or the factory was closed. All power-operated industries are supposed to be shut once a week as a measure of power conservation and so, whether they like it or not, workers get one unpaid holiday every week.

As mentioned earlier, according to the Factories Act, any unit which uses power and employs more than nine workers or has twenty or more workers but does not use power is deemed to be a factory and consequently, workers in such units are entitled to various rights like Employees State Insurance, Provident Fund, leave with pay and so on. In the case of a leading exporter, there were more than 500 workers in his four-storied building but the Manager told me that there were only thirty-five workers who were regular employees. The others were on piece-rate wages and employed by contractors. The factory owner did not incur any legal liability on their account although they were producing goods for him with raw materials purchased by him, using his machinery and doing the work in his premises. This situation may be said to be typical of other manufacturer exporters as well.

Two encounters I had are worth recounting for what they tell. In one factory, a worker told me in the presence of the owner that he was deeply indebted to the latter for the factory owner had spent about Rs 2000 on private medical treatment for the worker's wife when she had an accident. He told me in all sincerity that had it not been for the owner's assistance, his wife would have lost an arm. When the worker left, the owner said to me:

> I spent this money which I needn't have but I've got the loyalty of this man for life. He is a skilled worker and can supervize new recruits. He will never leave me to work for another man even at a higher wage. He keeps a check on other workers and reduces my burden of work. The money I spent is nothing compared to the returns I get.

One Works Manager said:

> If the employer is good, the workers will work well. We pay our workers monthly wages plus commission for production as well as Provident Fund, bonus, leave, Employees State Insurance, etc. People don't realize that if you treat workers well, they will never let you down. Our work is highly skilled. If we did not have permanent workers, we would lose a lot by training new recruits. This way we save money. And since we pay extra for exceeding production targets, the workers work well.

The instances cited above were exceptions and certainly do not exemplify a general trend. But where workers are treated well, there is a clear understanding on the part of the management that such treatment is justified by the returns it gives.

People engaged in the job of polishing probably had the most harrowing experience in the brass industry. Some polishers said that if they worked continuously for thirty days in the month, they would be dead in two years because the work is so hazardous. For every fifteen days of work, they have to take a break for fifteen days. Employers, however, saw this as irresponsibility on the part of workers. The main reason, they said, for not employing time-rated workers was that they were so unreliable. Electroplaters told me that because the job was hazardous, they could not afford to work for more than twenty days in the month. I shall return to this question later.

Another story though not representative needs to be told.

In one factory I visited, workers employed in moulding, polishing and scraping were locked up in cages. When the employer took me to visit this part of his factory, the supervisor first unlocked the main grill door. As we entered, there were large rooms with grills on the windows and grilled doors. Each process was being done in a different room and the grilled doors were locked from outside. Since part of the structure was open for light, it was also grilled. There was a small tea-stall inside the premises and whenever workers wanted drinking water or tea, it was passed through the grills. After we left, I noticed the supervisor locking the doors behind us! The exporter explained that these measures were necessary because workers were by and large dishonest and would try and steal the raw material which was almost as expensive as gold!

PARTICIPATION OF CHILDREN IN THE WORK-FORCE

There are no precise figures available for the number of workers in the brass ware industry, whether adults or children. Estimates made by different agencies vary and sometimes quite widely. The District Industries Centre, a government source, estimated that in 1987 out of a total of 16,000 workers, 9100 were men, 900 were women and 5000 were children. In sharp contrast, a study by Kulshreshta and Sharma in 1980 puts the total labour force at 1,00,000 of which 24 per cent or 24,000 were children (Kulshreshta and Sharma 1980). Again, a study conducted in 1979-80 by IDS in Moradabad argues that of about 70,000 workers, 80-85 per cent are males, 10-15 per cent are children and the rest females (IDS 1983: 4-5). In other words, there are between 56,000-59,500 men, 7000-10,500 children and the rest are women.

An unpublished report of 1988 of the Labour Department of the Government of Uttar Pradesh refers to the findings of a survey begun in 1981 by the National Industrial Development Corporation (NIDC) and quotes them. These figures do not include registered factories but concentrate on small-scale units. According to the NIDC report (cited in Table III below), of

29,100 workers, 20,370 are men, 7566 are children and 1164 are women. Thus, nearly 70 per cent of all workers are men and more than 25 per cent are children.

The same report refers to the conclusions of a sample survey carried out in August, 1986, by the Labour Department itself. This survey concluded that while 75 per cent of children work as part of family labour, only 25 per cent of them are wage earners. It went on to estimate that the number of such children was between 1800 and 2000 from the point of view of rehabilitation under the National Child Labour Programme (Labour Commissioner, U.P. 1988: 3). This researcher was told informally that in the absence of adequate staff, less than a hundred families were interviewed.

Table III

Break-up of Units (Process-wise) of Brass ware Industry at Moradabad

Nature of job	Total No. of units	Men	Women	Children	Total
Shaping	425	1860	23	296	2179
Polishing	1190	4068	284	1387	5651
Casting	2510	6072	276	1872	8220
Welding	431	746	–	18	764
Enamelling	85	712	63	96	871
Scraping	890	4346	386	2193	6925
Electroplating	256	1853	212	1613	3678
Engraving	1560	721	–	91	812
Total	7650	20,370	1164	7566	29,100

SOURCE: Labour Commissioner, U.P.: Project Report for Rehabilitation of Child Labour in Brass ware Industry of Moradabad prepared by Labour Commissioner, U.P. January 9 1988, pp. 1–2 (unpublished).

The number of children working in the brass ware industry has been thus estimated as 1800-2000 (by the Labour Department), as 5000 (by the District Industries Centre), as 7000-10,500 (by the Industrial Development Services report) as 7566 (by the National Industrial Development Corporation report) and as 24,000 (by Kulshreshta and Sharma). Even allowing for natural increase in numbers since the studies relate to different years, such wide variations need to be explained.

When I spoke to different categories of people in Moradabad like entrepreneurs, exporters, workers and others not connected with the government, almost everybody said that about 90 per cent of people in Moradabad worked in the brass ware industry. According to the 1981 Census, the population of Moradabad town was 3,45,350. But when I asked about actual numbers, I was given a range of between 2,00,000 and 3,00,000 people as working in the industry. I was also given to understand that more than 25 per cent of the work-force is made up of children, even though the proportion of children varies from process to process. Even if one takes a lower figure of 1,50,000 as the number of workers, it would mean that there are about 40,000-45,000 children working in the industry.

Government reports and government officials tend to severely underestimate the size of the problem. For one thing, no systematic survey has been carried out by them. For another, if the belief is that only 25 per cent of the working children are hired labourers in need of rehabilitation, the size of the problem becomes automatically smaller. But twelve days of seeing and visiting several hundred small units in the by-lanes of Moradabad convinced me that in virtually no case were children working as part of family labour. To the last child, they were all hired by others. It is in the light of my observation of different processes and assessment of the proportions of children in each of them coupled with the discussions I had with a wide cross-section of people in Moradabad that I would estimate the number of workers to be at least 1,50,000 and the number of children as about 40,000-45,000. The number of workers in different processes and the share of children in them

have been calculated on a similar basis. Yet, I cannot claim that
the figures offered in this report are free of error but am con-
fident they are closer to the facts than official documents allow.

Seventy-five to 80 per cent of the children are Muslims from
the town of Moradabad and 20 to 25 per cent Hindus, usually
Scheduled Castes, from adjoining villages in a radius of five to
six kilometres from the town. The latter can be seen at the
railway station in the morning sitting on top of the carriages of
the Amroha and Chaumasia passenger trains. The age-range of
the child workers is between eight and twelve years. The
Bagvans, Jatavs, Lodhes and Khagis are the castes to which the
children normally belong.

I was told by village officials that while adults go on their
own in search of work, children are recruited by *dalals* (middlemen), who usually belong to the village and who get paid a
commission for bringing child workers. *Thekedars* (contractors) and workshop owners prefer children because they are
easy to control. The middlemen look out for children. Their
parents are offered an advance of Rs 100 or the equivalent of
a month's wages. If a parent takes an advance, the child has to
work whether he likes it or not. If he plays hookey, the wages
of other children from the same village are cut and this way
some control is maintained. As regards children who belong to
the town itself, their parents are induced into sending them to
work by the lure of an advance of say Rs 500. This lump sum
payment is a big incentive for parents and it is adjusted against
a child's wages over a few months. Unlike as in the case of
children in the rural areas, there are no middlemen involved to
recruit urban children into the work-force.

MOULDING

Of the 30,000-odd workers involved in moulding in the box
mould furnace workshops, about 50 per cent or 15,000 are
children below the age of fourteen years. Their main job, as
explained earlier, is to rotate the wheel which fans the underground furnace. These boys are known as *pankhawalas* (the

persons who fan the flames) and this is the first job given to a new child recruit. The *ghadiyawala* (the person who melts the raw material in the graphite crucible) is the boy who heats the oblong ingot on top of the furnace, breaks it into small pieces with a hammer and melts the required amount of brass. When the molten brass is ready, he lifts the graphite crucible containing the raw material with long tongs and passes it to the adult worker, who then pours it into the moulds. Sometimes, when the adult is holding the mould, he pours the brass into it and then replaces the crucible into the furnace. Often, the job of the boy who rotates the wheel also includes that of removing the crucible from the furnace and vice-versa. Both the boy who rotates the wheel and the boy who removes the crucible help grind the hot black mixture into a fine powder with their bare hands and help remove the hot moulded metal from the moulds. These are all continuous processes and if the child is not rotating the wheel, he is either removing the crucible or grinding the black powder or removing the hot moulded metal. There is not even a minute's rest in a ten-hour day for a child working at a box mould furnace workshop.

The jobs described above in these workshops are done only by children. Employers justified the use of child labour for these tasks by saying that unless children began this work at an early age, they would never be able to become moulders in their adulthood; a high degree of skill was said to be involved. Yet, I interviewed several adult moulders who had not done such work as children. In fact, in the 600 odd box mould furnace workshops I visited, I found that the moulders were almost always under 30 years of age. People told me that children who work in box furnace workshops from a young age either do not survive as adults or become too ill to work. Tuberculosis (TB) is the most common consequence. In one unit I visited, as I was taking photographs, the child poured the molten metal into the mould and suddenly the room filled with fumes and everybody began to cough. It took me full fifteen minutes to recover from such a brief exposure and these children work in these conditions for ten hours a day, day in and day out! The moulder who employs children knows that his working life is limited and therefore tries to maximize his profits in the short time available to him by hiring children. The other costs of production like coal, sand, molasses, oil, etc., are beyond his control.

POLISHING

The other process in which a large number of children are working is polishing the semi-finished goods. Polishing employs about 25,000 workers of whom about 12,000 are children. Unlike the lock industry where children can be seen working on the buffing machines in large numbers, in the brass ware industry children spend their time applying chemicals on the wares to be polished, dipping wares in acid baths before they are polished, putting *masala* (a term used for describing a mix of ingredients) — on the buffs so that they could be used again. Many children working in polishing units are from the adjoining villages. I was told that while children working in the box mould furnace workshops invariably belonged to the city, children engaged in polishing work often came from outside. It was explained that polishing was a relatively unskilled activity into which untrained recruits could enter, while moulding required some training; living and growing up in the urban environment was supposed to help.

I visited six villages around Moradabad city from which people came to work in the brass ware industry. Dhakka village is five kilometres from Moradabad city. The total population of the village is 2000, of which 250 people go daily to work in the multi-purpose workshop units and about fifty are children below the age of fourteen years and about 150 are adolescents below eighteen years. The work of polishing and moulding is also done in the village and many people work here. All the workers working in the village and in the city are Muslims. Kundanpur village has a total population of about 3000. This village is about four kilometres from the city. Most of the workers go to the polishing units in the city. Approximately

250–300 workers commute daily on cycles or walk to work. There are no multi-process units in the village so they all work in the city.There are at least 160 children below the age of fourteen years. Most of the children had already left for work when I visited the village at seven in the morning and could come back home only as late as nine at night but sometimes only at eleven. Since they were afraid of walking home alone, they would wait for their friends and then come together. A common sight in the morning is young children holding on to their small tiffin-carriers as they set out to work. None of the children interviewed earned more than Rs 100 a month. The children said they continued to work as long as they were asked to by the unit owner.

Dhimri village is six to seven kilometres from Moradabad with a total population of 5000 people. From this village, only children below the age of fifteen years go to work. Approximately 200 children commute daily. They are either Muslims or Satar by caste and belong to families of landless labourers or people with small amounts of land.

Menather, another village, is five kilometres from the city with a population of 5000 people. About 100 workers commute to work of whom fifty are children. Most of the workers are Muslim. Jayantipur village, which is six kilometres from the city, has a population of 3000. Out of 250 workers who go to work, 150 are children. Many children and adults work in the polishing units set up in the village. While the adults are mainly Bagvan by caste, the children are mainly Muslims. In Bhadora village, about three kilometres from the city, 150 workers go to Moradabad and they are either Bagvans or Muslims. Pandit Nagla is another village about three kilometres from Moradabad. While parents are engaged in agricultural work, children, about 150, go to work. They are either Muslims or belong to the lower castes of Jatav, Lodhe and Khaagi.

Most multi-process unit owners prefer children from the rural areas because they are cheaper than children of the city. Most children working in polishing workshops were in the age-range of twelve to thirteen years, earned about Rs 100 a month and were kept on a monthly salary. The younger children, between the ages of eight and nine, earned Rs 60 a month and their wages were cut any day they did not come to work. The adults were paid on a piece-rate basis. The children who worked with moulders earned Rs 100–150 a month once they had gained experience and reached the age of twelve or thirteen years. Nine or ten year-olds earned Rs 3 a day and still younger seven to nine-year-olds earned Rs 60 a month. No child below the age of fourteen years earned more than Rs 200 a month irrespective of the kind of work he did or the number of hours he worked.

ELECTROPLATING

Out of 20,000 workers engaged in electroplating, about 5000 are children. The main job that children are involved in is in the tying of articles with wires which are then submerged by adults in chemical tanks containing potassium cyanide. Once the goods are plated, the wires are removed also by children and the wares are taken out into the sun by children where they cover each article with ammonium chloride powder so that all the moisture is absorbed. In the evening, the children carry the dried goods inside the workshop.

WELDING

There are probably 10,000 workers engaged in welding, of whom about 7000 are children. It was common in the lanes of Moradabad to see children working as helpers to adults, who were welding. The adult usually wore protective glasses to prevent injury to his eyes but the child, who passed him the goods and watched him carefully, did not use anything at all. The workshops where welding was carried out were very small and there was not enough space for the children to sit. The adult would sit outside the workshop and the children sat inside, often on top of the cylinder because there was not enough space on the workshop floor. If the cylinder exploded, as has sometimes happened, it was the child who would be injured. One other feature of welding workshops was that the number of children was very large per adult. One frequently saw one adult and three or four children in one workshop, though there were also units where there were no children at all. Children working in welding workshops were very young. Most of the children were in the age-range of six to nine years.

ENGRAVING

A few thousand children work in the processes of engraving designs and colouring. Children involved in these tasks more often than not help their fathers and contribute their mite to the labour of the family. The explanation for this phenomenon is that both engraving and colouring are highly skilled activities which require long periods of training. Parents who want a quick return by way of the child's wage cannot afford to wait the necessary time if their children were to take up these occupations. Because of changes in market demand, engraving and colouring are not at a premium any more and the wages for this category of artisans have in fact fallen. There is no certainty of employment for those who enter these lines. The rest of the workers were employed in factories, etc.

WAGE LABOUR NOT FAMILY LABOUR

Except in the process of engraving and colouring, child labour in the brass ware industry of Moradabad is not a part of family labour as it is usually made out to be. The Child Labour (Prohibition and Regulation) Act of 1986 does not apply to those children who work as part of family labour. In any case, in Moradabad, almost all the children work as wage labour and going by visual impression children do not seem to be remotely related to the adults they work with.

At one box mould furnace workshop in Dhakka village, a man and a boy were working together. I presumed that since this was a village and the work was being done in the courtyard of the house, the man and boy would be related. Since the man was not old enough to be the father of the child, I thought he was the brother and said, 'I suppose he is your brother', pointing to the boy. To which he answered in the affirmative. A little later, while we were waiting for the moulds to be prepared, someone said:

> This boy has been working for at least six years. (The boy was about twelve or thirteen years). Even his younger brother works and he is only seven years old. Rasheed is the sole earning member of his family. His father is dead and mother unemployed with lots of little brothers and sisters to support. He now earns Rs 5 a day.

Then I asked, 'You mean you two are not related? This boy is not a brother?' He said, 'He is not a real brother, but in the vocabulary of the village, everybody is a brother'.

During the course of the study in Moradabad, I visited nearly a 1000 units of different types and found that parents and children worked together in less than ten or fifteen of them. Such detailed investigation is not normally done by inspecting authorities even if they possessed the will and manpower to do so. Hence the myth that most children who work in Moradabad work as part of family labour persists. Exactly the opposite is the case.

ATTITUDES OF PARENTS

I interviewed several parents about their attitudes towards the fact that their children worked. Many times I got the distinct impression that parents believed that children were born to serve and support them and saw nothing wrong in their not being in school or not being able to play. It is, of course, true that few parents could afford to send children to school or let them have the luxury of play. The attitudes of many parents reflected the expectations that society has of children with respect to their roles and, in particular, their filial duties.

When I asked Sunil's mother whether Sunil ever protested

about being made to work, she said: 'If he doesn't work, he will die. We don't have a government job that we can feed him ourselves without lifting a finger. Whatever he earns is spent on him.'

At Bara Shah Shafa, Khajoor ki Sarai, Feel Khana and Lal Masjid, there are many polishing workshops. At one that I went to, two boys of twelve and fourteen years were working. The younger one told me that he lived on the premises and cooked his food on an electric stove. The room he lived in was small and most of the space was occupied by a wooden bed on which the two boys slept. A section of the room was partitioned and two buffing machines installed. These boys got up at 6 a.m. and by 7 a.m. when I visited, they were busy at work. Alam said that he earned Rs 250 a month and went home once in eight days. He was the sole supporter of his family of six brothers and sisters and a mother. His father, a rickshaw-puller died two years ago, and since then the boy had started working. I was told that most of the children who lived on the premises were those who had come from the rural areas. About 10 per cent of all working children lived in the workshops.

HEALTH HAZARDS

The two most hazardous processes in the brass ware industry are moulding and polishing and it is in these two processes that child labour is all-pervasive. I saw 600 box mould furnace workshops and this was the recurring pattern. For every adult, there were two children. The work in the box furnace work-shops is extremely dangerous. The child is employed to do two types of jobs. He rotates the wheel which is called a *pankha* (literally means a fan. In this context it is the rotation of the wheel which is called a *pankha* to keep the furnace fire burn-ing). In some box mould furnace workshops there were only two workers, an adult and a child. In these workshops, the child would rotate the wheel. After the temperature had reached a certain level, the child tested it by opening the top of the underground furnace and throwing a little powder into it. If the raw material — molten brass — was ready, blue and green flames would shoot up from the mouth of the furnace. The child then took a large pair of tongs and lifted the crucible of molten brass from the furnace and handed it over to the adult who poured the molten brass into the already prepared moulds. The boy then returned the crucible into the furnace with raw material and helped the adult to open the hot moulds and remove the pieces. As soon as this was done, he and the adult would grind the hot sand till it was very fine. Then, while the moulds were prepared by the adult, the child went back to sit at the wheel to fan the flames.

The job of the moulder is a very delicate operation and if there is a slight mistake or accident the boy can get very badly injured and can even lose his limbs. He wears no protective gear and stands barefoot on top of the furnace to either put in the crucible or to remove it. The temperature in the furnace is about 1100° C. As one exporter/manufacturer, explaining the processes in his factory, said: 'See how dextrous this young child is. He has to be. Because even if a drop of molten brass falls on his foot there will be a hole in it.'

The child is not only in danger of getting badly burnt but both he and the adult worker inhale the fumes and gases which are let off from the furnace and again when the molten brass is poured into the moulds. Local people and government officials said that all moulders developed tuberculosis. A local doctor, Anwar Husain of Peerzada, said that almost every brass-worker suffered from TB or other upper respiratory tract infections after a few years. This could be avoided only if the worker looked after himself and ate well. But since they cannot afford good food, the combination of poor nutrition and bad working conditions reduces the life span of workers by half. No one worked for more than ten or fifteen years and none lived beyond the age of forty years. In fact, in the 600 or so moulding units I visited, the workers were remarkably young!

In Bhurra Mohalla, commonly referred to as Jatavon Ka Mohalla, near Prince Road, about 100 families live there and almost 500 people are engaged in polishing work. Some of them polish steel utensils and others polish brass. There are hundreds of polishing machines installed in the locality; most of them are owned by workers who save and after a few years get a machine and then use hired help, mainly child labour. I talked to at least thirty people, many of whom had lost members of their families. Draupadi was a middle-aged woman whose child had started working at the age of eight and died the previous year at the age of twenty-five years. He was a polisher. Mangal Sein is sixty, and works as a cobbler. His four adult sons are dead. The youngest died the week before my visit, after vomiting blood. Just across the lane from Draupadi's house, a young adolescent boy had died the night before and the family was taking the body for its last rites. People in Jatavon Ka Mohalla said that 60 per cent of all polishers get ill and approximately 20–30 per cent of them die soon after. A young adolescent boy, Prakash said: 'I used to work on the machines, but since I started vomiting blood, I hire other workers, mainly children.' On being asked why people sent their children to work when they knew that the child would die, the answer was: 'The child is going to die in any case. If he doesn't work, he will die of starvation in a few days. If he works, then death is at least postponed for a few years.'

Everyone told me that death, and a very painful one at that, was inevitable for polishers at a very young age but there was no alternative. Chandrasen said: 'What can I say but that every family has lost one or two adolescent boys or adult sons? Now we have started taking this for granted.'

Local doctors admitted that brass-workers were prone to TB but they felt that this was largely due to poverty, malnutrition and congestion in their living quarters. They were not willing to admit easily that these problems were particularly acute for brass-workers, especially those working in box mould furnace workshops and in polishing work. Some reluctantly agreed that there was a correlation between work and TB as even in the city, it was mainly brass-workers who were affected. In the villages where people lived in relatively open spaces, the incidence of TB was negligible but those who were diagnosed as having the disease were brass-workers. In fact, Moradabad is one of the two cities with the highest rate of TB in the state. The local doctors were certainly not in a position to make a distinction between TB and pneumoconiosis or silicosis, the latter being clearly an industrial disease.

Doctors in Moradabad felt that workers who came with chest problems did not get themselves treated. There was such fear in the minds of workers about TB that if their problem was so diagnosed, patients rarely came back even though the disease was curable. This was so partly because the first advice the doctor gave his patient was to change his occupation and to improve his diet. Workers cannot afford to act upon these recommendations.

While local doctors said that the most common medical complaint of workers was chest diseases, workers themselves said that accidents at work were not unusual. Said Rafiqbhai: 'Accidents are very common. Sometimes, the crucible slips and your hands and feet get badly burnt.'

The most hazardous process was considered to be that of moulding in a box mould furnace workshop. One young man, pointing to six children working in his workshop, said: 'None of these children will survive beyond the age of thirty. They will die of TB.' Hafizbhai Namunewale said, 'Most parents who send their children to work are not even aware of what will happen to the child. They only realize it when a child gets injured and hurt. But by that time, it is too late to repent. And of course, poverty forces parents to turn a blind eye. If a *ghadiya wala* drops the *ghadiya* (crucible), he injures himself but that is not the end of the matter. The *dhalaiya* (moulder) will take the hot *chimta* (tongs) with which the child holds the *ghadiya* and brand him on the back as punishment! The child will shrivel up in pain and complain to his parents. The mother will put some ointment on the wound but will send him right back to work the next day! Ansari Sahib said:

> Children who work on polishing machines are at considerable
> risk. Not only do they inhale all the metal dust and *masala*,

but if a piece slips, it can severely injure the child. One of the main jobs the children do in polishing units is acid washing of goods before they are polished on buffing machines. You can't enter the room where this is done — all by children. You can actually see the green and blue vapours rising from the acid tubs. We people, who are workers, find it impossible to enter such a room. You won't be able to stand even outside the door. The stench is tremendous and the eyes burn. With polishing the person gets chest diseases. He suffocates to death.

I asked Hafizbhai whether the problem of child labour was better than before or worse. He said:

It's better. At least 5 per cent of parents are beginning to realize the harmful effect of work on the child. Look, you can see what happens to the child working as a *ghadiyawala*. His health deteriorates so fast. He is breathing in fumes from the furnace ten to twelve hours a day. Have you been near a *darja bhatti*? You won't be able to stand there for a few minutes. And this child spends his life in front of it. Within a short time, he gets weak. His legs become absolutely skinny. Parents can see this. Every other day the child has fever. It is only desperate parents who send their child to work at a *bhatti* (furnace).

Most people interviewed said that accidents were very common amongst children but I did not see any injured children myself. I was told:

Only when the child is well can he come to work. These days major accidents are relatively few. In the earlier days, when the *bhattis* used to get scrap as raw material — most of it from the ordinance factories — sometimes whole *mohallas* used to explode killing adults and children. Now this kind of thing is rare because the raw material is centrally processed at factories which make *sillis* and *gullis* and this danger is relatively less.

But in Rasheedbhai's locality just recently, a child was killed and several adults injured in an explosion. In a box mould furnace, a child was breaking up scrap brass from an ordinance factory with a hammer. One of the pieces was a live grenade which exploded on his face. He died instantaneously. But this is rare.

People, particularly local doctors, are reluctant to talk about health hazards to strangers for fear that they will get into trouble for not reporting obvious medico-legal cases. Parents do not talk about them for other reasons. Khalid Begum said: 'If the poor think of ill-health and illness, how can they work? Accidents are very common. My son lost four fingers. He was under treatment for a long time. Now he's alright.'

Ruksana Begum had also joined the conversation. She said:

> Only a few months back, Mumtaz's fifteen-year old son died. He had just started working as a welder with a stove welding workshop. God knows what happened, but there was too much gas in the stove and it burst. The boy caught fire and he died before he could be given any medical attention.

Suraiya narrated the story of her neighbour's son in Feel Khana who lost his arm in the belt which rotates the buffing machine in a polishing unit:

> Poor thing, he was only twelve years old. The story is that his clothes got caught in the machine. He tried to disentangle them and his hand got caught. Now he's OK. He can even work with one arm.

Khalida said smilingly:

> Accidents can happen any time on any job but you can't stop working. The disc of the grinder sometimes breaks and eyes get damaged. The crucible slips and hands and feet get burnt. But if a mother was to think of all these factors, how will she send her child to work?

I asked why most of the children were working in the three or four most hazardous jobs like moulding, polishing, electroplating and welding. Ruksana's answer was:

These jobs have quick returns. A boy who goes to work at a *bhatti* will get at least Rs 5 at the end of ten hours. This is not the case with skilled jobs like engraving, colouring, etc. For these jobs, you'll notice only those children who are working with their own fathers. The training period is long and there are no immediate monetary returns. It takes a long while before the child can earn enough. As it is, the rate paid to adult engravers is so little that children will get nothing for this. This work is the least harmful. Your clothes don't get spoilt. You don't inhale fumes and dust. The children who used to do a lot of engraving earlier have now virtually disappeared. Many men want these jobs because they are relatively easy, so where is the question of young boys getting them? It is only the very unskilled jobs that children get and unfortunately these are also the most hazardous.

It is clear that the majority of child workers in the brass ware industry are engaged in intrinsically hazardous occupations. With the current technology, one does not see any way in which their health can be protected or the health hazards significantly lessened.

EDUCATION

None of the working children I met were educated. They worked a minimum of ten hours a day and their parents said they were not in a position to pay for their education. I talked to Sayeedbhai a painter. His older son was busy colouring a brass plate. He has not been educated. But the younger boy goes to school. He does not want to send his child to work. He said:

> You can't sacrifice your family for work. It is bad enough that one son has not been educated and therefore he has to work at this job. But this little one will study. He can always learn the craft. After all, he belongs to a family of artisans. In any case, education will only improve his ability to work.

Others gathered around and said the same thing: 'Education

is very important if one day you want to become an entrepreneur. To manage the business, the child will have to be given education.'

I asked why some parents send their children to work and others do not. And the unanimous responses were: 'If you can't feed your children, where is the question of paying for their education?' But when I said that primary school education was free for children, they said:

Are there enough schools in Moradabad? Our children don't get admission into government schools and we can't afford to pay Montessori school fees. If there were more schools, half our problems would be solved.

I asked whether parents did not send their children to school because they felt education was irrelevant and made them work instead. The answer was,

If today the government comes up with a scheme to provide education to all children and sets up schools, all these children working in *darja bhattis* (box mould furnace) would leave work and go to school. No one sends their children to work because they think that education is irrelevant. But if there are no schools, then children are sent to work.

The attitudes of parents sometimes differed. Zakiabi's husband has deserted her. She lives with her four sons in her sister's house. Although she did not work herself, she sent all her children to work, though they were under twelve years. She said, 'Their father has deserted us and gone away so they'll have to work. If he comes back, he can educate them.'

She was so upset about having been deserted that she felt that it was the duty of her children to work and support her. Her young seven-year old son was working in a box mould furnace workshop. He had never been to school. When I asked him how many years he had worked, he said that he did not know how to count but he had been working for several years. The other workers said that he had worked for three years.

In Kathghar, Jamalbhai was working at a box mould furnace

workshop with two boys aged eight and ten years. The three together earned Rs 40 a day. The boys were not his sons. He said, 'I have only four daughters so the question does not arise. But if I had a son I would send him to school. This is no work for a child.' But in Peergave, Kathghar, Lal Masjid and Idgah, none of the working children had been to school. Some parents felt that, 'If they study, they will die of starvation.' They could not afford the opportunity cost of sending a child to school because every penny earned was crucial for bare survival of the family.

Hafizbhai Namunewala was adamant and said that the problem of child labour was closely linked to the problem of illiteracy. He said, 'I'll give it to you in writing that educated parents do not send their children to work. It is only illiterate parents who put their children to work at an early age.' He went on to add:

It is a vicious circle. If you are uneducated, you don't even understand the implications of what you are doing. You only think of today. It is almost impossible to explain to uneducated people the value of family planning, for instance. This only makes the problem more difficult to handle. For them, if a child is bringing in one or two rupees at the end of the day, it is good enough.

His son, Mushahid, interjected: 'Education is the most important thing. If you are uneducated, you don't even know the meaning of the word '*bhavishya*' (future).' Hafizbhai said:

We have had a law to ban child labour for so long. Has it ever been implemented? Do you know the laws in Japan? You cannot employ a child there. What prevents the government from enforcing the Child Labour Act and forcing parents to educate their children?

I replied that government officials often say that banning child labour is impossible because the economic condition of the families of working children will become worse. Hafizbhai had this to say:

It is true that many families rely entirely on their children. But not always because of economic necessity. In our neighbourhood, there are families where the father spends the whole day playing cards. The mother does housework. The only income of that family is from the children. Do you think that this should continue? Parents can also be callous. I met a woman this morning who was very upset because her twelve-year old son collapsed in a factory due to heat stroke and she had to spend Rs 30 on doctor's fees and medicines. If parents do not know what is good for their children, then surely the state has to intervene. The consequences of all this are very serious. These are the very children who as adolescent boys become irresponsible citizens. They have so much anger within them. They are the easiest targets for anti-social activity.

Some Muslim social activists confirmed this:

The child who is denied education and made to work is really frustrated. It comes out in little things like his inability to read the film posters. He feels ashamed that he has to ask another child which film is showing. And this alone can build up into a tremendous anger. There is so much violence in our *mohallas*, in our families — because of this.

Rahim Khan, designer, has educated all his children. He said:

The evidence of what education can do for you is all around us. Look at the exporters, they have become multi-millionaires before our eyes. Their children are in boarding schools. And look at us artisans — uneducated — how easily we are being exploited. If you are educated, you know what the laws are, the government policy is. Even if government has a programme for helping the artisans, they don't know about these things. Exporters have got so many concessions and income-tax exemptions that overnight they have become multi-millionaires. One of our biggest exporters has recently imported a twelve-seat Toyota from Japan. A car which will cost only Rs 60 on diesel from Moradabad to Delhi. They have four gunmen and guard dogs. Their imported German dog costs them Rs 3000 a month on food and sleeps in an air-conditioned room with one attendant. It is more than what they will spend on ten workers. How have they become so wealthy but by exploiting the uneducated workers?

The people gathered around were very resentful of those who had made it big. Many of them felt that the main road to upward mobility was education. It was the very first step. Without it, the question did not arise. One or two people were of the view that:

> The only way to implement a ban on child labour is to use police force. You have to make education compulsory. You provide school books, clothes, etc. Parents will protest. Employers will protest. But sooner or later they will realize that this is all for the good of the child.

Abidbhai said:

> It is very important to educate women. If you educate a boy, it is like educating one person. But if you educate a girl she in turn will educate her children. The condition of a family depends a lot on the women. Parents need to be educated on the harmful effect of work on the health of their children.

Hafizbhai added, 'Give education to children and their eyes will open up automatically.' Mukhtiarbhai spoke bitterly of the problems of education in Moradabad. He said, 'There is nothing called a school teacher here. In front of my house there is a government school. There are supposed to be four teachers but not one comes.' According to him, most of the schools are grant-in-aid schools getting funds from the government and run by registered societies. At the time of school admissions and just before examinations, they demand money in the form of donations on the slightest pretext. The private schools are not recognized by the government and their certificates and diplomas are of no use for college admissions. Muktiarbhai had a valid point regarding the medium of instruction which is Hindi:

> The medium of instruction in Moradabad is Hindi because that is supposed to be our national language. Yet university

education in places like Delhi is all in English. Our children
are handicapped. And if truly the intention is to use Hindi,
then why is all the literature on the subject of imports and
exports in English? All the information we need about government policies and programmes regarding trade are in English.
How are we supposed to understand that? Those who are
educated in English are obviously at an advantage. Now anybody who makes it as an entrepreneur sends his child to
Nainital or Dehra Dun for education. Even the better-off artisans are trying to send their children there. But very few
can afford it.

Surinder Singh, an activist in Moradabad, but not working with
brass workers, had ideas about the kind of education working
children need:

I was a child worker myself so I know what it means to be a
working child. My father died when I was seven years old
and my mother forced me to work. My clothes were always
torn and dirty and I was very ashamed of myself. It was only
after I had worked for some years, saved some money and
bought some clothes that I went to a teacher I knew in the
village to let me come to school. Even then, the first day, I
was scared. I didn't have the nerve to enter the school, so I
stood outside the gate the whole day. It was only when the
teacher I knew came that I went with her. Working children
have very low self-esteem. They will not even go and talk to
a child who is better dressed — because that signifies superior
status. The teacher in our society is glorified as the guru —
close to god — a position that we can never hope to attain.
The image must change if children are going to enjoy school.
The teacher must come down from her pedestal. Any scheme
to provide education to working children must take this into
account. Children must be given uniforms so that some semb-
lance of equality can be maintained. If education is to be
provided after work, it has to be qualitatively different from
that given to non-working children. It must be fun. There
must be a component of entertainment in it for it to be
successful.

The most horrifying consequences of working in the brass ware industry for children is that their lives are shortened by the hazards they are exposed to. Those who survive are often ill. Their life-chances are bleak because of their illiteracy and the question of bettering their lot simply does not arise; they are thus destined to remain poorly paid and unskilled workers for whatever is left of their lives. Given the nature and kind of work, part-time education is not a practicable proposition and it will be impossible to monitor such a scheme. The only solution is to lessen the awesome human cost and pay those parents who cannot afford the money to send their children to school.

TECHNOLOGY AND EMPLOYMENT: SOME OBSERVATIONS

One of the objectives of this study was to see whether any changes in technology could be recommended from the point of view of discouraging the use of child labour and promoting the employment of adults. On a visit to Bangkok in Thailand in 1988, I was able to visit four factories manufacturing brass ware. At each factory there were only eight to ten workers employed but the premises of these factories were almost as large as some of the biggest factories in Moradabad. When I looked at the processes in these factories, it became apparent that the technology used in Bangkok was virtually the same as that used in Moradabad. However, there were no children working in the brass ware factories in Bangkok.

It is relevant to mention here the differences in the technology employed between Bangkok and Moradabad. For one thing, the moulds and the crucibles used were of much larger size and could not therefore be handled by children. In one factory for example, where large statues of the Buddha were being made, I saw a crucible being lifted by two men with the aid of wooden supports. Clearly, such heavy weights could not be lifted by children. When I enquired with the factory supervisors as to why children were not employed, they gave three types of reasons. They pointed out that children were not fit by virtue of their physical attributes to work for the industry, that the work was hazardous and therefore not suitable for children and, finally, that child labour could be obtained in Bangkok only on a monthly wage as most children came from outside Bangkok to work and not on piece-rate wages. In one of the factories I visited where smaller decorative brass pieces were being manufactured, the activities and the machinery were virtually identical to those in Moradabad. Even then, no children were to be seen.

It is not as if there is no child labour in Thailand in general or Bangkok in particular. In fact, Bangkok attracts working children from the poorer Northern and North-Eastern provinces of Thailand. Several studies point out that there are over two million working children in Thailand, a significant proportion of whom are to be found in Bangkok (Bond 1982: 2; Udomsakdi 1986: 36). But perhaps there are better options available for children than working in the brass ware industry and therefore no child works in this industry. It is therefore necessary to look at the relationship between technology and the employment of children in a larger socio-economic setting.

When I spoke to manufacturers and exporters in Moradabad, they informed me that the technology employed in Taiwan and Korea in the brass ware industry was far more sophisticated than that used in Moradabad. The level of mechanization was much higher. In these countries, brass ware is manufactured by the die-casting method where an initial model or die is made and fixed on machines and thousands of pieces are then churned out. Clearly, in more developed capitalist economies, technologies of mass production are more in vogue. Since I have not studied the growth and development of the brass ware industry elsewhere, it is not possible to make further generalizations regarding the situation in those countries.

If one was to posit that increased mechanization in the brass ware industry of Moradabad is a desirable goal from the point of view of discouraging the use of child labour, the first question that needs to be answered is whether there is any incentive for an entrepreneur to take such an investment decision. It was pointed out to me in Moradabad that there have been periods as long as four or five years — such as, for example, after the 1980 riots — when trade saw a sharp decline because there was virtually no production. To regain one's position in the international market is a difficult task and it is only in the last couple of years that the industry is on the upswing. Apart from other factors like the inherently unstable international market, the uncertain communal situation of Moradabad is a risk to be constantly borne in mind. Such reasons inhibit technological investment and change. Moreover, we have to ask whether it is not cheaper for the entrepreneur to continue at the present technological level when labour in general is cheap and child labour particularly so. The answer, it would appear, in the context of the uncertainties of production and the market, to stick to cheap child labour unless pressure is brought upon the industry through importers.

Let us look at a small technological change that is possible. In the moulding units, there are usually one adult and two or three children. One child is exclusively engaged in rotating the wheel which fans the furnace. In very few units I noticed that a low horsepower motor was installed which rotated the wheel and eliminated the need for one child. When I asked other entrepreneurs why this simple device was not more widely used, I was told about — and in fact experienced — the extremely erratic power supply available in the town. Since power shortage is a way of life, most people preferred to keep a child worker fanning the furnace for, otherwise the entire production process would grind to a halt whenever power failed. And every day there would be no power for three or four hours. This background helps one to understand why even such small technological changes are not introduced.

In the polishing units, which along with the moulding units are the largest employers of children, the buffs on the polishing machines wear away in course of time. These buffs can be replaced by purchasing them in the market but until it becomes absolutely necessary to replace them, recycled buffs are used for as long as possible. In every polishing unit, one or two children spend most of their time extending the life of these buffs by putting gum, emery powder and some mixture on them. We may infer that the entrepreneur has calculated that it is cheaper for him to employ these children to recycle these buffs rather than buy them from the market. This story illustrates the relatively weak financial position of the entrepreneur who owns a small polishing unit. One cannot expect substantial investment in new technology from persons of such standing, unless those who get this work done also share their profits more equitably. Pressure can again be brought upon these small entrepreneurs only through the industry and that also when there is pressure upon the industry from the buyers of such goods.

I have in the section on the female worker referred to the fact that when there were technological changes in the process of scraping and polishing, women who usually did this work at home were substantially displaced from the labour force. Men took over this job on machines in factories and workshops. As a result, incomes of families in which women did this work saw a decline. To make ends meet in such families, young boys who might otherwise have been in school were sent out to work.

The earnings of the children helped in a small way to reduce the budgetary gap of the family. Evidence for the relationship between the displacement of female workers and increase in the incidence of child labour was to be found in interviews with female members of different households I visited. These events illustrate some unforeseen consequences of technological change which can, as shown above, increase the incidence of child labour.

Even if it were feasible to introduce mechanization in the brass ware industry in the background of the hurdles described above, it is necessary to ask whether increased mechanization is a desirable goal considering the prevalence of unemployment and under-employment. Technological changes on a large scale would almost certainly diminish opportunities of employment for adults even if such changes made children unsuitable as workers in the brass industry. Perhaps a better alternative would be to bring pressure upon the industry as a whole from the buyers of these goods and entrepreneurs, both big and small are forced to improve working conditions for labour welfare as well as to ensure that no child labour is employed. When there is a continued demand for the goods and non-availability of child labour, it is likely that the prospects of adult workers will improve.

THE IMPLICATIONS OF GOVERNMENT POLICY FOR THE BRASS WARE INDUSTRY

What holds good for the lock, gem, glass and pottery industries is also the case for the brass ware industry of Moradabad — everywhere, child labour is being passed off as family labour, despite facts to the contrary. And this is precisely because of the provision in the Child Labour (Prohibition and Regulation) Act. The fact that work is carried out in residential premises lends credence to the belief that the industry is 'cottage oriented' and that fathers pass on their skills to sons. The Labour Department of the Government of Uttar Pradesh organized a sample survey in 1986 and found that only 25 per cent of the children were wage workers and that, therefore, protection was required only for 2000 children. My estimates were that there were between 40,000–45,000 children working in the industry, the vast majority of whom are wage workers. The sight of adult males working with children reinforces the view that children work as part of family labour. Patient investigation is needed into these appearances and governmental survey staff are notably untrained for this type of work. When governmental teams visit, they are blandly told of non-existent family connections for people are afraid of violating the law for fear of being penalized. In the short time available, data collectors take what they are offered at face value. It bears repetition that while the work of engraving and colouring is done in family units, at least 75 per cent of the child labour force is engaged on work like moulding, electroplating, welding and polishing. These are all extremely hazardous occupations and, if properly investigated, would fall squarely within the purview of the Child Labour Act.

One plank of the National Child Labour Programme (NCLP) is to effectively implement the various laws enacted for the benefit of working children. But the labour office in Moradabad is grossly understaffed with only one labour inspector for the whole city. No organization, however sincere, could even get the facts straight — much less implement the law — when it is so thinly peopled. It is necessary both to sensitize the labour enforcement machinery to the problems of workers — both adults and children — as also to increase significantly the number of personnel deployed so as to be able to cover the large area of the industry.

The Government of India has laid down the framework of the NCLP and left it for the local authorities to implement. A bureaucratic tendency to accept what has come from above has led to a plan divorced from reality. The identification of hazardous and non-hazardous activities has been left for the Deputy Director of Factories (Medical) of Uttar Pradesh to decide at a later date. In the meanwhile, it is planned to give vocational training to children in the age-groups of ten to twelve years and twelve to fourteen years in the trades of engraving, polishing, foundry, gas welding, packing, soldering and electroplating and as machinists and tuners. These are all important processes in the brass ware industry. Polishing and foundry work may seem relatively easy but are extremely hazardous as are the jobs of welding, soldering and electroplating. To suggest that children between the ages of ten to twelve years should start with polishing and foundry work would be an express violation of Article 24 of the Indian Constitution. However, given the way in which the Child Labour Act is formulated, if these processes are taught in government-aided schools and institutions, these children would not come under the purview of the law. Thus what may be against the spirit of the Constitution may be perfectly legal!

But it would seem that the proposal under consideration to train twelve to fourteen year old children in soldering, electroplating, gas welding, etc., in factories would also violate Section 67 of the Factories Act. The section unequivocally states that children below the age of fourteen years should not be allowed to work in any factory. The scheme for such training, if approved by the Government of India, was to start in 1988-9 giving stipends and food to the children to be trained in local workshops.

Even if it were not the intention, a scheme to train children in the listed trades will result in providing skilled labour to the brass ware industry at no cost to the industry itself. Had free primary education been offered instead, these children would have had better life chances than their current dismal prospects of remaining workers forever.

Under the NCLP, there is a plan to improve the working conditions in the workshop where children above the age of fourteen years are working. In the areas of child labour con- centration, the removal of slums, improvement of sanitation and construction of approach roads are components of the plan in general. For anyone who has visited Moradabad, this scheme appears to be unrealistic for the improvement of working con- ditions would be close to being impossible unless the entire city is demolished and rebuilt. Obviously, this is not a prac- ticable proposition.

When this case study was written in 1988, a scheme, the Peetal Vasti or colony for brass-workers was being set up outside the city centre by the U.P. State Brass Ware Corporation. This would enable the artisans to move out of their congested living and working quarters to a space allocated outside the city centre. Here, perhaps plots could be allotted only to those families who undertook not to send their children to work but to keep them compulsorily in schools in Peetal Vasti. If the problems that poor children face in schools are taken care of and if an enforcement system devised, then such a scheme might well be viable.

Ultimately, the only solution to the problem of child labour in the brass ware industry is a complete and unequivocal ban on its use. This step would be in keeping with the stated policy of the Government of India, which says that it will not allow children to work in hazardous occupations. The National Institute of Occupational Health could do an epidemiological study to verify the extent of the problem of health hazards to child workers. The ban would have to be enforced only when the government is ready to provide free, compulsory primary education with the added incentives of free meals, uniforms and books. Exporters, to whom various concessions are given by the government, could be prevailed upon to pay a cess to help fund such a programme.

8

Traditional Crafts and Child Labour

There is an old and popular belief that certain craft-oriented industries would die out and the skills be lost permanently if child labour was to be banned. The picture painted is one where traditional occupations pass on from father to son, generation to generation. That picture does not fit the facts any longer. While it is true that there are still artisans in a few crafts who earn their living with the help of family labour and cater to the needs of local markets, they are not representative. In many traditional industries, the artisan has been displaced either wholly or in large measure by the entrepreneur and the trader/financier. The artisan who would buy his raw materials, process them and then sell them — functioning more or less as an autonomous producer with some interest in small-scale agriculture — has been adversely affected by industrialization, the injection of capital and the growth of new markets. Skills previously the preserve of a few families are now widely available in the labour market because of state-sponsored training programmes which cover many industries. Moreover, new technology has rendered many of these skills irrelevant. The artisan has been transformed into a factory worker by the large-scale nature of production.

Consider, for example, the case of the carpet industry of Mirzapur-Bhadohi-Varanasi in Uttar Pradesh. Eighty per cent of the carpet production in India takes place in that belt and is primarily export-oriented. The industry employs 200,000 workers, of whom 150,000 are children, not counting those working as part of family labour (Juyal 1987: 26). Juyal observes that traditionally most of the weavers came from low peasant groups like the Binds. These groups were small or marginal owner-cultivators and combined weaving with agriculture, more so because the looms remained idle for long intervals and did not provide regular employment. . . . Weaving is, by and large, still a 'supplementary' occupation for the small cultivating class (ibid: 20).

The growth and potential of the industry led to major structural changes. Juyal points out that:

> . . . some new leaders (like the Mishras, Dubes, Rajputs, etc.) have sprung up. They are all from the dominant castes in the agrarian structure of the region, with no background of trade, commerce, industry or artisanship (ibid: 22).

As a result, Juyal goes on to observe:

> Thus, far from being an industry of self-employed weavers, there has been increasing concentration of ownership of looms in the non-artisan class. The looms may be placed together in factory-like 'sheds' or in domestic premises, or even in the cottages of the weavers on a dispersed basis. But the fact remains that the emergence of this non-artisan owner class is, in fact, a major contributory factor to the exacerbation of the problem of child labour; more so the migrant-captive type drafted from outside the village or locality (ibid: 11).

As regards the imparting of skills, the rapid expansion of the industry was largely a result of the 600 carpet-weaving training centres that were set up by the Government of India, and which annually trained about 30,000 child weavers. The Government of Uttar Pradesh contended that carpets woven by the 'nimble fingers' of children were of superior quality to others (GOUP 1986b: 2). V.R. Sharma, a carpet manufacturer, admitted in an unusually frank interview:

> It is a myth that child labour is essential and the children are

capable of weaving better carpets than adults. The carpet manufacturers would have no objection whatsoever if children are not allowed to work in the industry. But children are being employed to help their families (*Indian Express*, 16 June 1987).

According to this prominent employer's perspective, the skills related to carpet-weaving could be passed on to others in training programmes.

I have already noted earlier how the traditional potters of Khurja run only twenty-five establishments today as against 300 run by rank outsiders; in the pottery industry as well, government-organized training programmes have helped the growth of the industry. Where it expanded because of an increased demand, new recruits were helped by government training programmes, as in the case of the carpet and gem-polishing industries. In the lock industry where the village artisan is still visible, factories account for the major share of production and the social background of factory owners — largely Punjabi Hindus — is quite different from that of the traditional Muslim craftsmen.

Sivakasi, in the State of Tamil Nadu, is the home of the match industry and employs 45,000 children. A study conducted for the Government of India by the Madras Institute of Development Studies (MIDS) had this to say about the reasons for child labour:

Although the 'nimble fingers' argument is widely accepted even by those who otherwise are opposed to child labour, the study indicates that there is no truth to it. Examination of the seventeen processes in match manufacture shows that children are employed in all twelve of the piece rated or contracted operations. . . . The major operations of frame-filling, box-filling and labelling and band-rolling are, of course, the principal employment generators. These are all simple tasks requiring a speed of movement and co-ordination of action but no special aptitude, which children might possibly have, and adults lose. In fact, not only were adults employed in all these sixteen operations, but they outnumbered children in the surveyed units and most crucially, their modal rate of physical production was more than that of children. There is no reason, therefore, to accept the 'nimble fingers' argument either on the grounds of adults' inability to work or due to their allegedly lower *pace* of work (MIDS 1985: 53).

It is a common myth in Firozabad that glass bangle-making and glass-blowing are hereditary occupations and therefore children should work so that this ancient craft is not lost. But skilled workers denied this. According to them the glass industry was only sixty to seventy years old. They pointed out that earlier most of the craftsmen were Muslims and now a large percentage belonged to the Hindu community. The workers said that the myth of a hereditary occupation was important in justifying child labour on the grounds that if children were not to work, the art would be lost. Even the work of a *taarkash* (the man who threads hot glass onto a rolling pin) can be learnt by paying him a fee. This is, however, not to say that a *taarkash* will not teach his child if he wants to learn. But there is nothing inherited about these skills, and are not confined to particular families.

The argument regarding hereditary occupations does not pass muster in the brass ware industry either. I have already referred to the findings of a study (IDS. 1983: 29) to the effect that whereas 66 per cent of workers were self-employed in 1959–60, that proportion fell to less than 1 per cent by 1974. Here again the migration of traditional Muslim craftsmen to Pakistan at the time of the Partition of India and the reverse flow of Punjabi entrepreneurs with their capital, the changes in international demand and the new technology it called for together led to the transformation of a household or cottage industry to one where the factory and the workshop became dominant and wage labour became the norm. In order to seek protection of law, an image is still projected of the industry as retaining its household or cottage character.

CHILD LABOUR AND ADULT UNEMPLOYMENT

A recent study done by the Inter-disciplinary group of the Aligarh Muslim University (AMU) revealed that while there is a demand for child labour, there is also high adult unemployment and under-employment. This study was concentrated in thirty *mohallas* (residential localities) of the Upper Kote area where 46 per cent of the Muslim population was engaged in lock manufacture. The sample used was rather large. They did a preliminary house-listing of 4166 households with a total Muslim population of 24,657. Later, an in-depth study was done of 562 households, i.e. 5 per cent of the total number of households listed in the area by the Aligarh Municipal Board. In the course of this study, it was observed that: '. . . There are many children who are earning and many adults who are not able to find remunerative work' (AMU n.d.: 20).

It is stated emphatically in the draft report of this study on Muslim entrepreneurs that adult workers are not fully employed. The average number of days in the year that employment was possible was 264 days. Those artisans: '. . . Who are able to get work for eight to nine months a year regard themselves as fully engaged. A lock assembly worker feels himself fortunate if he gets work for the fourth day in a week' (ibid: 52).

This study defined permanent workers as those who were working for more than 180 days in a year. Temporary workers were those who were busy for at least 160 days and casual workers were those who had worked for less than ninety days in the previous year. It was found that:

> Even the so-called permanently employed artisans are unemployed for more than three months, whereas others are unemployed for periods longer than 105 days, ranging from six to nine months. Thus the state of underemployment of labour is true for all the artisans, more for some and less for the others (ibid).

It was also found that: '. . . The number of hours worked are highest 11.94 for the lowest income stratum earning less than Rs 500 p.m.' (ibid).

I have already noted in the case study on the glass industry of Firozabad how the black marketing of coal yields large profits and thereby permits factory owners to shut down their operations for several months in the year, a situation then is deliberately engineered in which workers are laid off for long periods of time leading to severe unemployment. Even when the factories are running, in order to force workers into docile submission, there is no security of employment and workers are frequently and arbitrarily thrown out. In view of large-scale unemployment there are always fresh recruits to take the place of those whose services are terminated. The large-scale employment of children can be attributed to the savings on account of wage cost, increased productivity and the greater docility and vulnerability of children at the hands of employers.

In the carpet industry, Juyal says there is evidence that child labour is enhancing unemployment and underemployment of the adults. Within the industry, they not only seem to displace adult workers but also depress the incomes of adults doing similar work (Juyal 1987: 33).

Vishwapriya Iyengar, on a visit to Sivakasi interviewed both parents and children, writes about Chinnadorai and his young ten-year old brother Devraj, who work at a match factory in Kalgumali. Says Iyengar:[1]

> Kadaval, their father, told me about Devraj. Like the others he too works ten to fourteen hours a day for Rs 4 to 5. . . . Returning from the factory he falls asleep without being able to eat any dinner. His legs ache and he has to drag himself to walk. His eyes smart without enough sleep and his chest is congested all the time. . . . Every morning at 2.30 a.m., he begs his mother to let him sleep a while longer. 'This work is killing me. It is too difficult for me. Please let me stay at home.' The mother shakes the child awake, 'Your father has no work. We have to work. There is no other life for us.'

[1] See also Kothari 1983a, b, c.

Kadaval feels helpless watching this day after day . . . (Iyengar 1986a).

In the carpet industry of Kashmir, writes Suraj Gupte, 100,000 children of school-going age are working. Gupte reports:

> One Bashir Ahmed Batt whose two sons, aged twelve and ten, have taken to carpet (weaving) has this to say: 'Can you beat it that the owners and the management refused to give me a job? They openly say that the young children suit them better.' Why? 'Low wages are the chief reason', he replies. 'To cap that, children are not the ones who would grumble against the bad working conditions or organize a protest rally' (Gupte 1985: 9).

In industries like the pottery industry of Khurja and the brass ware industry of Moradabad, there is tremendous demand for labour to the extent that factory owners have started hiring Bihari migrant labour but there is also adult unemployment amongst local people. The preference was for Bihari migrant workers because they were the cheapest and always available. People coming from the adjoining villages were considered unreliable because they would stay away from work during peak agricultural seasons and city labour was thought to be arrogant. But in all units except for the very big factories using modern technology, child labour was the preferred form of labour even when adults were unemployed.

Some might argue that if child workers were not employed the production would discontinue, but given the low wages of adults, that argument has little appeal. It seems a clear case of the substitution of children for adults, on grounds of cost and ease of control.

THE VESTED INTEREST IN CHILD LABOUR

Defending Child Labour: The Industry's Viewpoint

As described earlier, there is virtually no control over hours of work, the conditions of work are appalling and the wages paid are meagre and well below a living wage in most of the case studies described in detail earlier. The prevalence of a high rate of adult unemployment goes hand in hand with an impressive demand for child labour. The obvious explanation for this phenomenon is that children are a source of cheap labour and can be exploited in ways that adults may not accept. Yet, child labour is sought to be justified by the unit owners on the grounds that if the children of the poor did not work, they would starve.

Recently, the premises of some lock-manufacturers who employ children were raided; this resulted in a furore and factory owners were up in arms. *The Lock Times*, a journal published by the All India Lock Manufacturers' Association (AILMA), Aligarh published an editorial titled 'Aparadhi Kaun?' or 'Who are the guilty?' In his editorial, Ramesh Arora, the General Secretary of AILMA, said that the blame for the existence of child labour rests upon the Government which has not been able to implement Article 45 of the Constitution of India which states that all children below the age of fourteen years shall be given free, compulsory, primary education within ten years of the commencement of the Constitution.

Arora's self-serving argument portrays factory owners as saints who come to the rescue of desperate parents mired in poverty. In his version of reality, compassion for the children on the verge of death and disaster compels factory owners to employ them even if it is against the law. Government officials emerge as heartless enforcers of labour legislation who penalize factory owners for their humane works (Arora 1986: 2).

By and large, factory owners and smaller *karkhana* owners were aware that child labour is illegal. They justify the employment of children with much the same arguments as the editorial cited above. At best, the justification is partial: if poverty is one side of the coin, then the profits of manufacturers is the other.

V.R. Sharma, the carpet manufacturer, contradicted himself first by saying that child labour was essential because otherwise the wage cost would go up by 50 per cent and later by saying that:

> the employment of children in the carpet . . . industry is necessitated not because of the requirements of the industry but because of the needs of the concerned children and their families (Sharma 1985: 4).

Simply put, employers prefer child labour because it is cheaper than adult labour and because children, unlike adults, cannot question the treatment meted out to them. Evidence indicates that the child's wage in any industry is a third to a half that of an adult for the same output, with the child working for as many, if not more, hours than the adult. Socialized into work at an early age, the child works without pause; an adult would balk at the monotony of the tasks performed. We saw earlier, how children in some industries are bonded, offering virtually 'free' labour and how in others with an apprenticeship scheme, they are not paid for months or even years.

The greater amenability of children to exploitation is succinctly described in a conclusion from a study of the match industry:

> Docility may create long-term economic advantages in that children are more likely to undertake unpaid work slipped in between piece-rated jobs, thefts of material and wastage which are elemental forms of protest may be smaller, and deductions from wages of fines and 'donations' may be more feasible. However, the non-economic advantages are probably greater. Docile workers will not protest if they are used like instruments of production, moved from operation to operation as the demands of the manufacturing process dictate. They will work as long as the management requires, particularly when they are on piece-rated occupations. Most important of all, they will not have the capability and experience to organize mass protests against wages and working conditions, even though their knowledge of their situation may be acute (MIDS 1985: 54–5).

Smitu Kothari was told by a foreman at the Standard Fire-
works Factory in Tayyalpatti village that 'we prefer child
workers. They work faster, work longer hours and are depend-
able' (Kothari 1983c: 1193).[2]

There are definite economic advantages in employing
children in the match industry although there is severe adult
unemployment in that area. Indicative of that, when the Tamil
Nadu government threatened to implement the ban on child
labour, the owners of match and fireworks factories protested
vociferously. The Secretary of the All India Chamber of Match
Industries, A.D. Amirthalingam, said that if child labour was
prohibited, the factory owners would go in for mechanization
or diversification of business (*Financial Express*, 17 October
1983). He added that the opponents of child labour were being
financed by a multinational firm, the chief competitor of the
Sivakasi match units, which together hold 30–35 per cent of
the market. He contended that there was no alternative to child
labour as there was an acute shortage of labour in and around
Sivakasi. He also argued that if the children were sent away
from the factories they would beg in the streets.

There are other factors which need to be kept in mind when
discussing the need for child labour by employers in the match
industry. According to the Madras Institute of Development
Studies report, factory owners employ *pannaiyal* or bonded
labour, where whole families are working for the employers in
a condition of slavery. As the report concluded, 'The open
admission of this practice provides evidence for the pre-in-
dustrial nature of employer-employee relations in the area and
has its effect on industrial relations in the match industry' (MIDS
1985: 58–9).[3] The second mechanism for controlling the labour
force is the provision of housing for workers (ibid.).

The report points out that those households which had a
large number of women and children were preferred in the
allocation of housing and also that if production targets were

[2] For a detailed account see Chandrasegaran n.d. and Mehta 1983.
[3] See also Kothari 1983a: 96–100.

not met, the families faced eviction. The conclusion drawn is that the aim of such measures was less to provide welfare than to ensure control (ibid.).

It must be noted here that children are herded into factory buses at 2 a.m. and return from work after dusk (Area Development Programme Report n.d.). The age of the youngest child found working by Kothari was three and a half years! (Kothari 1983c: 1191).

Thus, as the MIDS report points out:

> The crux of the problem of child labour is . . . the conditions of the households providing child labour. ι . ot only are they poor, their sources of income are unstable and the income itself fluctuates. They are dependent on agricultural wage work in an area of low agricultural potential. Most important of all, they find themselves unorganized in a situation where the manufacturers are organized, they are in a social milieu where the employer has almost unlimited rights, now found only in the most backward parts of the country. And finally, residents of their own village are liable to report on any action they may take to change the conditions in which they and their children are forced to work (MIDS 1985: 60).

The match industry is controlled by the powerful Nadar lobby. Kothari points to the fact that the eleven families of Sivakasi and Kovilpatti are responsible for over 70 per cent of the production in the non-mechanized sector and together, their output is more than that of the mechanized sector (Kothari 1983c: 1196).

Similarly, although there are 200 fireworks factories in the Sivakasi area the distribution of production again favours the Nadars; five of whom (with more than five units each) manufacture fireworks worth more than Rs 50 million. A few others have a turnover of over Rs 5 million (ibid.).

The carpet industry is another major industry where there is vested interest in keeping child labour. When the Government of India introduced the idea of levying a cess on employers of child labour, the carpet industry was alarmed. The Carpet

Council News, which is a monthly published by the Carpet Export Promotion Council, frankly admitted in its September 1986 issue that the intended comprehensive legislation on child labour would decrease production and increase costs and that the aim was to prevent such legislation from going through (Chadha ed. 1986: 2).

V.R. Sharma, a large-scale carpet manufacturer, wrote in 1985 that the major cost in the production of carpets was the labour cost. He argued that if the government were to try to bring this industry under protective labour laws and impose a cess on employers of child labour, it would be disastrous for the industry. He noted that a major part of the work in the carpet industry was done by children below fifteen years. He said that such legislation would bring an end to the flexibility that existed. That wages would rise by at least 50 per cent and that consequently the industry would close. He also felt that such legislation, besides being impossible to implement would increase corruption amongst the labour laws enforcement staff. He concluded that irreversible damage would be done and the result would be to 'have killed the hen that lays the golden eggs' (Sharma 1985: 4). Needless to say, the much discussed cess that the government was intending to impose was not included in the new Child Labour Act.

The glass, lock, carpet and match industries are not the only industries that have a vested interest in child labour. Venkatramani reports from Coimbatore, where more than half the cotton hosiery in the country is produced, that Tiruppur's 200-odd hosiery units have an annual turnover of Rs 900 million and an export turnover of Rs 280 million. Tiruppur shares the hosiery market with Calcutta. However, Tiruppur's hosiery is 2 or 3 per cent cheaper than Calcutta's and the main reason for this, as explained by T.V. Ratnam, Director of the South India Textile Research Association, Coimbatore, is that: 'Labour is only 10 per cent of the total production cost in the hosiery industry. But the employment of child labour gives Tiruppur an edge over Calcutta in terms of costs' (Venkatramani 1983: 60). Factory owners do not deny using children.

'Child labour may be illegal, but what can we do?' asked Mohan P. Kandaswamy, President of the South India Hosiery Manufacturers' Association '. . . From the drought-hit villages surrounding Tiruppur, children continuously flock to the town, literally begging for work. And we are also in dire need of labour' (ibid.).

Venkatramani quotes N. Duraiswamy, partner in Fancy Knitting Works to the effect that the industry would collapse without children. He recounts a colourful phrase used by one U.R. Nurugaswami, 'children are the life-breath of the garment-making units' (ibid.).

B.N. Juyal, writing about the silk textile industry of Varanasi, cites the admission of some employers that the entire industry would be in serious trouble but for the continued availability of child labour (Juyal et al 1985: 108–110).

It will thus be seen that in a wide range of industries, employers are willing to admit the economic value of children to their industries. While one can understand and even sympathize with the need of poor parents to place an economic value upon their children, it is utterly reprehensible that in the eyes of their employers, the value of children lies primarily in the cheapness of their labour.

9

The Female Child

Most debates on child labour leave the specific problems of the girl child unanswered. Part of the reason is that while boys can be seen working in workshops and factories, in some of the most hazardous working conditions, girls, with a few exceptions, work at home and are therefore invisible to the casual observer. This invisibility has serious negative consequences in terms of her status within the family which in turn determines her role in the family and society. Girls accompany parents to the fields and help with sowing, transplanting, weeding, harvesting and scaring away birds. And in addition to their domestic work, they are also involved in large numbers in the unorganized sector industries such as match, coir, carpet, lock, *beedi* (local cigarettes), gem polishing, *zari* (gold thread embroidery) making, ground nut shelling, etc. In the urban areas they work as domestic servants, rag-pickers, newspaper vendors, etc.

About 42 per cent of the Indian population consists of children and nearly half of them are girls. And about 40 per cent are girls in the age range of zero to fourteen years. A fact that struck me when looking for material on the girl child was the lack of documentation on the subject. While much has been written about the differential status of girls and boys with respect to health, nutrition and education, not much is known about the working girl. Part of the reason for this is that all accounts of women's work has focussed on the adult woman and even gender sensitive researchers have found the girl child invisible. This follows quite naturally from the fact that till very recently women did not include the work they did at home as labour and most of their work was categorized as household activities. Their self-perception was linked to the perception of the outside world and the fact that they worked for sixteen to twenty hours a day was not seen as work at all, not by their families and certainly not by them. When sixteen to twenty hours of women's work went unrecognized, it is not surprising that the work done by girls was not seen as 'work' at all!

The singling out of the female working child as the focus of research as against the working child per se has often been questioned. This, by implication means that the emphasis put on gender discrimination is, to say the least, invidious. This argument is further buttressed by the suggestion that the children who work in factories, mines and other hazardous employments in India are largely male children and that there-fore it is invidious to speak of the female working child when the brunt of exploitation is visibly borne by male children. I have in this chapter tried to underline the differences between the female working child and her male counterpart in respect of attitudes of parents, access to education, the type of work done and its implications for the adult worker and so on. For reasons of space, I have not dwelt upon the differences in the situation of the female working child which are linked to regional variations, caste and community.

The bulk of the female working child population is to be found in the rural areas. Significantly, while the work of girls in rural India is very visible, this is not so in the urban unor-ganized sector. Here, girls are found to be working in some concentrations of child labour but not in others. For example, of the 45,000 working children in the Sivakasi match industry in Tamil Nadu, approximately 90 per cent are girls below the age of fourteen years (Nair 1983: 15). Girls are found in large numbers in the coir industry of Kerala and home-based in-dustries like incense-making and *papad* (an Indian savoury) preparation (Jhabvala and Sebstadt 1980–1: 29; Krishna Kumari 1985). Girls are involved in substantial numbers in the *beedi* industry (*Economic and Political Weekly* 1981: 1305) and gem polishing industry of Jaipur, and the making of paper bags and garments, cotton-pod shelling, groundnut pod shelling, hand-embroidery, grain-cleaning, block-making, sub-assembling electrical and electronic items (Bhat 1987: 30). There are, at a rough estimate, approximately 6000 girls working in the gem polishing trade of Jaipur (Burra 1987a). Hundreds of girls are working in the lock industry of Aligarh, the brass ware industry of Moradabad in Uttar Pradesh (Burra 1989), the carpet industry of Jammu and Kashmir (Nangia 1988), the carpet industry of Rajasthan and the *zari* embroidery industry of Varanasi (Juyal 1985). But these are essentially invisible children who do not go to work in factories and in workshops and therefore do not come under the purview of the law. I shall return later to this theme. A large number of girls are to be found in domestic service, rag-picking, newspaper-vending and so on (Karlekar 1982; Patil 1986; and Juyal et al 1985). Most of them accompany their parents to work as they cannot be left behind at home.

SEX TYPING OF WORK

From a review of the literature, it appears that there is a strong sex typing of roles as regards the work that female and male children do in agriculture, household and the unorganized industry. My concern here is less with an anthropological under-standing of this state of affairs as its consequences for the future of male and female children.

All studies indicate that the burden of household duties falls largely upon the female child. In fact, the bulk of the female working child population is to be found in the rural areas where children are engaged in looking after younger siblings, cooking, cleaning, fetching and carrying. This releases adults for more productive and remunerative work. In the rural areas, little girls can be seen carrying small pots on their heads, following their mothers or elder sisters to the well. Water carrying, which is little more than play to begin with, nevertheless makes a useful contribution to the volume of work which has to be done in every household. Older girls accompany parents to the field to help them in activities such as sowing, transplanting, weeding and harvesting, collecting fuel and scaring away the birds. They also accompany their mothers to the market-place with small loads on their heads or backs.

Sex typing of work takes place in the unorganized sector where certain jobs are considered 'female' jobs. In the Jaipur gem polishing industry, *bindai-ka-kaam* was traditionally a female job. and even today some 6000 girls are to be found working with their mothers. They pierce holes in beads for necklaces. In the brass ware industry of Moradabad, polishing goods by hand was also considered *auraton ka kaam* or women's work. Leela Gulati writes that there is a clear-cut sex differentiation between the work that male and female children do in the coir industry. While both boys and girls are employed in rotating the spinning wheel, cleaning and willowing the fibre, ratt rotating,

> . . . in the beating of husks one sees only girls, hardly ever a boy. Only two boys and fifty-eight girls are employed in husk beating. However, while one sees girls of all ages, both the boys engaged in this operation, are in the age group of nine to eleven (Gulati n.d.: 14–15).

And finally, Gulati says:

> What can safely be generalized is that even in the two operations, spinning and husk beating, while girls tend to outnumber boys in a big way, [but] . . . [this is] especially so with respect to husk beating which is possibly one of the messiest [jobs] (ibid.: 27).

This is also the case with the match industry of Sivakasi where, according to the Madras Institute of Development Studies report:

> The picture that emerges is that boys . . . are exposed to the jobs requiring greater skills. The girls on the other hand are left to the vagaries of the job market as the piece rated occupations they are to be found in, require little mental skill and competition is accordingly greater (MIDS 1985: 21).

In the Indian context, the evidence suggests that girls are engaged in low-paid or no-wage unskilled jobs which do not necessarily lead to skill formation. In the case of boys, B.R. Patil points out in his study in Bangalore, jobs are closely related to apprenticeship training and skill formation (Patil n.d.: 9).

It seems as if the sex typing of roles restricts women to low-paying jobs. This becomes clear when one notices how *bindai ka kaam* (the piercing of holes in beads) in the gem polishing industry of Jaipur, which was always considered a female job, suddenly becomes a male preserve when the operation becomes mechanized and ultrasonic machines are made available. The process is exactly the same except where women work by hand and earn not more than Rs 4 or 5 a day, men can earn more than Rs 25 a day. Surprisingly, even in households where there are no young males available, hired labour is employed to do this work, rather than let the young girls work on the machines which are installed at home. Families believe that women cannot operate machines.

With respect to the brass ware industry of Moradabad, the situation is the same. About fifteen or twenty years ago, I was told, most of the work in the brass ware industry was done by females. They constituted more than 50 per cent of the total work-force. Today, their participation has fallen to less than 10 per cent. The reason for this state of affairs is that with the greater demand for goods, there has been an introduction of machinery in many of the processes which were formerly the preserve of women and girls. Thus the job of polishing, particularly of goods which were coloured, known as *kathai*, was done almost exclusively by women and girls. Today, men do this work in workshops on machines and earn three times more than the women did at home. Another female preserve was the job of *chilai* (scraping), and most of the women and girls were engaged in this work. But with the introduction of the grinder machine, the women and girls have more or less lost out. Only those jobs that cannot be done on the machine are given to women to do at home. Thus changing demands and consequent technological changes deprive women and girls of incomes they can ill-afford to lose (Burra 1989).

Thus, whichever industry one looks at, the pattern is repeated — boys go to work in skill-based industries and girls in unskilled low wage work. Wherever mechanization is introduced, leading to higher wages, boys take over the work girls were doing earlier.

ECONOMIC VALUE OF CHILDREN AND ITS IMPLICATIONS

Even if it is a commonplace observation in some circles that the value of domestic and household work is not properly computed since it does not bring in a wage and is not productively oriented, it still needs to be reiterated and is doubly important because it affects the attitudes of parents of female children and confers upon the latter a status that is lower than that of their male siblings. Many studies have documented the significance and value of such work.

Very rarely is the household work of girl children computed and the attitudes of parents are importantly dependent on this factor. Two recent studies have tried to do precisely this.

According to Ishrat Ali Siddiqui, a study by two experts from the Indian Institute of Science, Bangalore shows that the average girl child spent 29 per cent of the total time gathering fuel-wood, and 20 per cent on fetching water. In eastern Uttar Pradesh, where women spend between one and four hours daily on household work in addition to a back-breaking day in the field, at least 30 per cent of the household burden is shared by girls between the age group of six to eleven years. And in a country where women share 45.57 per cent of the agricultural work, more than 20 per cent is shared by girl children (Siddiqui 1985: 4).

Arun Bhattacharjee argues that:

. . . The social belief that a female child is an economic liability can be countered by the argument that in rural India a girl works for nine hours a day and an average of 315 days in a year in the fields and at home, providing the family an annual labour which at minimum wages could have cost Rs 2200 to hire. By the time she ceases to be a child she has provided economic help to the family worth Rs 39,600 surviving on food below nutrition level and struggling against prejudice and discrimination (Bhattacharjee 1985: 2).

In the journey of life, the destination of the female child is marriage. The perception of parents that the female child will ultimately leave her natal home and not be a source of support to them importantly determines the ways in which she is treated. On the other hand, the male child is perceived as the one to be relied upon in old age since he retains his links with the natal home and such is his role in most parts of India. According to a pilot study conducted by Maitreyi Chaudhuri amongst agricultural labour households in a village of Bolpur-Sriniketan Block in Birbhum district of West Bengal, one of the possible reasons for sex bias in child nutrition may be the traditional belief regarding the greater economic value of male children. In this study it was found that in no agricultural household were aged parents economically dependent on daughters or on the sons-in-law or daughters' sons (Chaudhuri 1985: 4-5).

ATTITUDES OF PARENTS TO DAUGHTER'S EDUCATION

The attitudes of parents to their daughters are not merely a result of not being able to place an economic value on the latter's contributions to the family; in India, the giving of a dowry at the time of marriage makes the girl a positive burden in comparison with her brothers. One manifest consequence is that education is denied to her. This is very evident from the Census data of 1981 which shows that female literacy is barely 24.8 per cent as against 46.9 per cent for males (*Census of India* 1981 Series-I India, Part II, Special: 78, 92). But the attitudes of parents to girls' education are etched more sharply in the case studies discussed below.

Female children are kept away from the educational process as Malavika Karlekar shows in her study on women sweepers in Delhi (Karlekar 1982). Her respondents felt that daughters could help the family by looking after younger children so that mothers could be released for wage-earning.

Of the entire sample, there were only four girls who were studying beyond Class VIII and two happened to be the daughters of two clerks. Further, six mothers admitted that while they had sent out their young daughters to be sweepers, their sons were still in school (ibid.: 120).

Says Karlekar:

If most mothers were somewhat motivated to keep their sons in school, far fewer were so inclined for their daughters. Apart from the opportunity-cost argument, women accepted the conventional stereotypes for their daughters; in addition they were pessimistic about the chances of their daughters achieving occupational or social mobility through education (ibid.: 121).

The attitudes of mothers to their daughters getting an education is clear from interviews with mothers. Phoolbathi, a sweeper, told Karlekar that:

. . . Nearly all our girls work as sweepers. Why should I waste my time and money on sending my daughters to school where she will learn nothing of use. . . . So why not put my girl to work so that she will learn something about our profession as well as be able to cook. My elder girl who is fifteen years old will be married soon. Her mother-in-law will put her to cleaning latrines somewhere. Too much of schooling will only give girls big ideas, and then they will be beaten up by their husbands or be abused by their in-laws (ibid.: 122).

B.R. Patil's study of working children in Bangalore city found that:

. . . The female working children have a relatively poor education background compared to the boys. This is primarily because the girls start working at an early age and poorer families do not give much importance to the education of girls (Patil n.d.: 5).

This study found that a larger number of girls are sent to earn an income while boys more often than not go to work partly at least to learn the trade (ibid.: 9). In the coir industry of Kerala where 19 per cent of working children have never been to school, Leela Gulati observes:

> A higher proportion of girls than boys are illiterate, the percentages being 21 per cent and 15 per cent for girls and boys respectively. But the percentage of school drop outs is higher among boys than girls. This can be taken to mean that a larger proportion of working girls than boys do not get sent to school at all but of the girls who start going to school the proportion of those who drop out works out to be less than the proportion of similar boys (Gulati n.d. 8-9).

An interesting finding of Leela Gulati's study on child labour in the coir industry of Kerala is, that while the proportion of illiterates is higher amongst girls than boys, the percentage of school drop outs is higher among boys than girls (ibid.).

The Report of the National Commission on Self-Employed Women and Women in the Informal Sector in India drew attention to the attitudes of parents — particularly mothers — to their daughters' education. In Rajasthan, this Commission met 215 women of which only four were literate and the women said quite frankly, 'We do not want to send our daughters to school after 1st standard, because they need to be trained in work' (Shramshakti 1988: lxvi-lxvii).

In state after state, the National Commission found that while women were willing to send their sons to school, that was not the case with their daughters. In Achbal in Kashmir, there was a meeting of 100 women and it was found that only eleven girls went to school as against 150 boys (ibid.: lxviii).

Part of the problem of child labour is that when parents do not get even minimum wages themselves, they can hardly afford not to use their children. In the case of home-based workers, the vicious cycle continues.

> . . . where the child is a girl, [it] results in the child being prevented from going to school, leading to the inevitable cycle of no education, low skills and low earning capacity, thus perpetuating home work with its exploitatively low wages (ibid.: 114).

This was also the experience of Maria Mies in a study of rural Indian women (Mies 1986: 15, 64–7). Malavika Karlekar writes that in a Bombay slum, illiteracy was three times as high among the women and girls than among the men. Women in migrant settlements in Delhi were prepared to send their daughters for a few years to primary school, but wanted their sons to finish school. The author noted that:

> . . . Parents tended to have unrealistic educational and employment aspirations for their sons. . . . They did not consider education very important for their daughters (Karlekar 1982: 122).

GENDER DIFFERENTIALS

In most cases, there is rigid sexual division of labour and women are forced to do wage labour and housework. And the only way this can be done is by using female children. Thus what Leela Gulati says about the Indian situation would apply also to other countries in the region where there is discrimination between male and female children. She says:

> In my studies I found that (a) boys stayed longer in school than girls; (b) boys were not expected to do virtually any household chores; (c) boys were allowed much greater freedom to spend whatever wages they earned; and (d) boys got relatively better food in terms of claim to rice against tapioca.
> On the other hand, I observed that (a) a girl has to do all the supporting household chores even when she goes to school; (b) she is withdrawn from school when she is needed

full time in the house; and (c) she has to contribute most of what she earns to the house when she goes out to work.

Possibly, the reasons for this attitude on the part of the women are that (a) they hope to be looked after by their sons in their old age; (b) while the sons bring in a dowry, the daughters are a liability; and (c) a son can hope to move into a better paid skilled, and sometimes possibly a regular, permanent job, whereas the daughter will work all her life for a low wage and be hard up (Gulati 1981: 169).

There are many problems with the education of girls. Some of them relate to the inadequate number of separate schools, availability of schools, shortage of women teachers in the rural areas, early marriage among girls, social beliefs that education must be linked to employment opportunities and since these are not available to girls, education is not necessary for them; and the social status of women. More effort needs to be put into making parents aware that children of both sexes are equal. With respect to gender disparities community participation is crucial in generating awareness about the importance of girls' education.

The clear differential between the level of literacy as between boys and girls has several important implications. The most immediate result is that the universalization of primary education will remain a distant dream when half the child population is treated in a discriminatory fashion. In many Asian societies, the work that girl children do has some common features: a large part of it has to do with domestic chores and the maintenance of the household and this is not normally recognized as 'work'. The contribution of girl children in assisting their mothers in home-based industry goes similarly unrecognized; the work that girl children do is generally of an unskilled nature and thereby confers low status upon them; their lack of skills and training effectively blocks avenues of upward mobility. The gender-typing of work and the gender-typing of roles interact upon each other and perpetuate an already unjust situation in which girls receive less education and nutrition within the family, are married at an early age and because of low skill levels, cannot improve their lot. In turn, they will enlist the aid of their female children in the struggle for survival.

THE UNORGANIZED SECTOR

There are almost 100,000 women lace-makers in the Narsapur *taluka* (an administrative unit of a district) of the East Godavari district of Andhra Pradesh and most of them started crocheting at the age of five to six years (Mies 1982: 54). The system that prevails is that each woman or girl works at small pieces on specification at home and these are collected by the agent and given to other women to join. There is thus no unity amongst workers. Girls work ten to eleven hours a day on lace-making and together with their domestic chores, they work thirteen to sixteen hours a day (ibid.: 121).

A recent study by Sudesh Nangia about child weavers in the carpet weaving industry in Jammu and Kashmir revealed that more than 50 per cent of child workers in the handicraft industry were girls and this was so more in the rural areas, than in the urban areas (Nangia 1988: 12). A similar observation was made by M.L. Pandit in an unpublished study of child labour in the handicrafts industry of the Kashmir Valley. Says Pandit:

> Comparisons of male and female child workers with total male and female handicraft workers reveal an important aspect of female employment. Male child labour accounts for 24.74 per cent of total male work-force. The corresponding proportion for female child workers is 46.83 per cent (Pandit n.d.: 12).

One of the reasons given for this trend by Pandit is that girls are kept back at home to work while boys are sent to school.

In the slate industry of Markapur, an unpublished study revealed that out of the 800 child workers employed in factories and commercial establishments, girl child labour was found to the extent of 70 per cent. By and large girls worked while boys were sent to school. Girls worked in the open mines from 8 a.m. to 1 p.m.

In the match industry of Sivakasi where approximately 45,000 children are employed, 90 per cent are girl children below the age of fourteen years. According to the Madras Institute of Development Studies, boys are involved mainly in skill developing jobs while girls are given unskilled jobs. The report observed that:

> . . . female workers both adults and children, are far more
> widely employed in the match industry, than male workers.
> They are universally employed in piece-rated work and are
> not used in any kind of work requiring supervisory capability.
> On the other hand, there are cases of boys serving as appren-
> tices or helpers in functions in which at least a small number
> will continue after growing up (MIDS 1985: 39).

The great preponderance of girls in the match industry is due to the fact that the wages in the match industry are much lower than the agricultural wage rate and less than half in most cases of earnings from non-agricultural wage work (MIDS 1985: 40). According to this study:

> . . . While the daily earnings from match work are about
> Rs 3.50 to Rs 4.00 per day, they amount to 75 per cent and
> 50 per cent respectively of the female and male agricultural
> wage rates (ibid.: 54).

No one other than a child, and that too, a female child will work in the match industry at such low wages. Thus, in the match industry, the larger number of girls in the work-force can be explained by the fact that the wages are so low and the work so unskilled and monotonous that even boys are not expected to work. Moreover, in view of the fact that the bulk of the work-force is made up of Scheduled Castes, there are no cultural and social constraints with respect to sending girls out to work.

It is not only in the maintenance of the household that the work of the female child goes unrecognized. A recent book on home-based industry tellingly makes the point that women engaged in productive work at home are invisible to most observers (Singh and Viitanen 1987). If the work of women in home-based industry is invisible, this statement is more true, if that is possible, for their female children. Guy Standing, in a recent paper, characterizes this method of organization of production as one way of evading stringent labour legislation.

Factory owners resort to giving work out on piece-rate wages to women at home because this is one way by which they can cut costs. The recent Report of the National Commission on Self-Employed Women has stressed the need for regulating the wages and working conditions of women who are largely self-employed. A point made time and again in the report is that employers pay women low wages because they know that they will be helped by their children — mainly daughters. There is ample evidence to show that, in part, the exploitation of the female child is directly a result of the exploitation of women. A report on *beedi* workers of Nizamabad in Andhra Pradesh states:

> In most places these days it is customary for even the poorest to at least enroll their children in school, even if they are sent to school only when there is no work to be done at home. But Sanghatana activists did not find a single (female) child of a *beedi* worker attending school. They stay at home to do the work their mothers cannot do. And once they are sufficiently grown up they go to the factory to 'help' their mothers. It is true that the . . . Act prohibits child labour (Section 24) but if children insist on filially helping their mothers, what can the poor seth do? And if, in the process, the seth also acquires well-trained new recruits whose training pays for itself, is he to be blamed? (*Economic and Political Weekly* 1981: 1305).

In most home-based industries, like the *agarbatti* (incense sticks) and *beedi* industries, the adult female worker is paid at so low a rate that, just in order to earn a pittance, she enlists the help of her female children. Ela Bhat writes about home-based workers:

Their earnings for an eight-hour working day are not more than Rs 3 as in the case of skilled zari workers in Delhi, and as low as Re 1 for lace-makers. Home-based workers earn the lowest of all categories of workers. Jennifer Sebstadt in her study on self-employed women finds that in Ahmedabad the average monthly income for home-based workers is Rs 130 as compared to Rs 250 for vendors and Rs 170 for labourers (Bhat 1987: 30).

The Report of the National Commission on Self-Employed Women brings this out forcefully. Examples from all over the country indicate that women are paid such abysmally low wages that in order to earn a living wage they are forced to use their daughters. A kite-maker, Rasulanbanu in Ahmedabad, made kites for a factory and was paid Rs 40 for 500 kites. It took her two days to make this many with the help of her neighbour (whom she paid Rs 2) and her daughters (Shramshakti 1988: xxxix). According to this report:

> In West Bengal, at Midnapur and Howra Haat, traders give material to women for stitching on piece-rate. They distribute this kind of work to villages all around Calcutta. For stitching twelve petticoats, they pay Rs 8. Gita can sew twenty a day in eleven hours if her daughters help her. Thus she earns Rs 300 a month — before she deducts her costs for thread, lace and maintenance of her sewing machine (ibid.: xl).

In the examples cited, the girl child is rarely seen as a worker by the parents and is therefore exposed to cumulative inequality. Very rarely, as in the case of Sivakasi, is the girl child sent to workshops and factories to work. One reason for the large number of girl children in the match industry is that the work in the factories is poorly paid and does not lead to skill-formation. Interestingly, another possible reason for the large concentration of girl children in Sivakasi is that the bulk of the labour force belongs to the Scheduled Castes where restrictions on the movements of females are not so severe. In all other concentrations of child labour in India such as the glass industry of Firozabad, the lock industry of Aligarh, the gem polishing industry of Jaipur, the pottery industry of Khurja, the slate industry of Mandsaur and the brass ware industry of Moradabad, the work-force is largely Muslim and the system of *purdah* (female seclusion) inhibits the female child from going to workshops and factories. In view of the hazardous nature of the jobs undertaken by boys in these places, by virtue of cultural and social constraints, the girl child is in fact saved from tremendous health hazards. In the case of the diamond-cutting industry of Surat, the exclusion of the girl child is probably due to the fact that the child workers are largely migrants from the adjoining villages and stay on the premises. The carpet industry of Mirzapur-Bhadohi and Varanasi is notorious for its high incidence of bonded labour and migrant labour — both factors inhibiting the use of girl children. In the carpet industry of Kashmir, girls work on looms as part of family labour.

While piece-rate wages and the system of sub-contracting keep women and girls in low-paid jobs, whenever technology is improved in order to increase production, women find themselves unemployed. In the Jaipur gem polishing industry, the job of piercing beads was essentially a female job at which hundreds of women and girls were employed. This work is still done manually by them. But due to the increased international demand for gem stones, an ultrasonic machine has been introduced to do the same work. Though it is a relatively simple gadget, nowhere in Jaipur are women seen doing this work on machines. The wages paid to men working on machines are many times more than that of women and girls doing the same job manually because the output of the latter is much less. While in Jaipur, women are clearly losing out to men over machines, in the Moradabad brass ware industry the situation is somewhat different. Earlier, the work of polishing by hand or *kathai ka kaam* was done exclusively by women and girls at home using chemicals. Again, due to a demand for brass ware abroad, indigenous polishing machines have been introduced in Moradabad and polishing — which was exclusively a female job — has now become entirely a male preserve. In this particular case, the chemicals used in polishing were extremely harmful for those using them and even the new polishing machines are dangerous. In a sense, therefore, the introduction of technology and the displacement of the female worker has been to her advantage in the case of Moradabad (Burra 1989), even though she might well have chosen otherwise.

SOME CONCLUDING OBSERVATIONS

It is apparent from the evidence presented above that there is a clear-cut differentiation between the male and the female working child both in the stereotyping of work according to gender, and in the attitudes and aspirations of parents. For a complex of social and cultural reasons, the girl child is under-valued by parents. Several consequences follow from this attitude. The girl child is seen as an economic burden and is, therefore, exploited even by her own parents. She is made to work very hard at home and outside but her economic contribution is never recognized. So no value is placed on her need for education and as she grows up, her lack of education limits her opportunities in the labour market and she is relegated to low-paid, unskilled jobs. The exploited girl child becomes the exploited adult woman: she also often does not see her work as an economic activity but as under-valued domestic work. The observations of the National Commission on Self-Employed Women and Women in the Informal Sector with respect to child labour, and particularly that of the girl child was:

> While the argument in support of child labour is that it enables the child to supplement the meagre household income, it only results in the piece-rated wages being fixed very low in the full knowledge that the home-based worker, who is more often than not a woman, will be 'assisted' by other members of her family, particularly the children. This vicious trap will have to be broken in two ways, one, by so fixing the piece-rate, as indicated by us under the Section on the Minimum Wages Act, that it enables a woman worker to earn a just wage for an eight-hour work-day and the other, by prohibiting child labour totally and at the same time enforcing the con-

stitutional mandate of compulsory universal elementary education (Shramshakti 1988: 114).

In fact, if one looks at official policy one finds that:

> Home-based piece rate workers are not included as workers in the Factories Act and so are not covered by most labour laws. Furthermore, most trades are not listed under the Minimum Wages Act and even where they are, home-based workers are not mentioned (Bhat 1987: 31).

Ela Bhat writes: 'There is no official policy to ensure employment for home-based workers or to improve their lot' (ibid.). Sometimes, if the girl goes to work in a factory in place of her mother and is injured, she is not even paid compensation because she is seen as a stand-in for her mother. Anil Awachat reports a case in a powerloom factory in Ichalkaranji, Maharashtra, where a thirteen-year old girl had got caught in the machine. When she bent down to reconnect a broken thread, her plait got caught in the wheel and she got sucked onto the belt. Her hand had to be amputated. She could not get the compensation due to her because:

> . . . It was her mother who was supposed to be at work, but a lot of women enter their names on three or four musters and send their daughters in their place at a couple of factories. Naturally the owner said, this girl is not even on the muster, why should I give her any compensation? (Awachat 1988: 1735).

The National Child Labour Policy seeks to have a beneficial impact upon the health, education and nutrition of the working child in a setting where different labour laws are better implemented. It covers only visible children and the policy, like the law, overlooks the female working child by default.

In conclusion, we might say that there are significant differences in the situation of the female working child from that of its male counterpart in the household, in agriculture and in the unorganized industry. These differences manifest themselves in a variety of ways: the gender typing of work, the value imputed to such work and its impact upon the attitudes of parents and access to education. By virtue of certain cultural restraints, the female child in the unorganized sector is spared the health hazards that the male child faces in mines, workshops or factories; the same stereotypes keep her at home helping her mother. When she is out of sight, she is out of mind. Devalued as a child, denied equal access to education and devoid of skills, she carries into her womanhood all the accumulated burdens of her past. The task of programme, policy and law is to offer the female child the possibility to grow, to change and to be free.

10

Consequences of Child Labour:
Education and Health

INTRODUCTION

When children work, both their education and health suffer. How does this happen? The Indian school system has a single point entry and consists of a sequential and full-time format of institutional instruction by full-time and professional teachers. One of the most comprehensive critiques of such a system in relation to the circumstances and needs of rural and agricultural society has been formulated by the noted educationist, the late J.P. Naik. He argues for a radical transformation in the traditional model of formal education. Despite the advantages of the single point entry method such as the creation of the homogeneous age-group cohort which rises, year after year, to successively higher classes, it means that the child who is unable to enter school at class I at the age of six years remains outside it forever. Though in principle the same child could enter class I at age eleven years, he would have to be with much younger children and despite his readiness to go faster, he would have to learn at the same speed. Most likely he would become a drop out. Naik (1975a: 117) says:

> What such a child needs is specially organized classes where primary education is imparted through special techniques suited to his more mature mind. But there is no provision in our system for this purpose.

Naik recommends a multiple-entry point at different ages say nine, eleven, fourteen and so on. According to him, an elastic schooling system which permits children to enter it as and when they wish to or are in a position to do so would attract large numbers of children who would otherwise have remained illiterate (ibid.).[1]

J.P. Naik makes a number of constructive suggestions to orient the school system to the needs of rural working children. For one thing, the school calendar should be so adjusted as to allow time off for agricultural operations like sowing and harvesting; for another, to reduce stagnation on account of children failing examinations, flexible systems which condense the curricula of classes I to IV into a shorter period of about two years for children over eleven could be devised. Another important recommendation he makes is to have pre-schools or creches attached to primary schools so that girls could bring their younger siblings there and look after them, as well as get an education. Instead of relying upon full-time professional teachers who raise the costs of the school system, Naik suggests simple solutions like employing local carpenters, tailors, singers and young persons who could teach for part of the time. Such a step would also generate additional local employment at lower cost. In summary, Naik's contribution has been to suggest that the school system be re-oriented to cater to the needs of working children in an agricultural society in a practicable way and at a low cost.

The lack of adequate infrastructure apart, the most common explanation for parents not sending their children to school is that they are too poor. It is argued that the economic contribution of the child to the income of the family — whether by bringing in a wage or by doing household maintenance work and thus releasing adults for productive work — is so important that the family cannot afford to lose this economically productive time for his or her schooling. Clearly, there is some substance in such reasoning, as poor families exist on the margins of survival.

[1] See also Naik 1975b and 1982.

Yet, such an argument fails to take into account the exploitation by vested interests of young children. Many studies document the role of vested interests and the impact they have upon the lives of children. It is also true that working children in India, by and large, belong to the poor regions of the country, the socially disadvantaged sections of society and some minority groups. There is a vested interest in seeing that the children of the poor do not avail themselves of the facilities for education. Large numbers of children are lured away from schools by middlemen who offer a better life if they agree to work. In what follows, examples are given from the match and carpet industries of how this process operates. This probably happens in other industries using child labour, but very little documented evidence was available. My own research in the five industries of glass, brass, lock, gems, pottery did not look at this aspect in great depth.

VESTED INTERESTS

In many of the large concentrations of child labour in India — such as Sivakasi in the State of Tamil Nadu — where the match industry is housed and where approximately 45,000 children are working, Smitu Kothari, a social activist, observes that, '. . . In village after village we found cases where children were induced to leave school to support the family economically' (Kothari 1983b: 13).

The educational status of children in the match factories of Sivakasi is dismal. UNICEF supported a sample study to investigate it. They conducted their survey in sixteen factories which were employing 4725 children. Of these 4725 workers, 544 were working at home. The figures are startling as they reveal that of the 4181 children studied, 3323 or 79 per cent were totally illiterate. Children numbering 474 or 11 per cent of the sample had received education up to the primary level. There were 384 drop outs accounting for the balance 9 per cent. When the research team looked at the wage register, they found that 81 per cent of the children had received payments after affixing their thumb impressions and only 19 per cent had signed their names. Thus in one of the largest concentrations of child labour, Sivakasi, nearly 80 per cent of the children were illiterate and most of them came to the factories from the rural areas in factory buses which left the village at 3 a.m. or 4 a.m. to return only after dusk. These children, mainly girls, are from Scheduled Castes and work ten to fourteen hours a day at break-neck speed in order to earn a pittance of Rs 2 or 3 per day (Area Development Report n.d.: 25–7). The average age of the working child is between eight to twelve years. According to the Area Development Report, 'It looks as though the mid-day-meals programme is the chief motivational link for most children to attend schools in an irregular fashion' (ibid.: 27).

If one looks at the educational status of children working in the carpet factories, the situation is similar. Prembhai, a social worker, was asked by the Supreme Court of India to investigate the incidence of bonded child labour in the carpet industry of Mirzapur-Bhadohi-Varanasi in the State of Uttar Pradesh. He interviewed 858 children who had migrated from the adjoining district of Palamau in the State of Bihar and found that only one child had been to high school. Thirteen children (1½ per cent) had been educated from class IV to VIII. Sixty-five children (8 per cent) had received education from class II to class V; seventeen children (2 per cent) were barely literate. And the bulk of 762 children, that is almost 89 per cent, were completely illiterate (Prembhai 1984: 51).

School authorities in the carpet belt are extremely concerned that children are being sent to work rather than to school. Parents are being bribed by middlemen with small consumption loans and an assurance that the child will learn a skill; they are then made to work fourteen to sixteen hours a day under the most unhygienic conditions which are also akin to semi-slavery. The situation in the carpet belt of Mirzapur-Bhadohi-Varanasi is so grim that local teachers were really concerned about what would happen to those children who were being made to leave school in large numbers. Prembhai observes in his report that teachers, educational administrators and village elders all reacted negatively to the impact of the industry. People told him that *harijans* were taking their children out of school to enter the industry and there was a discernible trend in the migration of children to those areas where the industry operated. One *harijan* leader told him that the industry was blocking the development of *harijans* and promoting illiteracy amongst them (ibid.: 135).

There are approximately 150,000 children working as carpet weavers in the Mirzapur-Bhadohi carpet belt (Juyal 1987: 26). The number of working children in the carpet belt went up when the Government of India set up carpet training centres in the Mirzapur area and other places and offered a stipend of Rs 60 a month to the trainees. A large number of children were forced by their parents to leave school and join the training institutes (Menon 1986: 65). Once the children had dropped out of school, there was no question of returning. When there was a slump in the carpet industry, these children were the first to be retrenched. These illiterate or semi-literate children were forced to take on jobs in roadside restaurants, as domestic servants and so on.

The match industry of Sivakasi and the carpet industry of Mirzapur-Bhadohi-Varanasi are both illustrations of the consequences of using children for their labour. It is not accidental that in both cases the children concerned belong to the socially lowest segment of society, i.e. the Scheduled Castes; these children are forced into relations of bondage with their employers, who suborn the parents by advancing small sums of money by way of loans and the children are bonded till the loan is returned at usurious rates of interest. Apart from the exploitative working environment, one glaring result of children's work is their almost complete illiteracy.

CLASS BIAS IN EDUCATION

It is demonstrable that children who work belong to the lowest strata of society and children who stay out of school also belong to the lowest rung in the class structure. Poromesh Acharya, in a study of child labour in four villages of two districts of West Bengal, found that of the total non-enrolled children in the age-group six to sixteen years, 70 per cent belonged to the two lowest agrarian classes, namely poor peasants and agricultural labourers (Acharya 1982: 18–19). Though the situation may well have changed for the better today, the statistics are revealing.

According to Acharya, more than 92 per cent of one set of respondents (who were lower middle and poor peasants as also agricultural labourers) replied to the relevant question by saying that their non-enrolled children were either gainfully employed or did household work during school hours (ibid.: 19).

Acharya makes an important statement regarding the attitude of the upper strata of rural society towards free compulsory education. He explains the opposition towards making elementary education compulsory by referring to the fear of the *jotedars* and the rich peasants that the traditional order would be disturbed. He observes that the continuing illiteracy of the labouring groups helps the reinforcement of the traditional patterns of authority in village life (ibid.).

Acharya's study found that the rich peasants did not want compulsory education because it would be inconvenient for them although all the children of the *jotedars* in the age group six to eleven years and 84 per cent of the children of the rich peasants of the same age-group were enrolled. Acharya does not mince words when he says:

> The reasons are very simple. They are against compulsion as they fear that universal and compulsory enrolment would deprive them of the easy supply of child labour. In that case, they would need to hire adults at a higher wage instead of child labour, which would lead to an increase in their cost of agricultural production (ibid.: 20).

U.P. Arora also has a similar observation to make regarding the need for child labour by rich peasants in the State of Karnataka. Arora argues that teenagers are subjected to *jeeta* (bonded labour) by landlords because they are always available for any type of work. He notes that the wards and relations of landlords increasingly go to the towns and cities to pursue a higher education and, consequently, there is a demand for more working hands (Arora et al 1977: 17).

Other studies are also pointers to local vested interests who do not want the children of the poor to get an education. The Rural Wing of the National Labour Institute conducted a study on bonded labour. Investigators interviewed some owners of bonded labourers in Andhra Pradesh about education for working children. Their response was:

> Once, they are allowed to come up to an equal level, nobody will go to the fields. Fields will be left uncultivated everywhere. We have to keep them under our strong thumb in order to get work done (NLI Rural Wing 1977: 542).

As in the case of unorganized industry, the cases cited above from backward sectors of the agricultural economy bring out the importance of the need of upper segments of the population to maintain illiteracy and thereby their hold on a docile and submissive labour force. When one studies the links between child labour and education, it is helpful to remember the social contexts in which child labour flourishes at the expense of education. The working child suffers from the spiralling disadvantages of being illiterate, coming from economically poor classes and belonging to socially backward communities.

WORKING CHILDREN AND SCHOOLS

There is a point of view frequently propounded by professionals in the field of education and policy-makers that the existing school system is irrelevant to the needs of working children. It is argued that sterile curricula, rote-based learning and the poor quality of teachers, amongst other ills, plague the school system and that, therefore, neither the parents of working children nor the children themselves are keen to gain access to it. I have tried to argue that this is a profoundly mistaken idea. Rather, evidence from the field suggests that parents have a deep

interest in educating their children. Education alone can provide mobility to the socially and economically disadvantaged
sections of society. More correctly it is straitened economic
circumstances which prevent the fulfilment of this aspiration;
inadequate school infrastructure tilts the balance in favour of
work.

In all the industries I had the opportunity of studying, it was
clear that the children of the master craftsmen and the better-off
artisans went to school regularly and spent perhaps a couple
of hours a day learning the trade. It was the children of the
lowest level of workers, the underemployed or of the unemployed who did not attend school and constituted the bulk
of the child labour force. By and large such children belonged
either to the Scheduled Castes, lower castes or the Muslim
community. These groups represented a combination of economic and social disadvantages. When one looked at the lives
of these children as they grew to adulthood, it was apparent
that the absence of schooling closed the route to upward
mobility and, once again, perpetuated the disadvantages in the
next generation. Interview after interview, without exception,
revealed widespread awareness about the importance of an
education to improve the prospects of children. Almost to a
man my respondents have great aspirations for their children
but the absence of an adequate school infrastructure offering
quality education combined with the costs of schooling served
to deny them the fulfilment of their hopes. In the cases where
the economic circumstances of the worker improved because
of some reason or the other, the first thing they did was to
remove their children from the work-force and put them into
school even if they substituted them with children of an even
poorer group. It would seem then to be a myth, sometimes
sedulously cultivated, that poor parents are simply not interested in a formal education for their children. In every industry
workers knew about how sections of the better-off, like the
entrepreneur, the trader and the exporter, send their children
to schools to learn English so that they would be able to deal
better with the outside world.

IMPACT ON HEALTH

It is ironical that the conservative approaches of experts have grown with fresh information regarding the deleterious effects of work on the health of young children. Many discussions on health hazards for working children start with opening statements like: 'Not all work is hazardous to children' (Gore 1985: 2-3) or 'work can in fact be beneficial to the child' [2] (Pitt 1985a: 12). More recently, an important study conducted in Bombay has argued that working children are in fact healthier than non-working children because of the food they get to eat.[3] In fairness, it must also be said that those who have written extensively about health hazards to working children and have argued that not all work is harmful (Pitt 1985b: 23) have also admitted that not enough information is available on the subject.

By and large children who are examined at the work-site are amongst the fittest. What about those who have fallen by the wayside — injured or ill or even dead as a result of overwork, exhaustion and so on? I shall try to establish the significance of such omission later in the chapter. To leave them out of the count is to be unscientific and leads to a distorted version of the facts. Such selectivity leads to what may be termed the 'pragmatic' view increasingly favoured these days by experts. This pragmatism bodes ill for the vision of health as a fundamental human right.

This chapter seeks to draw attention to the different types of hazards faced by working children and proposes a scheme of classification for them. Firstly, children are employed in intrinsically hazardous occupations where they may contract silicosis, pneumoconiosis, byssinosis, etc. by working in the slate, lock, glass and powerloom industries, for example.

---

[2] Pitt refers to studies which claim that working children are less sick than others because employers favour the healthy. He however, does not endorse this view.

[3] See Usha Naidu and S. Parasuraman's study of health situation of working children in Greater Bombay (1985).

Secondly, some hazards find their origin in the poor working environment. Thirdly, a few occupations may be considered safe but the vulnerability of children makes these occupations hazardous for them. Hence, one has to examine (a) whether hazards are intrinsic to the nature of the work itself or (b) whether they arise from the working environment and conditions of work or (c) whether the work is simply unsuitable for children.

Any occupation which allows the worker to come into contact with harmful substances like chemicals (as in the balloon, match and fire-works, lock and brass ware industries) or fire (as in the glass industry) or cotton fluff and dust that damage the lungs (as in the powerloom industry) may be termed intrinsically hazardous. These occupations would be hazardous for all workers, both adults and children. But since children are still in the process of growing and attaining their full physical stature, their growth is likely to be affected. We will now consider some examples of intrinsically hazardous occupations.

The Balloon Factories of Dahanu

In the balloon factories of Dahanu in Maharashtra, children's work includes mixing rubber with chemicals, colouring balloons and testing each balloon with gas. A thick pall of dust and chemicals pervades the rooms which are small, cramped and ill-ventilated. According to Geeta Menon, the children work nine hours a day, six days a week, 'Medical reports state that inhalation of such acids continuously over a period of time can burn respiratory lining and cause pneumonia, bronchopneumonia, cough, breathlessness and even heart failure . . .' (Menon 1985: 212).

A more recent newspaper article reported that when visitors visited the balloon factories of Dahanu, they were told not to enter for fear of choking on the ammonia fumes (Sharma 1992). The children who work there have to inhale ammonia, ascetic acid fumes and french chalk for more than eight hours a day and six days a week. Some children are barely eight years old!

The Match Industry of Sivakasi

Vishwapriya Iyengar writes about the health hazards to children in the match industry of Sivakasi in Tamil Nadu.

> Children mixing chemicals in the boiler room get lungfulls of toxic fumes, suffer high degrees of intense heat and run the risk of being badly injured in fire accidents. Children who stamp frames on the metal sheet too suffer heat, toxic fumes and excessive strain on the arms and shoulders which have to remove and place the heavy frames with great rapidity. Delay of a second . . . can cause the entire frame to go up in roaring flames which cause instant death (Iyengar 1986a: 5).

Smitu Kothari, writing about the match and fireworks industry, says that the working conditions are unsafe and detrimental to the health and well-being of children. Children are away fifteen hours a day, of which twelve are spent working in cramped environments with hazardous chemicals and inadequate ventilation. Says Kothari:

> 'Dust from the chemical powders and strong vapours in both the store room and the boiler room were obvious at practically every site we visited' (Kothari 1983c: 1192).

The match industry of Sivakasi is one of the most hazardous industries in the country where children work. Children interviewed by researchers tell about the strain of heat and the heavy frames which make them feel dizzy and faint. The children have to be very alert or else there is a danger that they will set fire to themselves. Fire accidents occur when the match heads rub against the frictional surface in the course of putting the box together too quickly (Iyengar 1987: 28–33).

The main risk in the match industry is a result of the chemicals used. The Area Development Programme Report for Ramanathapuram district, which was prepared for UNICEF, lists a wide variety of chemicals used in the match industry. These include tetrophosphorous trisulphide, amorphous red phosphorus, potassium chlorate, antimony trisulphide, zinc oxide, calcium sulphate and so on (Area Development Report n.d.: 11).

Given the kinds of chemicals used, it is not surprising that accidents are frequent (*The Hindu*, 31 January 1988).

The fire-works factories are particularly dangerous. It is only when newspapers report accidents that we hear of the health hazards in the industry. Kothari reports that in February, 1982, a cracker factory in Chellapathi village, twenty kilometres from Sankaran Koil, went up in flames. Six children were charred to death in the fire. They had been engaged in stuffing cracker powder into fire-crackers when the accident occurred (Kothari 1983c: 1192). In another accident thirty-two children were burnt to death in an electrical fire in a cracker factory (Singh 1982). More recently in July 1991, thirty-six people were killed in a blast in a fire-works factory near Meenampatti village about five kilometres from Sivakasi. Within seconds about fifteen buildings of the factory were charred. The newspaper reported that the minimum age of the victims was sixteen years. But even if they were younger, the bodies were beyond recognition and neither parents or employers would admit of child labour in a banned industry. The proprietor, of course, fled the scene of action (*The Hindu*, 12 July 1991).

Not only are working conditions hazardous, the children are brought from home in factory buses at 3 a.m. in the morning. The buses are packed to the brim. In an accident, thirty-seven children lost their lives when a bus, over-loaded with child workers, was swept off in the river Arjuna in a flash flood at Thirumagal. Interestingly, when the bus was stuck under a bridge the children wanted to get out but were prevented from doing so in order to prevent the bus from being swept away in the flood (Garg 1980). Gurbir Singh (1982) reports that after the bus tragedy, Mrs Jayalaxmi, a Lok Sabha (Lower House of the Indian Parliament) member, had called for a probe into the Sivakasi industries alleging that the number of deaths was very high. She said, 'the agents of the factory buy the parents off and conduct mass cremation or mass burial in some secluded places.'

The attempt of employers is to pay a paltry sum to the parents and hush up the incident. Accidents in the match and fire-works industry are fairly frequent though they do not get reported because of the political vested interests of the employers who are able to contain the information locally. But researchers in the field tell another story.

A review of the literature from other industries shows that similar types of health hazards exist in other industries as well. In many industries — such as powerlooms — workers suffer from byssinosis. This disease is caused by cotton dust and fibre which get embedded in the lining of the lungs and cause fibrosis of the tissue. This reduces the normal capacity of the lungs and puts pressure on the surviving tissues. A patient of byssinosis is highly susceptible to bronchitis and tuberculosis. There are an estimated 15,000 children working in the powerloom industry of Bhiwandi in Maharashtra (Barse 1985).

The Slate Pencil Industry of Mandsaur

In Mandsaur district, Madhya Pradesh, where the slate industry is housed, silicosis is a very common occupational disease among the workers. The verdict of a team of doctors headed by the Mandsaur hospital's civil surgeon, Dr J.N. Narodia, is that there is no cure for silicosis. Dr Narodia explains how and why silicosis is dangerous:

> . . . Silicon dust . . . is very light and flies about, unlike, say, coal dust in a coal mine which is heavier and falls to the ground. The silicon dust rises and enters the lungs, forming silica patches. This reduces the elasticity of the lungs, causing fibrosis. As a result the vital capacity of the lungs, that is the oxygen exchange rate, is reduced, since the surface area which absorbs oxygen is less due to the silica patches. The patient does not get oxygen and develops symptoms of chest diseases, like TB. If the patches are large enough . . . the person suffocates to death. The only treatment possible is not for silicosis but to check secondary infections like pneumonia, etc. (Mitra 1986: 105).

Approximately 1000 children are employed in Mandsaur (Rao 1980: 1883) and cut plates of shale into small pieces with electrically operated saws, a process which emits dense clouds of a fine, light dust that the workers constantly inhale. The result is silicosis or pneumoconiosis, a lung disease similar to, but much deadlier than tuberculosis. According to Amiya Rao:

> . . . The medical check-up conducted by the Social Service Club of Indore earlier this year (in 1980) has revealed that most of the child workers have got this disease (silicosis) and will soon die. 'We can't do a thing', says the Civil Surgeon. 'The disease causes fibrous changes in the lungs. Lungs are gradually eaten away, patients suffer respiratory trouble, begin to spit blood and then die a painful death' (ibid.).

Nirmal Mitra reports:

> Children at the age of twelve and even less, are forced into the fatal work to sustain their dying parents, brothers and sisters, only to learn that they will die soon enough too — of the dust, fatigue and inhumanity. The story has been repeated year after year, for five decades now (Mitra 1986: 100).

The enormity of the health hazards can be appreciated when it is realized that in the village of Multanpura, which has 60 per cent of all the slate pencil factories in Mandsaur, there is hardly any old person and almost every third woman is widowed. They are known as 'pollution widows' because their husbands have died from inhaling the slate dust. Most of the workers in this industry will choke to death before reaching forty years of age! (ibid.).

Other Industries

Ninety-five per cent of the respondents in a study conducted by M. Mohandas among *beedi* workers claimed that their health problems were because of their occupation (Mohandas 1980: 1522). The *beedi* industry is one of the largest employers in the unorganized sector and the bulk of the work-force is made up of women and children.

Many occupations may not be hazardous in themselves but the environment makes them such. In many other cases, an intrinsically hazardous industry becomes more dangerous because of lack of precautions or because no care is taken of the surroundings.

Some occupations become hazardous because of working conditions and the working environment. For example, children work at their own or in the artisan's houses that are dark and ill-ventilated as their occupants cannot afford anything better (Burra 1986). Given the lack of precautions, the delicate nature of children and their long hours of work, their eyesight is damaged in gem-polishing, diamond-cutting, carpet-weaving, *zari* work (gold thread embroidery), etc. (Jani 1986; Juyal 1985; and Khan 1987: 5). The posture in which they sit for long hours while weaving carpets causes postural deformities and spinal problems (Boudhiba 1981: 11). Had the working conditions been ideal, perhaps some of these hazards could have been eliminated or their impact reduced. But the piece-rate system, in which payment depends on the output at abysmally low rates, generates extraordinary pressure on the child to work for periods of time which are beyond his or her physical capacities (Burra 1988; 1986). In turn, this intensifies the hazards.

Many other jobs may be in what is considered a non-hazardous environment for adults but the situation of a child worker makes them hazardous. Occupations like domestic work, working in *dhabas* (roadside eating places), selling newspapers, etc. may be safe for adults, but the fact that children are at the mercy of the employer and do not have the support of their parents or anyone else puts them in a very poor bargaining position and consequently in a hazardous situation. Recently a 15-year-old boy was set ablaze by his employer, a factory owner because he asked for leave to visit his home in Bihar. He died of burn injuries (*The Pioneer*, 8 April 1994; *The Times of India*, 8 April 1994).

There are differing views on whether working in *dhabas* or as domestic servants is hazardous work or not. A survey in Bombay conducted by Usha Naidu showed that working children were better off than non-working children in these two sectors. This analysis was based on height and weight measurements and working children were found to have an edge over non-working children. The explanation proffered was that working children were given food on the premises. While this may well be true, often children are given the left-overs from the plates of clients. But there is another side of the picture, the grim reality of which makes the child very vulnerable.

A large number of children working in the *dhabas* and as domestic servants live on the footpaths or on their employer's premises. By virtue of being children, they are at the mercy of their irate customers and employers. Often they are vulnerable and fall prey to the anti-social elements of the urban jungle (Ganguly 1984; Rai 1984; and Pillai 1985).

Children are also sexually abused and made to pimp for the under-world of thugs and gangsters that people the more sleazy and shadowy portions of the city. Sudhindra Shukla writes about the exploitation of the *dhaba* boys that leads not merely to physical but also to mental torture. Says Shukla:

> It was a small, dark, dingy cafe or *dhaba* as it is known in Delhi. A grimy, peaky boy, ill-clad barely twelve years old, was handing out cups of tea to a dozen odd customers in the shop. I, too, was there. Balancing several cups in his two small hands this small boy was hurrying to serve the yelling customers, when a man rushing into the *dhaba* dived towards the wash basin, bumping into the boy and upsetting the tea cups. The tea spilled and the man's clothes were stained, so was his temper. He lashed out at the boy slapping him hard, leaving him in a trance (Shukla 1984).

The story related by Shukla is by no means unusual. Children interviewed by me in the Aligarh Observation Home said they were severely beaten up by their employers for breakage of crockery. It was quite common for children to slip on wet floors of the *dhabas* carrying heavy loads of food and tea, thus not only incurring the wrath of the customers but also losing their wages till they had paid for the breakage.

Another factor that makes working in *dhabas* unsafe for children is that many of these tea-stalls or roadside hotels become gambling dens at night. The child worker who may be serving tea in the daytime is often made to carry bottles of liquor or peddle drugs among the clients at night (Anklesaria 1984).

Many children who work in *dhabas* live on the premises because they have either run away from home or have been sold by middle-men to the employers. They are at the mercy of the employer who often pushes them beyond their physical capacity (Singh et al 1980: 125–6). This exploitation often includes sexual abuse. *Dhaba* owners very rarely employ slum children because these children are not available round the clock. Says Shukla:

> A few days ago I chanced to meet such boys working in cafes of Bombay . . . (They said) that many had to succumb or submit forcefully to sodomy, victimized either by the proprietors, the senior boys or the local goondas. All they say is *kya karega saab, naukri karneka hai, seth log ka baat nahi manega to naukri to jayega, phir bahut maar bhi khane ko milega* (What to do sahib, have to work. If we do not obey the bosses, we will not only lose our jobs but will be given the beating of our lives) (Shukla 1984).

Amit Sengupta, writing about working children, says:

> In Old Delhi, Jama Masjid, Chandni Chowk, Ghanta Ghar and Paharganj I met children and adults who said there are many among those who rule the pavements, shops, *dhabas* and mohallas in these places who can rape children, sodomize them, and leave them in the grip of disease . . . . (Sengupta 1985).

In the same way, children working as domestic servants face very great hardships. Young boys of seven and eight years are often seen at five in the morning walking the employer's dog or buying milk. Many of these children work from dawn to late at night, cooking, cleaning, washing and running errands. They are often not given adequate food and, if caught eating what they are not given, are subject to corporal punishment. Not only are they severely punished for mistakes but often accused of theft when the employer has merely misplaced his things (Boudhiba 1980: 2; Ratnani 1985: 31; and *Indian Express*, 22 February 1988). They sometimes end up with police records. It is this vulnerability which makes the working of children as *dhaba* boys or as domestic servants hazardous.

Health hazards are obviously of varying kinds. Horror stories abound and there is no saying that children in domestic and *dhaba* jobs are better off than those in rag-picking or children working in unregulated workshops and factories. The degree of the hazard varies. In some cases, the hazard is obvious and in others it is insidious. In March 1994, I met ten-year old Rama Rao who had been beaten black and blue by his employer, the wife of an Air Force Officer, ostensibly for eating chocolates. When I saw him, he could not open his eyes and his head was misshapen. She had branded him with tongs. Rama Rao used to get up at 5.30 a.m. to fill water, sweep and swab the house, wash the utensils, fetch and carry. He was allowed to go to bed only late at night. Rama Rao's employer had bought him for Rs 600 from his parents. Whenever the employer beat him, she would turn the T.V. on loud so that neighbours would not hear his screams. Rama Rao was finally rescued by the neighbours and kept in safe custody by an NGO. He now goes to school. He was physically abused as a child at home so he did not want to go back to his parents. (*The Times of India*, 5 March 1994) Article 24 of the Indian Constitution, which is a fundamental right, states clearly that children below the age of fourteen years will not be allowed to work in any hazardous employment. But till such time as the word hazardous is not defined, children in many sectors will not even come under the purview of the law.

The classification of health hazards suggested above makes it clear that we cannot club together all categories of working children. The Government of India has taken the view that since children work on account of poverty and since governmental resources cannot match the magnitude of the problem, at the very least, children should not be permitted to work in hazardous occupations. But what has the government done about this? A look at the Status Report on Child Labour prepared by the National Institute of Occupational Health (NIOH) at Ahmedabad for the Child Labour Technical Advisory Committee (CLTAC) is revealing. Its major finding is that there is inadequate information about the health hazards working children face. The NIOH itself has investigated the slate pencil industry and it is reported that there are no epidemiological studies for other child labour concentration areas. The Status Report has not even put together all the data available in the form of newspaper and magazine articles and reports prepared at the behest of the Union Labour Ministry.

Regarding the glass industry, the Report has this to say:

In this industry there is a serious risk of physical injury, burn hazard, and exposure to silica containing dust. According to an NIOH study report (NIOH 1983-4) there was prevalence of 4.76 per cent silicosis cases among eighty-four workers studied in the batch house of a glass sheet factory. On the other hand an ITRC study at Ferozabad (ITRC-1984) could not detect any silicosis cases. Hence, well planned and quickly executed studies at Ferozabad are needed before taking any action (Ramaswamy et al 1987: 13).

Yet the Union Labour Minister himself along with some members of Parliament had personally raided factories in Firozabad and had found that some children were badly burnt and some others had even lost an eye (*Amar Ujala* 1987). Moreover, the glass industry has been thoroughly researched and an impassioned documentary has been made on the subject by film-maker, Meera Dewan. The authors of the Report seem to be blissfully unaware of all this work on the glass industry. Even if the Report was based on inadequate homework, it would have been in the fitness of things for the CLTAC to have sent teams of doctors and others to observe how the lives of children are quietly burning themselves out in the glass factories of Firozabad.

It is this insouciance and casual attitude that allows the Report to say about electroplating operations (commonly used in the lock industry of Aligarh and the brass ware industry of Moradabad):

> In these, cyanide solutions are handled. Hence, there is a necessity for regulating the conditions (Ramaswamy et al 1987: 16).

Shouldn't children be banned from working with potassium cyanide, a deadly chemical, into a solution of which they dip their hands for the better part of a ten hour day, in the lock industry, for example? The lack of attention to work done in the past is reflected in the recommendations that more studies on the glass and brass ware industries are warranted. It is overlooked that these industries were banned, presumably for good reasons, by the U.P. state government under the Employment of Children Act, 1938.

The CLTAC has met in a perfunctory way and come up with piece-meal recommendations. One hopes that the CLTAC will visit the child labour concentration areas and sieve more thoroughly the evidence available in so many published articles and reports. The reports of the Children's Employment Commission and the Public Health Commission in England in the nineteenth century provoked considerable public debate for the wealth of data they made available on hazards to children, which ultimately led to the reform movement to end child labour in England. Will the CLTAC take the cue and grasp the opportunity to bring to light the horrific conditions under which children work and live in so many parts of the country?

11

What can be done . . .

The classic defence offered by apologists for child labour is that it is caused by poverty. In one sense, this is an unexceptionable assertion. In another sense, such a statement deflects attention from the quiescence and inactivity of the state. Most importantly, the causal relationship sought to be established between poverty and child labour masks the systematic exploitation of children in some areas of work. It has been the argument in this book that the prevalence and persistence of child labour itself reinforces, if not creates, poverty.

All evidence from the field indicates that children who are working in industry from an early age burn themselves out by the time they are thirty or thirty-five years old. They have not had any education worth the name and their health is severely impaired. Often, in situations like these, such persons are heavily indebted as well. The circumstances of unemployment — if not unemployability — combined with their inferior position in the hierarchies of caste and class pre-dispose them to putting their own children to work in turn. And so the downward spiral of exploitation and poverty wends its way.

All categories of children, whether they are working as part of family labour, working in hazardous industries or working as bonded labour are, in one form or the other, child labour. But it is important to make these categorizations and distinctions because there are differences in the degrees of exploitation. Unfortunately, when one uses the term 'child labour' to define all these different categories, the solution that comes to mind is to use the traditional tool of labour legislation and 'ban child labour'. It is then of course expected that once the legislation is in place, child labour will disappear. Looking at child labour as merely a 'labour problem' also means that most of the solutions presented are in the form of asking for equal wages for adults and children, unionizing children so that they can demand equality from the system, improving working conditions, etc.

Historically, however, abolition of child labour was closely linked with the introduction of compulsory education. This was the experience of several countries described very vividly by Myron Weiner (1991) and it was also discussed at length in the Legislative Assembly Debates in the early part of this century. Compulsory primary education means that for at least a part of the day children would mandatorily have to remain in school.

Free and compulsory primary education is a necessary, if not sufficient, condition for the elimination of child labour. The use of the word 'compulsory' has made people very ambivalent. A number of questions come to mind: Does it mean that parents who don't send their children to school will have to go to jail? Will it increase the poverty of poor parents? Will it create needs in the poor that cannot be fulfiled? These questions are valid. Compulsory education does mean that there is an element of enforcement, but nowhere in the world have parents been sent to jail. It could be, for instance, in the Indian context, that it becomes the mandate of Panchayati Raj institutions to enforce compulsory education down to the village level.

Another common fear is that poor parents who are dependent upon the income of their children would in fact suffer enormous economic hardships, if compulsory education was to be introduced. The process of introducing compulsory education is in itself a gradual one. Most countries started by making it compulsory for children in the age group of six to nine years to be in school, and then gradually raised the age limit for compulsory education. If one looks at the problem with the data available on child labour, one finds that children start actually earning a wage only after they are ten years old and above. The economic value of children below ten years is very limited.

Another common misconception is that compulsory education means that children will not be allowed to work at all. Children in all societies which have introduced compulsory education have combined schooling with work, but the priority has been *education first and work later* and not the other way round. The acceptance of compulsory primary education implies the acceptance of a norm that learning is primary for children and not working. And that learning should not be in workshops, factories or mines but in schools.

Through the introduction of compulsory primary education, one could hazard that at least 70 per cent, if not more, of children who are currently outside the school system, would go back to school. There would still be some categories of child labour such as children working in factories, workshops and mines, children who are bonded to feudal landlords and factory/workshop owners and street children who have left their homes for the towns and cities to fend for themselves, who would not necessarily be affected by compulsory primary education. For example, it can be nobody's case that the introduction of compulsory education can eliminate the phenomenon of bonded children in feudal agriculture. Land reforms, rural development programmes including public works, income-generation schemes and the availability of credit are some of the important measures that are necessary to tackle the problem of bondage. Without such measures, attempts to enforce any law prohibiting child labour in feudal agriculture would not seem to have much chance of success.

Consider next, for example, the case of street children. Their situation is relatively unamenable to either the introduction of compulsory education or the implementation of labour laws. For a variety of reasons — poverty, discord, violence or child abuse in the family, kidnapping and so on — street children have left their homes to seek refuge in the town and city. It is in dealing with such children that Non-Governmental Organizations could play a major role in terms of providing shelter, access to counselling, health services, non-formal education, protection against urban predators and so on. In this case, the role of the state could be supportive of well-intentioned, voluntary effort. The experience of institutionalizing such children in state-run facilities has not been salutary. City administrations can become facilitators in the provision of urban basic services and criminal law needs to be humanized so that such children are not seen as vagrants, juvenile delinquents or anti-social elements.

With respect to the category of child labour working in factories and workshops, there is a categorical ban on children working below the age of fourteen years in factories under the Factories Act. This ban, however, is widely flouted by some entrepreneurs who use a strategy of artificially partitioning the area with curtains made of gunny cloth. Another method used in the match industry of Sivakasi is to sub-contract some aspects of the production process in order to circumvent the law. It is common knowledge that in many industries, units are not registered as factories in order to escape the stringent provisions of law. Then we have a situation — in the lock and pottery industries, for example — where many units employ child labour but claim that they are not factories. It is unrealistic to expect an under-staffed labour inspectorate to distinguish in law and practice what in fact constitutes a factory.

With respect to the working of children in workshops, there are a number of loopholes in the Child Labour (Prohibition and Regulation) Act, 1986, which makes it a completely ineffective instrument for the removal of children working in industry. One clear loophole is that children can continue to work if they are a part of family labour. It is worthwhile to go back a little and look at how protective legislation had been formulated in India for this section of the labour force. As has been mentioned earlier, the Royal Commission on Labour had been appointed in 1929 to look into the working conditions of the labouring classes. They had visited several industries and recommended that certain industries be banned for children. The Report became the basis of the Employment of Children Act, 1938, which listed those industries as banned. The only exceptions to the ban were in cases where children worked in family enterprises or in institutions sponsored by the state. The exception made for children working as part of family labour was justified at the time since the production process in many industries had the small artisan as the representative figure. The Partition of India in 1947, and the migration of Muslim artisans to Pakistan and the entry into India of Punjabis and their capital was to significantly alter the nature of the production process in north India. In time, the artisan of yore working at home with his family was to be replaced by the entrepreneur and his factory or workshop even as national and international demand rose sharply and called for a change in technology.

It was such a historical context that explained the proviso in the 1938 Act exempting child labour in family enterprises from the ban. But with the context having changed out of recognition, there is no justification for such an exemption in the Act of 1986. In fact, by granting such an exemption, the Act has become toothless for factory and labour inspectors are hardly equipped to determine the paternity of children at work, even assuming that they are in a position to inspect some reasonable proportion of premises where they work. Since people have become aware of the law, they freely claim parenthood of the children they employ.

The Child Labour (Prohibition and Regulation) Act of 1986 also has a Schedule attached to it which is largely the same as that found in the Employment of Children Act, 1938. In addition, the new Act lists in its Schedule certain chemicals and bans the working of children in processes that use these. This Act is based on the belief that child labour should be prohibited only in hazardous processes. The underlying assumption seems to be that by banning children working with such chemicals, they would not work in hazardous but non-hazardous processes would be permissible for child labour. Once again, it seems impractical to think that a labour inspector without the necessary qualifications and an infrastructure of testing laboratories can identify dangerous chemicals. The obvious conclusion to be drawn is that when an industry is hazardous, it should be banned for children, whether in factories or workshops or at any stage of the production process. If we look at the carpet industry, it is banned for children thanks to the Employment of Children Act, 1938, the relevant provision of which has been reproduced in the 1986 Act. As a result, both national and international pressure is growing to eliminate child labour in this industry. With such an unequivocal ban, there is no room for legal hair-splitting and semantic tomfoolery about whether a process is hazardous or not. Similarly, children are banned from working in the match and *beedi* (local cigarettes) industries, irrespective of the nature of its process.

The Child Labour Act of 1986 does not use the word hazardous anywhere. The implication is that children may continue to work in those processes not involving chemicals. Even though the Act does not use these terms, one could classify some processes as hazardous and the others as non-hazardous. I have already discussed the practical difficulties that will be faced by anybody who tries to monitor which processes children are involved in, once they enter a workshop. Moreover, even if they are working on what is ostensibly a non-hazardous process, they are certainly exposed to the risks and hazards of the environment in the workshop. For example, children may be packing locks in close proximity to a polishing unit and may well be inhaling the metal dust that causes lung diseases. Yet another case would be of those children who serve water in units cutting designs on glass bangles. Here again, even if such work seems free of hazards, these children are inhaling quantities of glass dust every day. In the pottery industry, we have historical evidence from Western countries in the nineteenth century that children who worked there suffered from stunted growth as did their progeny even after a generation or two! In the pottery industry of Khurja today, children appear to be doing only the innocuous task of lifting up and putting down unbaked pots but the hazard of working with damp clay containing silica may well manifest itself in a few decades. Standard textbooks on occupational health tell of the dangers of silica dust.

In many of the industries studied, adults and children complained of lung problems and the most common diagnosis was that they had tuberculosis. Medical personnel in these small towns I visited were clearly not trained in occupational health. Moreover, tuberculosis is a disease most commonly attributed to malnutrition, ill-ventilated residential premises and poor environmental hygiene, all of which are associated with poverty. Keeping these factors in mind, it is not easy without systematic medical research to link cause and effect. There is considerable empirical evidence that workers' lives are shortened when they begin work at a young age in unhealthy environments. All of the foregoing suggests, at the very least, the need for systematic and activist medical research in occupational health.

I have tried to show how impracticable and unrealistic it is to draw a distinction between hazardous and non-hazardous processes in a particular industry. What is necessary is for whole industries to be listed as banned for child labour which will make the task of enforcement far simpler and strategies of evasion far more difficult. The carpet industry, first banned by the 1938 Act, has attracted considerable attention from researchers, social activists and the media. Frequent exposes have led to increased consciousness about the horrific conditions under which children work in the carpet industry. It is increasingly being recognized — and even admitted by employers — that the theory of 'nimble fingers' is largely untrue and that adults can easily do the work that children perform. There is a growing lobby in the country demanding the enforcement of the ban on child labour in the carpet industry without attention being diverted to any fruitless debate on whether some processes in the carpet industry are non-hazardous. A new voice recently added to the protest against child labour in the carpet industry is that of importers from foreign countries. As the stories of oppression gain increasing circulation in world media, there is a rising and insistent demand amongst many importers that only those carpets will be bought which are certified as not to involve the labour of children. The pressure placed upon producers of goods meant for export has enormous potential: it is hoped that we will soon reach a stage when children will be in fact eliminated from the carpet industry. Again, national publicity has certainly helped the cause of child labour in the construction industry. Public interest litigation brought forth a Supreme Court judgement banning child labour in the construction industry and there is evidence in the bigger cities that this pernicious practice is certainly dwindling: employers seem to have weighed the pros and cons of employing child labour and decided against it.

One of the ways in which child labour has been promoted in the carpet industry has been through the setting up of training centres by the state governments in the Mirzapur-Bhadohi belt of Uttar Pradesh, in Kashmir and in Rajasthan. In doing so, the state governments have taken advantage of an exception provided to the general ban on children working in the carpet industry in cases where the institutions involved are state-run or state-funded. Even private entrepreneurs can get grants from the state ostensibly on grounds of training children in carpet-weaving. The reality in the field is that children much below the age of fourteen years — even as young as five years — have joined these private training-cum-production centres to avail of the stipend of Rs 100 to 150 a month. Many of the children have been taken out of school by their parents in order to get the stipendiary sum.

Children in centres run by state governments are usually around the ages of nine or ten years and they are expected to join the industry after the training year is over. Thus state policy directly contributes to violation of the law which stipulates that children below the age of fourteen years be prohibited from working in the carpet industry. When state governments lend legitimacy to the process of training of children in the carpet industry, private entrepreneurs can easily pass off their production centres as training-cum-production centres funded by the state.

Such a situation is rich with anomalies for on the one hand, the Child Labour (Prohibition and Regulation) Act, 1986, bans the working of children in the carpet industry (albeit with the exemptions referred to above) but on the other hand, the industries departments of some state governments are actively drawing very small children into the carpet industry. What is truly reprehensible is that this ostensibly developmental pro- gramme results in many children being taken away from school by poor parents enrolling them at these training centres. Once again, the state itself appears to be acting against the Constitu- tional directive regarding the provision of universal primary education. Another consequence of setting up such training centres is that the private trade in the carpet industry — no- torious for its rapacity and greed — gets trained child labour without investment since the state itself has funded the training process. In Rajasthan, carpet manufacturers/exporters are in close touch with the master weavers who train children under the state government schemes. Once the children are trained, these entrepreneurs plan to instal looms in the homes of these children in order to pass such activity as a traditional occupation of the family. A neat smokescreen is thus erected in order to circumvent the law. In a few years from now in Rajasthan, the situation is likely to resemble that in Mirzapur-Bhadohi where the induction of children in the carpet industry was aided and abetted actively by the training programmes of the state govern- ment. Today in Uttar Pradesh, it is extremely difficult for anyone at all, let alone an under-staffed and corrupt lower bureaucracy, to tell whether a carpet has been manufactured by children under the guise of family labour or not. It becomes a great deal more difficult to ascertain the truth in the face of the strong popular belief that such activity is largely done by families and at home.

The classification of child labour suggested above follows from a contextual understanding of the circumstances under which different types of children become involved with work. Certain legal and policy changes become unavoidable if all this is to be reversed. At the same time, with respect to child labour in factories and workshops, an area-specific and industry-specific approach will perhaps be useful. For example, in the gem polishing industry of Jaipur, I found that the work done by children is not intrinsically hazardous but they are exploited for many years under the guise of apprenticeship training. The gem industry in India is export-oriented and booming: surely, the government could negotiate with the industry using the carrot of incentive and the stick of disincentive so that all children in the industry get schooling and if there is any training, it should only be after school hours and only in the school premises. There should be no question of children undergoing training in factories or workshops for then there would be no control over the hours of work, etc., or their educational status. Unlike other industries I have discussed, children in the gem polishing industry will not burn themselves out by learning the work from a young age. In fact, since there is full employment in this industry and wages are above the statutory minimum, that child who picks up a few skills will be in a better position when he embarks upon a career on maturity.

In the match industry of Sivakasi, it has been suggested by the Madras Institute of Development Studies that the only way to enforce the ban would be to make piece-rate wages comparable to wages paid to agricultural workers. It has been suggested in their study that to make this viable, it may be necessary to adjust the excise duty so that the burden of extra wages does not fall upon the employers. There is also a substantial cushion in the high profits, some of which could be used to cover any increased wage costs.

In many industries like glass, lock, slate, balloon, brass ware, *beedi*, match and fireworks, hazards arise not only from the poor working environment but also because of the technology employed. As India opens up its economy and integrates into the world market, industrial collaborations with firms in developed countries are bound to rise. While granting approvals for such collaborations, it should be possible for the government to insert a clause to the effect that child labour will not be used in any process connected with the industry. As observed earlier, the emerging world-wide conscience about human rights is beginning to have an impact with some countries banning or proposing to ban the import of goods manufactured with the help of children.

In the wake of the liberalization of the Indian economy, increase in productivity has become one of the main objectives. Faced with international competition, some sectors of the Indian industry seek an advantage by the recruitment and use of cheap child labour. Sericulture, fish processing, food processing and genetic engineering of seeds are some of the sectors where there is a reported increase in child labour. A child labour impact assessment should therefore become mandatory for the clearance of all development aid projects so that they do not unintentionally create situations which worsen the situation of child labour.

It has often been pointed out that the single-point entry, sequential system of schooling and a school calendar wholly out of alignment with the peak seasons of agricultural activity are indices of the insensitivity of the school system to the felt needs of peasant societies. The prevailing pattern of schooling does not allow for the need of children to look after their younger siblings and perform sundry domestic chores. The role of the woman as part of the productive labour force has not been taken into account and the common presumption is that she is available full-time for housework. Flexible and shortened school hours with creches for younger children would go some way in meeting this difficulty. The provision of creches will certainly help promote girl children going to school in larger numbers. To make school more attractive, it should become the focal point for child-related services: midday-meals could reduce nutritional deficiencies and health and immunization services for children would find a ready clientele. The absence of an adequate physical infrastructure to make schooling available in the proximity of the village child, the reluctance of school teachers to work in remote, far-flung rural areas and their lack of training and motivation are important reasons for the poor state of the educational system. The increasing politicization of village school teachers in many parts of India sees them spending considerable time, money and energy in seeking comfortable stations of posting and avoiding places thought inconvenient. While school teachers are certainly poorly paid, they function largely without accountability to the parents, the village community and the educational and district administrations. This well-known catalogue of the shortcomings of the school system obviously calls for remedial measures.

Remedial measures apart, the Constitutional directive of providing free and compulsory education to all children below the age of fourteen has remained largely void of content. Except for states like Kerala, indicators like attendance and drop out rates offer little comfort. If Governments are serious about implementing the Constitutional directive, budgetary allocations will have to be significantly stepped up and the political will found to reach education to all. Universal primary education is not given the importance it deserves and instead, many governmental programmes offer palliatives like adult literacy programmes and the establishment of model schools catering largely to the rural elite, rather than tackle frontally the need for a good basic education.

It will be seen that the difficulties of working children can be dealt with only by the State in view of the nature and size of the problem. Voluntary effort can at best be a drop in the ocean. Here again, any attempt to impose and enforce child labour laws will be beset by difficulty given the complex socio-economic roots of child work. If the school system is re-oriented along the lines suggested above, and ways found to involve village communities in the running of schools thus making the school system more accountable to the people, most children of this category would both be able to attend school and still have time to help out in domestic chores. At that stage, the introduction of compulsory education would be important so that individual parents cannot unilaterally keep their children at home. There are already successful experiments in the field initiated by voluntary agencies which proves that this strategy can work. Panchayati Raj institutions could also see to it that all children go to school for at least part of the day.

Not much is known about the impact of women's work on the incidence of child labour. The Report of the National Commission on Self-Employed Women and Women in the Informal Sector observes that women in this sector rely heavily on their children for earning a living wage. Unless the issue of home-based, piece-rate workers is resolved and minimum wages and social security provided to this sector, children will continue to be exploited. Girls are particularly vulnerable for it is safer to keep them at home and make them work rather than send them out to workshops and factories. It is because they are unseen and unheard that they are doubly exploited. The boy goes out to work and brings in a wage: he is treated as a useful member of the family because he contributes to the family economy whereas the girl is only seen as a burden upon the family. She suffers in terms of her health, nutrition and education. Unfortunately, most Non Governmental Organizations (NGOs) working on women's issues have, till recently, neglected the problem of the female child and have focussed attention upon the adult woman. Most NGOs working with women in the informal sector have not known how to tackle the problem of the female child as their main concern for many years has been to help women improve their productivity and hence their incomes. A visit to any area where there are home-based, piece-rate *agarbatti* (incense sticks), *beedi*, garments, *papads* (an Indian savoury), coir and other workers will find girl children as little as six years working for long hours with their mothers. Undoubtedly, they learn some skills from their mothers but long and back-breaking hours are responsible for making them grow into helpless adult women who have little bargaining power. It is important to document through empirical research the extent and nature of this problem in order to find practical solutions. Certainly, compulsory primary education with midday-meals does provide some respite to working girls, particularly if schools provide creches as well.

One conclusion is that compulsory primary education will

to a great extent reduce the numbers of children working full-time, particularly those working in the rural areas and as part of family labour. If there is at all a blueprint for tackling the problem of child labour, it is education. It will still leave categories of children working in workshops, factories, on the streets and in bondage out of the school system. For these categories of children, a multi-pronged and multi-faceted strategy that takes into account educational needs and the particular demands of the area or the industry, needs to be devised. Independent research in the unexplored domains of child labour will help map the terrain. The coverage by media of child labour will increase awareness and consciousness amongst policy makers and others; the parents of child workers themselves are often unaware of the health hazards their children face and educating them about this with the help of audio-visual media is a priority. Voluntary effort by Non-Governmental Organizations can help in advocacy of the cause by bringing pressure upon the system to correct itself.

For a thorough examination of the issue of child labour in all its ramifications, a statutory Commission on Child Labour needs to be established. Such a Commission should have a clear mandate to make field visits and the power to summon witnesses, the funds to commission research, and the autonomy to live up to its mandate. There should be a requirement that the Commission's Reports be placed before the Parliament so that their findings and recommendations are given due weight. Hopefully, such a Commission will bring to the forefront of public consciousness the exploitation of child labour and thereby provoke discussion and debate as an impetus for change.

Bibliography

Acharya, Poromesh, 'Child Labour' in *Seminar*, July 1982, 275.

Anand, A.L., 'Export of Locks and Padlocks' in *Souvenir for Seminar on Locks*, Aligarh, 21 March 1982.

Anees, Mohammad, 'Epidemiology of Chest Diseases in Lock Workers in Aligarh (Uttar Pradesh)', Thesis for M.D. Department of Preventive and Social Medicine, Jawaharlal Nehru Medical College, (Aligarh: Aligarh Muslim University) 1978.

Anklesaria, Shahnaz, 'Child Delinquents: Rebels without a Cause', *Statesman*, 8 April 1984.

Arimpoor, Joe, 'Street Children of Madras: A Situational Analysis', Study conducted for Ministry of Welfare, Government of India and UNICEF (Noida: National Labour Institute, Child Labour Cell) 1992.

Arora, Ramesh, *The Lock Times* (Hindi) (Aligarh: All India Lock Manufacturers Association) August 1986.

Arora, U.P. et al *Social Cost of Bonded Labour* (Allahabad: Academy of Social Sciences) 1977.

Awachat, Anil, 'The Warp and the Weft-I' in *Economic and Political Weekly*, vol. XXIII, no. 34, 20 August 1988.

Awasthi, Dilip, 'Glass Industry. Cutting Corners' in *India Today*, 31 December 1986.

Banerjee, Sumanta, 'Child Labour in India' in *Mainstream*, vol. XVIII, no. 10, 24 November 1979.

Barse, Sheela, 'Child Labour Hit by Powerloom Closure', *Indian Express*, 15 November 1985.

——, 'Glass Factories of Firozabad-I. Children Playing with Fire', *Indian Express*, 5 April 1986a.

——, 'Glass Factories of Firozabad-II. Fleecing of Hapless Labour', *Indian Express*, 6 April 1986b.

Barse, Sheela, 'Glass Factories of Firozabad-III. Nelson's Eye to Workers' Safety', *Indian Express*, 8 April 1986c.

Bhat, Ela, 'The Invisibility of Home-based Work. The Case of Piecerate Workers in India' in Andrea Menefee Singh and Anita Kelles-Viitanen (eds) *Invisible Hands* (New Delhi: Sage Publications) 1987.

Bhattacharjee, A., 'The Girl Child: A Being that does not Exist for the Media', Paper presented at the NMC-UNICEF Media Workshop on the Girl Child, New Delhi, 12–14 October 1985.

Bhattacharya, T.P., *Status Report on Ceramic Industry at Khurja, U.P.* (Calcutta: Central Glass and Ceramics Research Institute) March 1982.

Bhowmik, Sharit K., 'Plantation Labour Act and Child Labour' in *Economic and Political Weekly*, vol. xxvii, no. 42, 17 October 1992.

Bond, Tim, 'The Abuse of Child Labour in Thailand', An M.R.G. Special Report presented to the Working Group on Slavery; A U.N. Sub-Commission on Human Rights, Geneva, August 1982, pp. 1–14.

Bouhdiba, Abdelwahab, 'Exploitation of Child Labour', Special Rapporteur of the Sub-Commission on Prevention of Discrimination and Protection of Minorities, E/CN4/Sub.2/479, 1981.

Burra, Neera, 'Child Labour in India: Poverty, Exploitation and Vested Interest' in *Social Action*, vol. 36, July–September 1986a.

——, 'Glass Factories of Firozabad: I — Plight of Child Workers' in *Economic and Political Weekly*, vol. xxi, no. 46, 15 November 1986b.

——, 'Glass Factories of Firozabad: II — Plight of Child Workers' in *Economic and Political Weekly*, vol. xxi, no. 47, 22 November 1986c.

——, *A Report on Child Labour in the Lock Industry of Aligarh, Uttar Pradesh, India*, Prepared for UNICEF (New Delhi) 1987a.

——, *A Report on Child Labour in the Gem Polishing Industry of Jaipur, Rajasthan, India*, Prepared for UNICEF (New Delhi) 1987b.

——, *A Report on Child Labour in the Pottery Industry of Khurja, Uttar Pradesh, India*, Prepared for DANIDA (New Delhi) 1987c.

Burra, Neera, 'You've Got your Facts Wrong Mr Tytler', *The Times of India*, 4 April 1988.

——, *The Informalisation of Employment: Child Labour in Urban Industries of India*, Labour Market Analysis and Employment Planning, Working Paper no. 25 (Geneva: International Labour Office) 1988.

——, *Child Labour in the Brass Ware Industry of Moradabad, India* (New Delhi: ILO/ARTEP) 1989.

Census of India, 1981, 'Primary Census Abstracts: General Population', Series 1, Part II 15 (1).

——, 'Provisional Population Totals: Workers and their Distribution', Series 1, Paper 3, November 1991.

Chadha, T.S. (ed.), *Carpet Council News* (New Delhi: Carpet Export Promotion Council) June 1986.

Chakrapani, S., 'Child Labour in Mandsaur, Slate-Pencil Industry', Recommendations made at Workshop on Child Labour in India (New Delhi: Indian Social Institute) 14–15 November 1985.

Champakalakshmi, R. *Measures for Improving the Working Conditions of Children in the Carpet and Glass Bangle Industries* Confidential document (New Delhi: Institute of Applied Manpower Research) (n.d.) pp. 1–26.

Chandrasegaran, K., *Study on Child Employment in Match Industries and Fireworks at Sivakasi* (Pondicherry: Government Law College) unpublished (n.d.).

Chanthanom, Suvajee, 'Child Servitude in India' in *Child Workers in Asia*, vol. 5, no. 5, July–September 1989, pp. 3–8.

Chatterji, Debasish, 'Child Labour in Glass Industry' in *Surya India*, June 1986.

Chaudhuri, M., 'Sex Bias in Child Nutrition', Paper presented at the NMC-UNICEF Media Workshop on The Girl Child New Delhi, 12–14 October 1985.

Chowdhury, Neeraja, 'Those Bonded and Branded in Boyhood', *Statesman*, 11 April 1984a.

——, 'Uttar Pradesh, Bihar Told to Probe into "Bonded" Child Labourers', *Patriot*, 24 April 1984b.

——, 'Bonded Child Weavers Released', *Patrika*, 10 December 1985.

Daniel, Christopher, 'Child Worker has Come to Stay?' in *Social Welfare*, vol. XXII., no. 8, 1976.

Das, M., 'Bonded Child Labour in Mirzapur: 75,000 Kids Exploited in Carpet Industry' in *Current*, 21 December 1985.

Dasgupta, Saibal, 'Child Labour. Dirt being Swept under the Carpet', *Times of India* (Bombay) 12 August 1992.

Devi, Mahasveta, 'Palamau: The Long Road to Freedom', *Business Standard*, 21 April 1984a.

——, 'MPs Concern over Child Labour', *Indian Express*, 25 April 1984b.

Gangrade, K.D. and Joseph A. Gathia, *Women & Child Workers in the Unorganized Sector* (New Delhi: Concept Publishing Company) 1983.

Ganguly, Piyus, 'Child Labour Rules Flouted with Impunity', *The Telegraph* (Calcutta) 16 April 1984.

Garg, R.B.L., 'Fair Deal for Children', *Patriot*, 28 November 1980.

Ghosh, A., *Street Children of Calcutta: A Situational Analysis*, Study conducted for Ministry of Welfare, Government of India and UNICEF (Noida: National Labour Institute, Child Labour Cell) 1992.

Gore, M.S., 'Opening Address' in Usha Naidu and Kamini R. Kapadia (eds), *Child Labour and Health: Problems and Prospects* (Bombay: Tata Institute of Social Sciences) 1985.

Government of India, *Legislative Assembly Debates (Official Report)* vol. I, Part I, First Session of the Legislative Assembly (Delhi: Superintendent, Government Printing Press) 1921.

——, *Report of the Royal Commission on Labour in India* (Calcutta: Government of India Central Publication Branch) 1931.

——, *Report of the Committee on Child Labour 1979*, Ministry of Labour (Nasik: Printed by the Manager, Government of India Press) 1981.

Government of Uttar Pradesh, *Report of the UP Labour Department on Child Labour in the Glass Industry of Firozabad*, (unpublished) 1986a.

——, *A Pilot Project on Child Labourers in Carpet-Weaving* (Varanasi: Government of Uttar Pradesh) (mimeo) 1986b.

Gulati, Leela, *Profiles in Female Poverty: A Study of Five Poor Working Women in Kerala* (Delhi: Hindustan Publishing Corporation) 1981.

——, *Child labour in Kerala's Coir Industry — A Study of a Few*

Selected Villages (Trivandrum: Centre for Development Studies) (unpublished) (n.d.).

Gupte, S., 'Child Labour' in *ICCW News Bulletin*, vol. xxxiii, no. 3, September 1985.

Iyengar. L.V.,'Where Children Labour and Fathers Despair!' *Indian Express*, 16 February 1986a.

———, 'Child Labour in the Match Units of Southern Tamil Nadu', Paper presented at a Seminar on Child Labour in India (New Delhi: Indian Social Institute) 9 August 1986b.

———, 'Pyre of Childhood: Child Workers in the Factories of Sivakasi' in Manju Gupta and Klaus Voll (eds), *Young Hands at Work: Child Labour in India* (Delhi, Lucknow: Atma Ram & Sons) 1987.

Jani, Gaurang, 'Child Workers of Diamond Cutting Industry in Surat — Some Observations', Paper presented at Workshop on Child Labour in India (New Delhi: Indian Social Institute) 9 August 1986.

———, 'No Sparkle in Gem Workers' Lives', *The Hindustan Times*, 26 July 1987.

Jhabvala, Renana and Jennifer Sebstadt, 'To Be Self-Employed . . . and a Woman', *Himmat*, vol. 17, no. 15, 1980-1.

Juyal, B.N. et al *Child Labour: The Twice Exploited* (Varanasi: Gandhian Institute of Studies) 1985.

———, *Child Labour and Exploitation in the Carpet Industry: A Mirzapur-Bhadohi Case Study* (New Delhi: Indian Social Institute) 1987.

Kapoor, Aditi, 'If We Move Slowly We Were Beaten, Carpet Children Recount Days of Captivity', *The Times of India*, 6 November 1992.

Karlekar, Malavika, *Poverty and Women's Work: A Study of Sweeper Women in Delhi* (Delhi: Vikas Publishing House) 1982.

Khan, Shamshad, 'Experiences with the Rehabilitation of Working Children: A Practical Approach', Paper presented at a Seminar on Child Labour and the New Legislation (Srinagar: Friedrich Ebert Foundation) 4-8 May 1987.

Khandekar, Mandakini, *A Report on the Situation of Children and Youth in Greater Bombay* (Bombay: Tata Institute of Social Sciences) 1970.

Khatu, K.K. et al *Working Children in India* (Baroda: Operations Research Group) 1983.

Kishwar, Madhu and B. Horowitz, 'Family Life: The Unequal Deal' in M. Kishwar and Ruth Vanita (eds), *In Search of Answers: Indian Women's Voices from Manushi* (London: Zed Books Ltd.) 1984.

Kothari, S., 'Exploiting the Young' in *India Today*, 15 January 1983a.

——, 'Child Labour in India: A Case Study of Sivakasi', Paper presented at AWDI-FES Seminar on The State of Unorganised Labour, 24–7 February 1983b.

——, 'There's Blood on those Matchsticks' in *Economic and Political Weekly*, vol. xviii, no. 27, 2 July 1983c.

Krishnakumari, N.S., *Child Labour in Bangalore City* (Delhi: Published by I.S.P.C.K.) 1985.

Kulkarni, M.N., 'Match-making Children in Sivakasi', *Economic and Political Weekly*, vol. xviii, no. 43, 22 October 1983.

Kulshreshta, D.K. and S.K. Sharma, 'Child Labour in Moradabad Metalware Industry', *The Economic Times*, 19 October 1980.

Labour Commissioner, U.P., 'Project Report for Rehabilitation of Child Labour in Brass Ware Industry of Moradabad prepared by Labour Commissioner, U.P.', (unpublished) 9 January 1988.

Marla, Sarma, 'Bonded Labour in Medak district (A.P.)' in *NLI Bulletin*, vol. 3, no. 10, October 1977.

——, *Bonded Labour in India: National Survey on the Incidence of Bonded Labour, Final Report* (New Delhi: Biblia Impex Private Limited) 1981.

Marx, Karl, *Capital Volume I*, Introduced by Ernest Mandel (The Pelican Marx Library, Penguin Books in association with New Left Review) [1867] 1982.

McDonald, Hamish, 'India. Boys of Bondage. Child Labour though Banned is Rampant' in *Far Eastern Review*, 9 July 1992.

Mehta, Manharbhai, 'How Children are Exploited in "Socialist" India' in *Organizer*, January 1983.

Mehta, Prayag, 'Mortgaged Child Labour of Vellore. Women Beedi Workers Tale of Woe' in *Mainstream*, vol. xxii, no. 1, 3 September 1983.

Menon, Sadanand, 'Sivakasi: The Little Japan of India', *The Times of India* (Sunday Magazine) New Delhi, 7 October 1979.

Menon, Geeta, 'Health Problems of Working Children: Some Observations' in Usha Naidu and Kamini Kapadia (eds) *Child Labour and Health: Problems and Prospects* (Bombay: Tata Institute of Social Sciences) 1985.

Menon, Ramesh, 'Child Workers. The Wages of Innocence' in *India Today*, 15 February 1986.

Mies, Maria, *The Lace makers of Narsapur. Indian Housewives Produce for the World Market* (London: Zed Press) 1982.

——, Assisted by Laliltha K. and Krishna Kumari, *Indian Women in Subsistence and Agricultural labour, Women, Work and Development 12* (Geneva: International Labour Office) 1986.

Mitra, N., 'Slave Children of Mandsaur' in *Sunday*, 15-21 June 1986.

Mohandas, M., 'Beedi Workers in Kerala: Conditions of Life and Work' in *Economic and Political Weekly*, vol. xv, no. 36, 6 September 1980.

Mundle, Sudipto, 'The Bonded of Palamau' in *Economic and Political Weekly*, vol. xi, no. 18, 1 May 1976.

Murthy, N.L. et al 'Child Labour in Agriculture: A Case Study in Andhra Pradesh' in *Mainstream*, vol. xxiii, no. 49, 3 August 1985.

Naidu, Usha and S. Parasuraman, *Health Situation of Working Children in Greater Bombay*, WHO sponsored Study Report (Bombay: TISS) 1985.

Naik, J.P., *Equality, Quality and Quantity: The Elusive Triangle in Indian Education* (New Delhi: Allied Publishers Private Limited) 1975a.

——, *Policy and Performance in Indian Education 1947-74*, Dr K.G. Saiyidian Memorial Trust, Jamianagar, New Delhi (New Delhi: Orient Longman) 1975b.

——, *The Education Commission and After* (New Delhi: Allied Publishers Private Limited) 1982.

Nair, R., 'Education: Why do more Girls Drop Out?' in *Kurukshetra*, 1-15 May 1983.

Nangia, Sudesh, *Child Workers in Carpet Weaving Industry in Jammu and Kashmir (with a special emphasis on girls)* (New Delhi: Project sponsored by UNICEF, Regional Office for South Central Asia) (mimeo) October 1988.

Nayyar, Rohini, 'Female Participation Rates in Rural India' in

Economic and Political Weekly, vol. xxii, no. 51, 19 December 1987.

Ninan, S., 'Carpet Boom Rides on Child labour', *The Indian Express*, 22 December 1983.

———, 'Weaving a Warped Future', *The Indian Express* (Sunday Magazine) 6 May 1984a.

———, 'Government is Firm on Ending Child Labour: Minister', *The Hindustan Times*, 3 May 1984b.

———, 'SC Notices in Mirzapur Case', *The Indian Express*, 9 May 1984c.

———, 'Dream that Turned into a Harrowing Nightmare', *Patriot* 11 April 1984d.

———, 'Kids Kidnapped to Weave Carpets', *The Indian Express*, 11 April 1984e.

Pal, Bulbul, 'Bangle-makers: A Fragile Existence,' *Express Magazine*, 4 May 1986.

Pandit, M.L., *Child Labour in Handicrafts of Kashmir Valley* (unpublished manuscript) (n.d.).

Pardesi, Ghanshyam, 'Dust unto Dust' in *The Illustrated Weekly of India*, 11 August 1985.

Parke, J.E., *Text-book of Preventive and Social Medicine* (Jabalpur: Banarasidas Bhanot) 1974.

Parmeggiani, Luigi, *Encyclopaedia of Occupational Health and Safety*, Third (Revised edition) vol. 2 (Geneva: International Labour Organization) 1983.

Patel, B.B., *Status Report on the Problems of Child Labour with a Focus on Diamond Cutting and Polishing Industry of Gujarat* (Carried out at the instance of Ministry of Labour, Government of India) (Ahmedabad: Gandhi Labour Institute) September 1987 (mimeo).

Patel, B.B. and Raksha Alagh, *Child Labour in India* (Incidence and Occupational Diversification across Social Strata) (Ahmedabad: Gandhi Labour Institute) (n.d.).

Patil, B.R., *The Working Children in Bangalore City* (Bangalore: Indian Institute of Management) (unpublished manuscript) (n.d.).

———, 'Child Workers in Bangalore-I', *The Financial Express* (Bombay) 3 January 1986.

Patnaik, Malabika, 'Child Labour in India: Size and Occupational

Distribution' in *Journal of the Indian Institute of Public Administration*, vol. 25, July–December 1979.

Pichholiya, K.R., 'Child Labour in a Metropolitan City: A Study of Ahmedabad' in *Indian Journal of Labour Economics*, vol. xxii, no. 4, January 1980.

Pillai, Ajith, 'Children of Shuklaji Street', *The Sunday Observer*, 1 September 1985.

Pitt, David C., 'Child Labour and Health' in Usha Naidu and Kamini Kapadia (eds), *Child Labour and Health: Problems and Prospects* (Bombay: Tata Institute of Social Sciences) 1985a.

——, 'Child Labour and Health' in P.M. Shah and Nigel Cantwell (eds), *Child Labour: Threat to Health and Development* (2nd revised edition) (Geneva, Switzerland: Published by Defence for Children International) 1985b.

Prasad, T., 'Preventing Exploitation of Children' in *Social Welfare*, August 1982.

Prembhai, *Report to the Supreme Court regarding Child Weavers of Mirzapur-Bhadohi-Varanasi* (Varanasi: mimeo) 1984.

Puri, Rakhat, 'India has 100 Million Bonded Labourers', *The Hindustan Times*, 30 September 1984.

Purushotham, P., 'A Profile of Beedi Workers' in *Social Change*, vol. 13, no. 1, March 1983.

Ramaswamy, S.S. et al *Status Report on Child Labour* (Ahmedabad: National Institute of Occupational Health) (mimeo) 1987.

Rao, Amiya, 'Silicosis Deaths of Slate Workers' in *Economic and Political Weekly*, vol. xv, no. 44, 1 November 1980.

Rao, B.V.R. and B. Malik, *Street Children of Hyderabad: A Situational Analysis* (A study conducted for Ministry of Social Welfare, Government of India and UNICEF) (Noida: National Labour Institute, Child Labour Cell) 1992.

Rao, Sudha V., 'Rural Labour: Case Study of a Karnataka village' in *Economic and Political Weekly*, vol. xix, no. 18, 5 May 1984.

Rai, Usha, 'The Forgotten Children of Delhi', *The Times of India*, 16 August 1984.

Ratnani, Jagdish, 'Tender Age, Big Shoulders' in *Onlooker*, 23 July–7 August 1985.

Reddy, Nandana, *Street Children of Bangalore: A Situational Analysis* (A study conducted for Ministry of Social Welfare,

Government of India and UNICEF) (Noida: National Labour Institute, Child Labour Cell) 1992.

Sadhu and Singh, 'Child Labour in India' in *The Indian Worker*, 6 October 1980.

Sarma, A.M., 'Child Labour in Indian Industries' in *The Indian Journal of Social Work*, vol. xi, no. 3, October 1979.

Sebastian, A., 'Child Migrants and Child Migrant Labour' in K. Srinivasan et al (eds) *Demographic and Socio-economic Aspects of the Child in India* (Bombay: Himalaya Publishing House) 1979.

Sengupta, Arindam, 'The Curse of Katni-Limestone Industry Workers Dying through Barbaric Exploitation' in *Probe India*, June 1983.

Sengupta, Amit, 'A Childhood Denied', *Patriot Magazine* (New Delhi) 28 July 1985.

Sharma, T.N., 'Potential of Village Pottery in India' in *Khadi Gramodyog* (Bombay: Directorate of Publicity, Khadi and Village Industries Commission) February 1978.

Sharma, V.R., *Impending Threats to the Hand-knotted Carpet Industry*, Mirzapur (unpublished) 1985.

Sharma, Subramaniam, 'The Killer Balloon' in *Business Standard*, 11 March 1992.

Shukla, Sudhindra, 'Little Ones Meandering in the Dark', *National Herald*, 25 March 1984.

Siddiqui, I.A., 'Focus on the Girl Child', Paper presented at NMC (National Media Centre) — UNICEF Media Workshop on the Girl Child, New Delhi, 12–14 October 1985.

Singh, Andrea Menefee and Anita Kelles-Viitanen, *Invisible Hands* (New Delhi: Sage Publications) 1987.

Singh, Musafir et al *Working Children in Bombay: A Study* (New Delhi: NIPCCD) 1980.

Singh, Gurbir, 'At Sivakasi', *The Economic Times* (Saturday) 10 April 1982.

Singh, N.K., 'Slate Pencil Industry: Deadly Bondage' in *India Today*, 30 September 1986.

Sud, S.K., 'Illiterate Child Labourers of Chandigarh', *Patriot*, 12 January 1985.

Sudha, B.G. and Smita Tewari, 'Child Labour in Rural Areas: Some Factors' in *Kurukshetra*, vol. xxxiii, no. 7, April 1985.

Thanga Raju, M., 'Child Labour in Rajasthan' in *Labour Gazette*, vol. 57, no. 1-2, December 1977.

Udomsakdi, Yupah, 'The Exploitation of the Child in Thailand', Paper presented at The Meeting of Experts on the Exploitation of the Child, 1984 at the Conference on Child Labour and Child Prostitution 1986, *LA WASIA*, 1987.

Venkatramani, S.H., 'Tamil Nadu: Vested Interests' in *India Today*, 15 July 1983.

Miscellaneous Articles

Amar Ujala (Hindi), 'Central Minister and Parliamentary Committee Found Children Working. Four Factory Owners of Firozabad Arrested', Agra, 25 January 1987.

Area Development Programme, 'Social Service Inputs for Young IMP's on Match Factories in Sivakasi Area' (Tamil Nadu: Area Development Programme) (mimeo) (n.d.).

AMU, 'Inter-disciplinary Study on Muslim Entrepreneurs in Aligarh' (Aligarh: Aligarh Muslim University), draft (n.d.).

BLF, *Proceedings & Resolution of First National Workshop on Eradication of Child Labour in Carpet Industry* (New Delhi: Bonded Liberation Front) (mimeo) 1991.

CRRID, *Communal Violence and its Impact on Development and National Integration*, Centre for Research in Rural and Industrial Development (mimeo) (n.d.).

Down to Earth, 15 September 1992, 'Interview with Bonded Child Carpet Weavers'.

Economic and Political Weekly, vol. xvi, no. 32, 8 August 1981, 'Beedi Workers of Nizamabad'.

IDS, *Moradabad Art Metalware Industry — Impact of Exports on its Structure of Workers. Contribution of Handicrafts and Handloom Production to Indian Development.* Product Review Paper: Art Metalware 4 (New Delhi: Industrial Development Services) cyclostyled, 1983.

MIDS, *The Match Industry in Sivakasi, Sattur. Towards Removal of Child labour* (Madras: Madras Institute of Development Studies) (mimeo) August 1985.

M.P. Chronicle, 17 April 1984, 'Of Bonded Kids & Indifferent Govt'.

New Age, 4 September 1986.

NLI Rural Wing, 'The Dark World of Jeeta Gadus' in *NLI Bulletin*, vol. 3, no. 12, 1977.

Patriot, 17 October 1983, 'Sivakasi to Resist Child Labour Ban'.

Shramshakti, 'Report of the National Commission on Self-employed Women and Women in the Informal Sector' (New Delhi: Department of Women and Child Development) 1988.

Target, vol. VII, no. 12 (New Delhi: Living Media Pvt. Ltd.) 1986.

The Financial Express, 17 October 1983, 'Child Labour Abolition: Sivakasi Match Units Threaten to Mechanise'.

The Financial Express, 11 August 1992, 'Bonded Labour — A Blot on India's Reforming Face'.

The Hindu, 31 January 1988, 'Eight Killed in Blast'.

The Hindu, 1 July 1989, 'Focus on the Little Ones in Bondage for Life'.

The Indian Express, 11 April 1984, 'Tribal Children of Raipur in Bondage'.

The Indian Express, 18 January, 1987, 'UP Welfare Scheme for Child Workers'.

The Indian Express, 16 June 1987, 'Duty Crippling Carpet Industry'.

The Indian Express, 22 February 1988, 'A Sordid Tale of Torture, Ill-treatment'.

The Indian Express, 1 July 1989, '75 m. Child Labour in 5 Asian Countries'.

'Cruel Exploitation of Child Labour at Sivakasi' in *The Indian Worker*, vol. XXVII, no. 50, 17 September 1979.

The Indian Worker, 31 March 1980, 'Labour in Parliament'.

The Indian Worker, vol. 29, no. 29, December 1980, 'Bonded Labour'.

The Pioneer, 8 April 1994, '15-year-old boy set ablaze by employer'.

The Telegraph, 22 April 1983, 'TN to Ban Child Labour'.

The Times of India, 7 September 1981, 'Child labour: These Hands were meant to Play'.

The Times of India, 31 January 1988, '8 Killed in Factory Fire'.

The Times of India, 26 March 1988, 'No Child Worker Below 14 in Khurja Potteries'.

The Times of India, 12 April 1988, 'Tytler Replies', Letters to the Editor.

The Times of India, 1 July 1989, 'Eradicate Bonded Labour: Bhagwati'.

The Times of India, 4 August 1992, 'Four Bonded Child Labourers Rescued'.

The Times of India, 5 March 1994, 'Mistreated servant boy rescued'.

The Times of India, 8 April 1994, 'Teenager burnt to death'.

UNICEF, *Children and Women in India. A Situation Analysis 1990* (New Delhi: UNICEF India Office) 1991.

——, *The Invisible Child. A Look at the Urban Child in Delhi* (n.d.).

Index

women, 13, 200, 204, 255
in brass industry, 147, 150,
151
in the gem industry, 81
upward mobility and, 214
work, 207
World War II, 113
work:
on contract basis, 61
free, 18, 199
hours, 39
on lot basis, 61, 82
opportunities, 139
overtime, 159
paid, 14
pressure of, 125
tiring, 127
unpaid, 14, 68, 90, 91, 199
workers, 142
child, 35n
full-time, 93
health, 5

life span of, 74
main, 10, 11
permanent, 32, 36, 64, 109,
128, 195
standard of living, 5
unskilled, 81, 128, 138, 154
work-force, 12, 154
children in, 43-7, 154, 236
working children, 3, 4, 31-4,
101-7, 123-7, 182, 205, 224
educational status of, 103-7,
225
needs of, 224, 229
problems of, 107
self esteem among, 182
Work Participation rate (WPR),
12, 13
of females, 12
workshops, 2, 11, 147, 155,
218, 245, 246, 247, 248,
255, 256
single process, 142